PENGUIN CLASSICS

GENERAL EDITOR, POETRY: CHRISTOPHER RICKS

SELECTED POEMS

WILLIAM BLAKE was born in Broad Street in 1757, the son of a London hosier. Having attended Henry Pars's drawing school in the Strand, he was in 1772 apprenticed to James Basire, engraver to the Society of Antiquaries, and later was admitted as a student to the Royal Academy, where he exhibited in 1780. He married Catherine Boucher in 1782 and in 1783 *Poetical Sketches* was printed. The first of his 'illuminated books' was *Songs of Innocence* (1789), which, like *The Book of Thel* (published in the same year), has as its main themes the celebration of innocence and its inviolability.

Blake sets out his ideas more fully in his chief prose work, *The Marriage of Heaven and Hell* (1791), which proclaims his lifelong belief in the moral primacy of the imagination. But in *Songs of Experience* (1794) he recognizes the power of repression, and in a series of short narrative poems he looks for mankind's redemption from oppression through a resurgence of imaginative life. By 1797 he was ready for epic; *Vala* was never finished, but in *Milton* and *Jerusalem* he presents his renewed vision of reconciliation among the warring fragments of humanity. Other striking poems of his middle years are the lyrics of the Pickering Manuscript, and *The Everlasting Gospel*, but in the last years of his life he expressed himself chiefly in drawing rather than poetry.

Little of Blake's work was published in conventional form. He combined his vocations as poet and graphic artist to produce books that are visually stunning. He also designed illustrations of works by other poets and devised his own technique for producing colour-printed drawings. Blake died in 1827, 'an Old Man feeble & tottering but not in Spirit & Life, not in the Real Man, The Imagination which Liveth for Ever'.

G. E. BENTLEY, JR, taught at the universities of Chicago (1956–60) and Toronto (1960–96), plus a year each in Algiers, Poona, Shanghai and Canberra. His research is chiefly on William Blake but his books include studies of Blake's friends John Flaxman, George Cumberland and James Edwards. His recent books include an edition of *William Blake's Writings*, 2 vols (1978, 2001), *The Stranger from Paradise: A Biography of William Blake* (2001, 2003), and *Blake Records* (second edition, 2004).

WILLIAM BLAKE
Selected Poems

Edited and with an Introduction and Notes by
G. E. BENTLEY, JR

PENGUIN BOOKS

PENGUIN CLASSICS

Published by the Penguin Group
Penguin Books Ltd, 80 Strand, London WC2R 0RL, England
Penguin Group (USA) Inc., 375 Hudson Street, New York, New York 10014, USA
Penguin Group (Canada), 10 Alcorn Avenue, Toronto, Ontario, Canada M4V 3B2
(a division of Pearson Penguin Canada Inc.)
Penguin Ireland, 25 St Stephen's Green, Dublin 2, Ireland
(a division of Penguin Books Ltd)
Penguin Group (Australia), 250 Camberwell Road, Camberwell, Victoria 3124, Australia
(a division of Pearson Australia Group Pty Ltd)
Penguin Books India Pvt Ltd, 11 Community Centre, Panchsheel Park, New Delhi – 110 017, India
Penguin Group (NZ), cnr Airborne and Rosedale Roads, Albany, Auckland 1310, New Zealand
(a division of Pearson New Zealand Ltd)
Penguin Books (South Africa) (Pty) Ltd, 24 Sturdee Avenue, Rosebank 2196, South Africa

Penguin Books Ltd, Registered Offices: 80 Strand, London WC2R 0RL, England

www.penguin.com

This selection first published in Penguin Classics 2005

025

Set in 9.25/11 pt PostScript Adobe Sabon
Typeset by Rowland Phototypesetting Ltd, Bury St Edmunds, Suffolk
Printed and bound in Great Britain by Clays Ltd, Elcograf S.p.A.

ISBN-13: 978-0-140-42446-1

www.greenpenguin.co.uk

FSC www.fsc.org MIX Paper from responsible sources FSC™ C018179

Penguin Books is committed to a sustainable future for our business, our readers and our planet. This book is made from Forest Stewardship Council™ certified paper.

Contents

SELECTED POEMS

Chronology

1757 *28 November*: Born to Catherine and James Blake and christened on 11 December at the parish church of St James, Westminster.

1757–72 Lived above the family hosiery shop at 28 Broad Street, Golden Square, with his brothers James (1752–1827), John (1755–?56), John (1760–?1800), Robert (1762–87, christened Richard), and his sister Catherine Elizabeth (1764–1841); none of his siblings married.

1761 First visions.

1762 *25 April*: Catherine Sophia Boucher born and christened on 16 May in the parish church of St Mary, Battersea; her father William Boucher (also spelled Butcher) was a not-very-successful market gardener, and her four brothers and eight sisters had a distressing tendency to die young.

1767–?72 Attended Henry Pars's drawing school in Beaufort Buildings in the Strand.

1772–9 Apprenticed to the engraver James Basire and lived at his house at 31 Great Queen Street, Lincoln's Inn.

1779–82 Probably living back with his family at 28 Broad Street.

1779 ff. Student at the Royal Academy.
Exhibited there in 1780, 1784, 1785, 1799, 1808.

1782–3 Engraved illustrations for Miguel de Cervantes, Laurence Sterne, Sarah Fielding, Tobias Smollett, Samuel Richardson in *Novelist's Magazine*, VIII–XI.

1782 *18 August*: Married Catherine Sophia Boucher in St Mary's, Battersea.

1782–4 Living at 23 Green Street, Leicester Fields.

1783 *Poetical Sketches* printed at the expense of the Revd Anthony Stephen Mathew and Blake's friend, the sculptor John Flaxman.

1784 'An Island in the Moon' written.

1784–5 Established a print shop at 27 Broad Street with fellow apprentice James Parker.

1785–90 Living at 28 Poland Street.

1787 Death of beloved brother Robert; thereafter Blake fills Robert's notebook with some of his most wonderful poems and designs, particularly *Songs of Experience* (1793) and 'The Everlasting Gospel' (?1818).

1788 First experiments with Illuminated Printing in *There is No Natural Religion* and *All Religions are One*, neither of them published.

1789 *Tiriel* written and illustrated; *Songs of Innocence*, *The Book of Thel* in Illuminated Printing published.

1790–1800 Living at 13 Hercules Buildings, Lambeth.

1790 *The Marriage of Heaven and Hell* probably published.

1791 *The French Revolution*, Book I, a proof printed in conventional typography but never published.

1793 *Visions of the Daughters of Albion*, *America* and *For Children: The Gates of Paradise* published.

1794 *Songs of Experience*, *Europe*, *The First Book of Urizen* published.

1794–7 Edward Young's *Night Thoughts*, with 357 folio watercolours (1794–6) by Blake, forty-three of them engraved by Blake (1796–7), published (1797).

1795 *The Song of Los*, *The Book of Ahania*, *The Book of Los*, twelve large colour prints printed.

1796?–1807? *Vala* (1796) or *The Four Zoa's* (1807) written and illustrated.

1799–1805 Bible illustrated for Thomas Butts with 135 temperas (1799–1800) and watercolours (chiefly 1800–1805). Butts was a clerk in the office of the Commissary General of Musters.

1800–1803 Moved to Felpham, Sussex, to work for three years under the patronage of William Hayley, a successful and complacent gentleman poet and biographer.

1801 Milton, *Comus*, eight watercolours, with another set painted in 1815.

1803 *16 August*: Charged with sedition and assault after a fracas with a soldier in his garden at Felpham. On 4 October A True Bill found against Blake on the charge of assault and sedition at his trial at Petworth, Sussex.

1804 *11 January*: Acquitted of charges of assault and sedition at trial at Chichester.

1803–21 Living at 27 South Molton Street, Westminster.

1804[–?11] *Milton* written and printed.

1804[–?20] *Jerusalem* written and printed.

1805–6 Job watercolours made for Butts, engraved and published (1826).

1805–8 Robert Blair's *The Grave*, with forty watercolours (1805) by Blake, twelve of them engraved by Schiavonetti, published by R. H. Cromek (in 1808, 1813, 1826 etc.).
1806–9 Shakespeare, Second Folio, with six watercolours by Blake.
1807? The Ballads Manuscript transcribed by Blake.
1807–8 Milton, *Paradise Lost*, twelve watercolours, with another set painted in 1808.
1809 Milton, *On the Morning of Christ's Nativity*, six watercolours.
1809–10 Private exhibition of his pictures held at the family hosiery shop; described in his *Descriptive Catalogue* (1809). Included temperas of *The Canterbury Pilgrims* and *The Ancient Britons.*
1810 Large engraving of the procession of Chaucer's Canterbury Pilgrims printed.
1812 Exhibited at the Associated Painters in Watercolour exhibition.
1814–17 John Flaxman, *Compositions from . . . Hesiod*, thirty-seven designs etched by Blake (1814–17) and published by Longman (1817).
1818 Meets the painter John Linnell.
1818 ff. Visionary Heads drawn.
1821-7 Living at 3 Fountain Court, Strand.
1821 Virgil, *Pastorals*, ed. R. J. Thornton, published with twenty-seven prints by Blake.
1821? *On Homer's Poetry [and] On Virgil* printed.
1822 *The Ghost of Abel* printed.
1824? Book of Enoch, five watercolours by Blake.
1824–7 Dante, *Divine Comedy*, 103 watercolours (1824–7?), seven engravings (1826–7) by Blake, published (1838).
1826 *Illustrations of The Book of Job*, twenty-two plates designed (1805–6) and engraved (1824–5) by Blake and published by Blake and John Linnell.
1826? 'Laocoon' engraved and annotated.
1827 *12 August*: Died in mid-song.
1831 *18 October*: Catherine Blake died in the arms of the wife of Blake's disciple Frederick Tatham.
1833 ff. Sale, loss and deliberate destruction of the books, drawings and manuscripts which Blake had left to Catherine and she to Tatham.
1863 Alexander Gilchrist, *Life of William Blake, 'Pictor Ignotus'* (published in 1863, 1880, etc), the first important book on Blake.

Introduction

William Blake was scarcely known to his contemporaries except as a competent engraver, an eccentric painter in watercolours – and 'an unfortunate lunatic, whose personal inoffensiveness secures him from confinement'.[1] His books were almost entirely unknown, partly because he never made more than a few copies of any of them – perhaps thirty at most – and partly because he sometimes preferred to give them away to friends rather than to sell them to the public, as with his *Poetical Sketches* (1783). Those who bought his books often relished them more for their designs than for their poetry – his early biographer Allan Cunningham said that *America* and *Europe* were 'plentifully seasoned with verse' among designs characterized by 'grandeur' and 'a magical effect'.[2] The very best poets and critics – Samuel Taylor Coleridge, William Wordsworth, Charles Lamb, William Hazlitt – treasured the poetry of *Songs of Innocence* and *Songs of Experience*, but most of those who saw Blake's verse scarcely attempted to appreciate its beauty and profundity. Robert Southey, the poet laureate, dismissed *Jerusalem* as 'a perfectly mad poem'.[3]

The best known of Blake's designs were those for Robert Blair's *The Grave* (1808) (see below), and the most widely accessible of his poems was his dedication in Blair's book 'To the Queen'. *The Antijacobin Review* for November 1808 said that

> The dedication . . . is one of the most abortive attempts to form a wreath of poetical flowers that we have ever seen. Should he again essay to climb the Parnassian heights, his friends would do well to restrain his wanderings by the strait waistcoat. Whatever licence we may allow him as a painter, to tolerate him as a poet would be insufferable.

BLAKE'S CAREER AND INFLUENCE

Blake had several creative careers, and in each he was extraordinarily original. His professional career was as an engraver, for which he served a seven-year apprenticeship. He was a skilful translator of designs to copper, and most of his life he earned his living by this skill. He was a technical innovator, and his techniques of relief etching and colour printing are unique to him and died with him. His greatest accomplishments were his twelve great colour-prints, separately issued on subjects such as Hecate and Nebuchadnezzar (1795), his twenty-two triumphant *Illustrations of the Book of Job* (1826), and his unfinished suite of seven marvellous engravings for Dante's *Divine Comedy* (1826–7). These are among the most wonderful prints ever created in England.

His greatest ambition was always as an artist: he drew pictures while sitting at his father's shop-counter as a child, and on his deathbed he coloured the finest copy of *The Ancient of Days*. His father sent him to Pars's Drawing School for boys, and later he attended the Royal Academy school. He exhibited pictures at the Royal Academy (1780–1808), at his own exhibition at his brother's house, the family hosiery shop (1809–10), and at the Society of Associated Painters in Water-colours (1812). Most of his designs were watercolours on paper of modest dimensions, about 12″ × 16″, but his tempera on canvas of *The Canterbury Pilgrims* (1809), by which he hoped to vindicate his reputation, was 18″ × 54″, and his huge lost tempera of *The Ancient Britons* (1809) was 10′ × 13′4″. Most of his pictures were illustrations of poetry, by both himself and others. Some, like *The Ancient of Days*, are enormously powerful. These are major accomplishments, though – like the poems – few of his designs were seen by the public of his time.

As with his art, Blake's career as a poet spanned his entire life. He began composing poetry as a child, and he was still making songs on his deathbed. His first surviving poem, which begins 'How sweet I roam'd from field to field', was composed before he was fourteen (1771), and his splendidly insolent and patronizing address 'To The Accuser who is The God of This World' may have been finished in 1826, the year before he died. Most of the early poems, such as those in *Poetical Sketches* (1783) and 'An Island in the Moon' ([?1784]), are lyrics and some of them are exquisite.

The verses in *Poetical Sketches* are, of course, the work of a boy, but a boy of brilliance. They exhibit a boyish enthusiasm for blood and gore, for the very new fashion for the Gothic, and for patriotism ('Soldiers, prepare! Our cause is Heaven's cause,' *Poetical Sketches*, 'Edward the Third', l. 55). In their adolescent enthusiasms, some of the verses combine echoes of the unfashionable Elizabethan poets and a dissenting hostility to Church and State:

> O what have Kings to answer for,
> Before that awful throne!
> When thousand deaths for vengeance cry,
> And ghosts accusing groan.
> ('Gwin King of Norway', ll. 97–100,
> *Poetical Sketches*)

Others are daring in their sexual suggestiveness:

> O deck her forth with thy fair fingers; pour
> Thy soft kisses on her bosom; and put
> Thy golden crown upon her languish'd head,
> Whose modest tresses were bound up for thee!
> ('To Spring', ll. 13–16)

And some are of breathtaking daring in prosody, with blank verse which may have scarcely a pause at the end of the line:

> Let thy west wind sleep on
> The lake; speak silence with thy glimmering eyes,
> And wash the dusk with silver.
> ('To the Evening Star', ll. 8–10)

Perhaps the finest of them is 'To the Muses', an 'elegy for the death of music which demonstrates by its sweetness that music is not dead':[4]

> How have you left the antient love
> That bards of old enjoy'd in you!
> The languid strings do scarcely move!
> The sound is forc'd, the notes are few!
> ('To the Muses', ll. 13–16)

The nineteenth-century poet Algernon Swinburne said that in 'To the Muses' 'the Eighteenth Century died to music'.[5]

The *Songs of Innocence* (1789) and *Songs of Experience* (1794) contain most of the lyrics by which Blake is best known, such as 'The Tyger', 'The Lamb' and 'London'.

In *Songs of Innocence*, 'everything that lives is holy'.[6] The poems have a simple vocabulary and apparent transparency which belie profound sophistication and defy simple analysis.

> The speakers of the poem . . . are babies, children, and adults, black and white, birds, insects, and animals; none is William Blake. All speak from a sense of protection, of safety, of being in their proper places in an ordered universe. Each, whether child or adult or ant, is guided by the glow-worm, 'the watchman of the night' and by 'God ever nigh', by 'angels bright Unseen . . . [*who*] pour blessing', and by 'Thy maker . . . [*who*] Heaven & earth to peace beguiles'.[7] Each is protected by something outside himself; it is the sense of protection, rather than the reality of the protection, which brings peace and joy. These innocents do not know that there is nothing outside themselves to protect them. It is not society but vision which sustains them. In 'The Chimney Sweeper', the unspeakably filthy and forlorn little boy dreams of 'an Angel who had a bright key' of vision which transforms the brutal world for him: 'Tho' the morning was cold, Tom was happy & warm'.
>
> The songs are about children, by children, and for children. Some, such as 'The Lamb' and 'Infant Joy', are in words of only one or two syllables, and the designs are simple, bold and beautiful.
>
> The *Songs of Experience* are songs of the unprotected, songs of betrayal or at least of a sense of betrayal – the laments of the victims. They are cries of honest indignation and social protest, the self-enjoyings of misery. Though invited by the bard to 'Arise from out the dewy grass' and 'controll the starry pole', the earth-bound lapsed souls are yet 'cover'd with grey despair' and lament that they are 'Chain'd in night' by 'Starry Jealousy', the 'selfish father of men'. With self-devoted earnestness, they 'build a Hell in Heavens despite'.[8]
>
> The pervasive miseries of social injustice are memorably mourned in 'London':
>
> I wander thro' each charter'd street,
> Near where the charter'd Thames does flow
> And mark in every face I meet
> Marks of weakness, marks of woe.
>
> But the illustration to the poem represents 'London blind & age-bent'. The 'Marks of weakness, marks of woe' must be within himself.
>
> . . .

In 'The Lamb' in *Songs of Innocence*, the little boy constructs a catechism for the lamb:

> Dost thou know who made thee?
> . . . For he calls himself a lamb . . .

The same syllogism, deducing the qualities of the creator from those of his creation, is used in 'The Tyger' in *Experience*, with terrifying effect:

> Tyger, Tyger, burning bright,
> In the forests of the night:
> What immortal hand or eye
> Could frame thy fearful symmetry?

The grammar, like the logic, becomes so involved that the limbs of the creator are scarcely distinguishable from those of his terrible, bloodthirsty creation. The poem moves from physical power (who 'Could frame thy fearful symmetry?') to moral daring (who 'Dare frame thy fearful symmetry?'), and any answer to the question is terrifying. Yes, it is the same God who created the meekness of the lamb and the terrors of the Tyger, or no, there are two creating Gods, one for the helpless lamb and one for the preying tyger.

. . .

The *Songs of Experience* are the complements to *Songs of Innocence*, not the answers to them. The singers of Innocence feel protected by powerful forces outside themselves, while the singers of Experience feel threatened by powerful forces they cannot control or propitiate. Neither set of singers has yet learned that the power of divinity lies not beyond us but within us.[9]

In about 1787 Blake invented a method of relief etching which permitted him to combine comparatively rapidly and economically his visual and verbal inspirations on the same page – what he called Illuminated Printing. Thereafter, all the poetry he published combined words and images inextricably intertwined. On the title-page of *The First Book of Urizen* a bearded old man, Urizen himself, copies *with each hand* from a huge opened book a text which is entirely illegible. *Europe* begins with a magnificent image of a bearded old man (like Urizen) leaning out from the sun to create the universe with light from his fingers, but the nature of his creation is indicated by the title-page facing 'The Ancient of Days', which depicts a huge serpent coiled beneath and across the words 'EUROPE a PROPHECY'. This awe-inspiring God creates a universe of terror. We should see both Blake's designs and his text to understand them fully as he intended us to do.

There is a remarkable intellectual consistency in Blake's works, from *Songs of Innocence* (1789) to *Jerusalem* (finished 1820). Many of these ideas are expressed most memorably in *The Marriage of Heaven and Hell* (1790). Here are plainly expressed his views on the nature of vision, the usurpations of institutional religion, good and evil, reason and energy ('Energy is Eternal Delight'): 'everything that lives is Holy'; 'All deities reside in the human breast'. From such seeds flowered many of Blake's most eloquent verses.

In his earliest printed poetry in *Poetical Sketches*, there are experiments with mythical themes peculiar to Blake, and most of his surviving poems are long, mythological narratives in unrhymed verse which challenge conventional belief about politics, religion, psychology and nature. Some of the early works, such as *The French Revolution* (1791) and *America* (1793), are explicitly political, centred in society; La Fayette and the Bastille in France are named in the first, and 'Washington, Franklin, Paine & Warren' in the colonies and celebrating the overthrow of temporal tyrannies in the second: 'Empire is no more! And now the lion & wolf shall cease'.[10] Later the focus of his poetry is not so obviously political, with less stress upon law and prison and more upon the tyrannies of the mind, 'the mind-forg'd manacles' of 'London'; we are prisoners with 'chains of the mind locked up'.[11] Increasingly the poetry turns from the psychological and mental limitations of man to the limitations of God, to 'the eternal mind bounded'.[12]

Blake created a number of myths of his own – as his character Los says, 'I must Create a System, or be enslav'd by another Man's'[13] – which are psychomachias or wars of the spirit. The early myths, for instance in *Tiriel* and *The Book of Thel*, are concerned with doomed psychological explorations of a fallen world. Later ones, as in *America* and *Europe*, deal with titanic political struggles for empire and dominion. In *The Book of Urizen* the myth turns to the divisions within our own souls, at first with the apocalyptic conflict between reason (Urizen) and imagination (Los). As the myth becomes more comprehensive, in *Vala*, *Milton* and *Jerusalem*, the prime elements of which we are made up are called The Four Zoa's – the Living Creatures of Ezekiel – and Los, the imagination, is identified with Christ, through whom we may regain divine unity. In Blake's myth, the first fall is not the fall of man but the fall and division of God into mental realms, pitting reason (Urizen) against imagination (Los). The words 'Christ' and 'Christian' do not appear in his poetry before *Vala* ([?1796–?1807]) and *Milton* (1804[–11?]), but thereafter they are central to his myth:

> Glory! Glory! Glory! To the Holy Lamb of God!
> I touch the heavens as an instrument to glorify
> the Lord!
>
> (*Milton*, pl. 11, ll. 28–9)

Blake became a devout believer in Christ as the embodiment of the human imagination, though he always deplored institutionalized Christianity, and 'he did not for the last forty years [of his life] attend any place of Divine worship'.[14]

Among Blake's contemporaries, Wordsworth, Coleridge, Lamb and Hazlitt were deeply impressed by his poetry, but his influence on poets of his time was negligible. However, his influence on some later writers has been profound, including poets as diverse as W. B. Yeats and Allen Ginsberg, and pop musicians of the twenty-first century such as Billy Bragg and Patti Smith. A number of plays have been written about Blake,[15] and several novels focus upon him, the most remarkable of which are Joyce Cary's *The Horse's Mouth* (1944) and *Rouze Up O Young Men of the New Age* (1983) by the Japanese Nobel Laureate Kenzaburo Oe (translated by John Nathan in 2002).

Blake also composed music and sang his own songs, including those in his *Poetical Sketches*. He rejoiced that in the village of Felpham 'I can be Poet, Painter, & musician as the inspiration comes',[16] but he did not know how to write down his tunes 'upon paper . . . in bars and crotchets'.[17] Though he 'was entirely unacquainted with the science of music, . . . his tunes were sometimes most singularly beautiful, and were noted down by musical professors'.[18] Even in old age he sang his own songs, and 'Just before he died . . . He burst out in Singing of the things he saw in Heaven'.[19] But none of his music has survived, and we know scarcely more of his songs than that he sang them all his life.

Blake's most extensive influence is probably on musicians, for there are many hundreds of settings of his poems, including those by Benjamin Britten, Allen Ginsberg, Mike Westbrook, William Bolcom and Finn Coren, and especially C. Hubert Parry's setting of 'Jerusalem' from *Milton* as a hymn.[20] Most of this music capitalizes upon the obvious lyrical and rhythmical qualities of Blake's verse, but there are also settings of 'An Island in the Moon', *The Marriage of Heaven and*

Hell and *Tiriel*.[21] And in 1931 Gwen Raverat and the great Blake scholar Geoffrey Keynes created *Job: A Masque for Dancing* with music by R. Vaughan Williams, which is still in the repertoire of the Royal Ballet in London.

Blake's reputation is growing right around the world, and his pictures, poems and life are studied extensively beyond the English-speaking world, from Spain and Italy to Japan and Korea; there are probably more publications about Blake in Japanese than in all other non-English languages combined. In the rebellious 1960s, students marched with banners quoting aphorisms from *The Marriage of Heaven and Hell*: 'One Law for the Lion and Ox Is Oppression' and 'The Tygers of Wrath are Wiser than the Horses of Instruction', and in the twenty-first century some courses for business executives in anger management are based on his ideas. William Blake's spirit is alive and well.

BLAKE'S LIFE IN ENGLAND

In most respects, Blake lived an extraordinarily quiet life. He was born on 28 November 1757 above his father's little haberdashery and hosiery shop in Broad Street, Golden Square, Westminster. Such general education as he received was probably at the knee of his mother, and he thanked 'God I never was sent to school To be Flogd into following the Style of a fool'.[22]

He would have liked to be a painter, but instead he was apprenticed at the age of fourteen to the engraver James Basire, with whom he lodged from 1772 to 1779. On the completion of his apprenticeship indentures, he embarked vigorously on the career as an engraver from which he derived his chief income most of his life.

At the same time, he enrolled as a student at the Royal Academy and exhibited pictures there in 1780, 1784, 1785, 1799 and 1808. However, he found few patrons for his work, and most of the pictures were bought by one modest man of extraordinary perceptivity and generosity – a white-collar Maecenas. This patron was Thomas Butts, a clerk in the office of the Commissary General of Musters, who devoted a very substantial portion of his known income to buying hundreds of Blake's pictures and some of his books.

Blake was best known in the world of art for his twelve illustrations to Robert Blair's poem called *The Grave* (1808) and for his own private exhibition of his pictures in 1809 in the premises of the family hosiery shop, where his brother also lived. The *Grave* designs were widely admired, but they were also savagely criticized for their attempt to represent spirits such as the soul departing from the body. The exhibition and its *Descriptive Catalogue* were seen by very few, but they attracted such virulent public criticism that many more individuals knew of the reviews than they did of the pictures.

The only sensational public actions of Blake's life were his trials in 1803 and 1804 on trumped-up charges of assault and sedition brought against him by a disgruntled soldier. This individual bitterly resented the indignity he suffered when Blake threw him out of his garden in Felpham and then trundled him down the main street of the village before his comrades in the Royal Dragoons and the astonished villagers. At a time when fear of an invasion by Napoleon was rampant, Blake was in real danger, but his neighbours and his patron stood by him staunchly, and his acquittal was received with cheers. These events are referred to repeatedly in his poetry, particularly in *Milton* (1804[–11]) and *Jerusalem* (1804[–20]).

Blake seemed strange to many because he profoundly disbelieved in the authority of Church and State, indeed of all institutions. He wrote of himself 'as a Worshipper of Christ' who 'believe the Bible & profess myself a Christian', but he prayed in private; 'I will not worship in their Churches'.[23] He spoke of 'The abomination that maketh desolate, i.e. State Religion, which is the Source of all Cruelty', and he said that the suppression of civil liberties in England during England's crusade against France showed that 'The Beast [of the state] & the Whore [of state religion] rule without control'.[24]

He and his devoted wife Catherine lived quietly in rented flats – and once in a whole house – in London except for three years when they moved to the little seaside village of Felpham, Sussex (1800–1803), where Blake worked under the patronage of the generous, genteel and popular poetaster William Hayley. When they returned to London, Blake settled into a life of growing obscurity and poverty, for many years largely withdrawing from his profession of engraver and apparently supporting himself with the occasional sale of pictures and books.

One of Blake's greatest frustrations was in connection with the engraver-turned-publisher R. H. Cromek. Blake had made forty designs in illustration of Blair's *The Grave*, and Cromek purchased twenty of them for the risible sum of twenty guineas – enough for the Blakes to live on for perhaps four months – with the proviso that Blake should also engrave them at a far more substantial price for a handsome illustrated edition of the poem. To save money, Cromek then reduced the number of designs to be published from twenty to fifteen and then to twelve. And, worst of all, he then took the commission for the engravings away from Blake and gave it to the more successful and fashionable Louis Schiavonetti.

Later Blake showed Cromek his design of the procession of Chaucer's Canterbury Pilgrims, and Cromek commissioned Blake's friend Thomas Stothard to paint a picture with the same very unusual subject and dimensions for £100. Blake was shocked into furious doggerel:

> A Petty sneaking Knave I knew.
> 'O Mr Cr—do ye do?'

He lost faith in connoisseurs and amateurs, 'The Cunning sures and the aim at yours'[25] as he called them, and he was also destroyed financially. Cromek made handsome profits on the edition of Blair's *Grave* and on the exhibition of Stothard's painting and the engraving of it, while Blake sank steadily into poverty and obscurity.

In 1818 he met John Linnell, a vigorous young landscape painter, who protected and fostered Blake for the rest of his life. In particular, Linnell published Blake's engravings for the Book of Job (1826) and the *Divine Comedy* (1838) and introduced him to a circle of adolescent disciples, including the painters Samuel Palmer, George Richmond and Edward Calvert, who in mockery of their youth called themselves 'The Ancients'. These new friends made Blake's last years rich in spirit, though meagre in gold.

One new friend was John Varley, an occasionally successful painter and astrologer, who was fascinated by the visions Blake said he saw and painted. He encouraged Blake to make midnight drawings of what have come to be known as Visionary Heads – representing the mighty or notorious dead, from Alexander the Great, Merlin and Edward I to the murderess Catherine Hayes (1690–1726) and Colonel Blood (?1618–80) who stole the crown jewels of England. These Visionary Heads confirmed contemporaries in their suspicion that Blake was mad, and often they are a severe test to moderns who admire his poetry and designs and like to think that he was more sane than his contemporaries. Among the more remarkable subjects are *The Man Who Built the Pyramids* and *The Ghost of a Flea*.

BLAKE IN PARADISE: THE LIFE OF THE MIND

> I have very little of Mr. Blake's company;
> he is always in Paradise.[26]

For Blake, 'Mental Things are alone Real'; 'What are all the Gifts of the Spirit but Mental Gifts?'[27] It is not what we see that is important but how we see it. 'A fool sees not the same tree that a wise man sees.'[28] Blake was keenly aware of the beauties of the natural world, of the evening star, the sunrise, the song of the lark, but to him they spoke of God's glory.

> 'What' it will be Questiond, 'When the Sun rises do you not See a round Disk of fire somewhat like a Guinea?'
> O no, no. I see an Innumerable company of the Heavenly host crying 'Holy Holy Holy is the Lord God Almighty!'[29]

Blake was a devoted reader of the Bible and profoundly Christian, but his understanding of the Bible and of Christianity were peculiarly his own.

> The Vision of Christ that thou dost See
> Is my Vision's greatest Enemy.
>
> . . .
>
> Both read the Bible day & night
> But thou readst black where I read White.[30]

For Blake, the only life that mattered was the life of the mind, the flourishing of the imagination, the visions of paradise. His first vision, when he was four years old, was of God who put his head in at the window, and when he was eight or ten he saw angels in the trees with spangled wings. His pictures and his poems were representations of what he saw in vision, in his imagination, and these visions were sharper and more memorable than the mere trees and streets with which most of us make do.

> He who does not imagine in stronger and better lineaments and in stronger and better light than his perishing mortal eye can see does not imagine at all. The painter . . . asserts that all his imaginations appear

to him infinitely more perfect and more minutely organized than any thing seen by his mortal eye.[31]

In a letter of 22 November 1802, Blake wrote:

Now I a fourfold vision see
And a fourfold vision is given to me;
Tis fourfold in my supreme delight
And three fold in soft Beulah's night
And twofold Always. May God us keep
From Single vision & Newton's Sleep.[32]

Eventually Blake created a religion of art, of imagination:

The Old & New Testaments are the Great Code of Art . . . The Whole Business of Man Is The Arts & All Things Common . . . Christianity is Art & not Money . . .

A Poet, a Painter, a Musician, an Architect: the Man Or Woman who is not one of these is not a Christian. You must leave Fathers & Mothers & Houses & Lands if they stand in the way of Art.

Prayer is the Study of Art.
Praise is the Practise of Art.
Fasting &c all relate to Art.
The outward Ceremony is Antichrist.
The Eternal Body of Man is The Imagination, that is
God himself.[33]

All his life Blake was sustained by his visions, by spirits who spoke to him, who dictated poems to him, and who were the subjects of his poems and designs. This is, of course, part of an ancient literary tradition, exemplified by Homer, Dante and Milton, in which the poet is inspired by a heavenly muse. But for Blake, the visions are literal, constant presences: the Archangel Gabriel visited him, the Virgin Mary spoke to him, 'The Prophets Isaac and Ezekiel dined with me'.[34] For Blake, the world of spirits, of the mind, is the only real world.

'I have Mental Joy & Mental Health
And Mental Friends & Mental wealth,
I've a Wife I love & that loves me,
I've all But Riches Bodily.

'I am in God's presence night & day
And he never turns his face away.[35]

Once young Samuel Palmer told Blake how sometimes he felt deserted by the power of invention. To his astonishment, Blake turned to his wife suddenly and said: 'It is just so with us, is it not, for weeks together, when the visions forsake us? What do we do then, Kate?' 'We kneel down and pray, Mr. Blake.'[36]

THE TECHNOLOGY OF VISION: ILLUMINATED PRINTING

Blake's visions and creations were holistic. He saw the visions and he heard the words together, and he wished to unite them on the page, the designs interwoven with the poetry. The publication of such works by conventional technology would have been difficult and expensive, involving the assistance and interference of typesetters and engravers, printers and publishers. How could he display to the public his illuminated visions without such assistance/interference?

For years he could not solve the problem. His earliest poetry was either in manuscript, as with 'An Island in the Moon' ([?1784]), or in conventional typography, as in *Poetical Sketches* (1783), which was privately circulated. In either case it was unillustrated and seen only by friends. Then, after the death of his brother Robert in 1787:

> In a vision of the night, the form of Robert stood before him, and revealed the wished-for secret, directing him to the technical mode by which could be produced a fac-simile of song and design. On his rising in the morning, Mrs. Blake went out with half a crown, all the money they had in the world, and of that laid out 1*s.* 6*d.* on the simple materials necessary for setting in practice the new revelation.[37]

The wished-for secret was to involve the adaptation of the ordinary tools of an engraver. Instead of gouging out the design on the copperplate with a graver, or etching the design conventionally in acid, Blake wrote his poems and drew his designs on the surface of the copper with a liquid impervious to acid. When the copperplate was covered with acid, the exposed surfaces were left in high relief, as in conventional typography. Composition of the text was far quicker and cheaper than in conventional typography, and creation and printing of the designs was far simpler, quicker and cheaper than with conventional engraving or etching. Further, Blake could compose directly on the copper, and the printing could be done on an ordinary flat-bed printing press rather than the specialized rolling press needed for conventional engravings. Such relief-plates could even be printed without a machine press at all; paper could be put on the inked copperplates and rubbed with a wooden spoon to make quite satisfactory impressions. At a time when the government felt threatened by the expression of democratic and seditious ideas and required the licensing of printing presses and publications, Blake's invention offered wonderful convenience and independence.

He called the process 'Illuminated Printing', and he described it in his prospectus 'To the Public' (1793):

> the Author . . . has invented a method of Printing both Letter-press and Engraving in a style more ornamental, uniform, and grand, than any before discovered, while it produces works at less than one fourth of the expense.
>
> The Illuminated Books are Printed in Colours [e.g., red or blue or green], and on the most beautiful wove paper that could be procured.
>
> No Subscriptions for the numerous great works now in hand are asked, for none are wanted; but the Author will produce his works, and offer them to sale at a fair price.

At first (1788–95) he printed in very small batches, up to a dozen copies at a time; thereafter he generally printed only one or two copies at a time, and eventually he printed only when he had an order.[38]

A huge advantage of this method of book-making was that every stage was in the artist's hands. He wrote the poetry, created the designs, made the ink, inked and printed the copperplates, made the colours and watercoloured the prints, stitched the leaves, and sold them, the early books at between 3s and 10s 6d (15–58 pence in today's money), the later ones at ten or even twenty-five guineas (£10.50 and £26.25 in today's money). Only the copperplates and paper had to be bought readymade. His wife Catherine helped him in the printing – probably Blake inked the plates and Catherine, the clean-hand person, printed them – and she helped him in colouring the prints and in stitching the leaves into sugar-paper (pale blue, rough paper) wrappers. In Blake's myth, 'first he [Los-Blake] drew a line upon the walls of shining heaven/And Enitharmon [Catherine] tinctured it with beams of blushing love'.[39] No one else was involved in creating the finished work – and no one else had to be paid for it.

A major drawback was that the process was very labour-intensive, especially in the colouring. Profits could be achieved only by not counting the time and skill of Blake and his wife – and probably scarcely even then. Paper was very expensive, often more than half the production cost of conventional books, and copper was far more expensive than paper. To save money on the copper, Blake often used the backs of copperplates.

An even bigger drawback was that, while Blake cared deeply about making beautiful books, he cared scarcely at all about selling them. When he and his fellow apprentice James Parker started a printing business in 1784, it failed as a joint venture within a year. As he wrote of the need to find engraving work, 'I suppose I must go a Courting which I shall do awkwardly'.[40]

The intricate and messy business of making ready for printing – setting up the press, adjusting the roller to get the pressure right, grinding the ink, dampening the paper, printing, drying the prints – all this was straightforward enough when printing was done regularly, but for occasional work it was very inefficient. In 1808 Blake wrote to his old friend George Cumberland that he had 'so long been turned out of the old channel [of printing] into a new one that it is impossible for me to return to it without destroying my present course . . . my time . . . in future must be devoted to Designing & Painting'.[41]

He did return to printing about 1811, but he could scarcely produce his books on a commercial scale. In 1818 he wrote:

> The few [copies] I have Printed & Sold are sufficient to have gained me great reputation as an Artist which was the chief thing Intended But I have never been able to produce a Sufficient number for a general Sale by means of a regular Publisher. It is therefore necessary to me that any Person wishing to have any or all of them Should Send me their Order to Print them . . .

Probably Blake lost money on his works in Illuminated Printing, even when leaving out of consideration the wages of the artist, author, printer, colourer and salesman.[42]

But Blake was not content to reproduce his works in Illuminated Printing mechanically. The individuality of his method, with every stage in his own hands, meant that each copy he produced could be unique. Early copies are printed on facing pages, as in conventional printing, the colours are added very lightly, and the emphasis is upon narrative and continuous text. Late copies are printed on only one side of the leaf, so that only the frontispiece and title-page face one another, the colouring is heavy and sometimes covers the text so completely that it is difficult to read, and the effect is of a collection of pictures with occasional text. The colouring of most copies printed after 1795 was unique, sometimes with very significant differences; one of the boys in 'The Little Black Boy' is sometimes black and sometimes pink, and elsewhere men who are young and clean-shaven in one copy are old with long white beards in another and naked men are given clothes. Plates were subtracted from or added to different copies, such as in the *Songs* and *Milton*. The order of the plates was often changed – each copy of *The First Book of Urizen* and of *Songs of Innocence* and *Songs of Innocence and of Experience* printed before 1818 is arranged in a different order – so that each copy of a work by Blake in Illuminated Printing may be unique.

As Blake wrote in *Jerusalem*, pl. 3:

> Every word and every letter is studied and put into its fit place; the terrific numbers are reserved for the terrific parts, the mild & gentle, for the mild & gentle parts, and the prosaic, for inferior parts; all are necessary to each other. Poetry Fetter'd, Fetters the Human Race. Nations are Destroy'd, or Flourish, in proportion as Their Poetry, Painting and Music are Destroy'd or Flourish!

Blake's works in Illuminated Printing are far more than words on a page. The very letters may flourish with blossoms or tiny figures, as on the title-page of *Songs of Innocence*. The designs on almost every page form a complement and extension of the poetry (or vice versa); for instance, in 'The Blossom', the poem speaks only of the Robin and the Sparrow, but the design shows winged humans, and in 'The Tyger' the fiery, deadly, 'fearful symmetry' of the beast in the poem is reduced in the design to a small harmless animal like a child's stuffed toy which is sometimes coloured pink or green. The Illuminated Books can only be appreciated as Blake intended when they are seen with their designs, and anything less than a facsimile is simplistic.[43]

'SINGING OF THE THINGS HE SAW IN HEAVEN'

Blake's last great works were his engravings for *Illustrations of the Book of Job* and for Dante's *Divine Comedy*. By the mid 1820s his health was failing, and he was 'All strings & bobbins like a Weaver's Loom', as he said in a letter of 1 August 1826. The following April he wrote to George Cumberland:

> I have been very near the Gates of death & have returned very weak & an Old Man feeble & tottering, but not in Spirit & Life, not in The Real Man, The Imagination which Liveth for Ever. In that I am stronger & stronger as this Foolish Body decays.

Even when ill he continued to create in words and designs. On 1 June 1825 he wrote: 'I am in Bed at work . . . I can draw as well aBed as Up & perhaps better but I cannot Engrave.' And in February 1827: 'I am still feeble & tottering . . . [but] I go on as I think improving my Engravings of Dante more & more.'

As he told Crabb Robinson on 7 December 1826, 'I cannot consider death as any thing but a removing from one room to another'.[44]

When he died on 12 August 1827, George Richmond wrote to Samuel Palmer:

> He died on Sunday Night at 6 Oclock in a most glorious manner. He said He was going to that Country he had all His life wished to see & expressed Himself Happy hoping for salvation through Jesus Christ – Just before he died His Countenance became fair – His eyes brighten'd and He burst out in Singing of the things he Saw in Heaven. In truth He Died like a Saint as a person who was standing by Him Observed –

Blake was one of those, like his heroic Los, the Imagination, who 'kept the Divine Vision in time of trouble'.[45] He lived by faith, for indeed he believed that the world is sustained by faith. As he wrote in 'Auguries of Innocence' (1807):

> He who Doubts from what he sees [107]
> Will neer Believe, do what you Please.
> If the Sun & Moon should doubt
> They'd immediately Go out. [110]
>
> . . .
>
> God Appears & God is Light [129]
> To those poor souls who dwell in Night
> But does a Human Form Display
> To those who Dwell in Realms of day. [132]

For Blake, God and the infinite are visible everywhere – not only in the Bible and in art but in the smallest fluxions of nature. In this faith he teaches us

To see a World in a Grain of Sand
And a Heaven in a Wild Flower,
Hold Infinity in the palm of your hand
And Eternity in an hour.[46]

WORKS IN THIS EDITION

This Penguin edition gives the complete texts of *America*, *The Book of Thel*, *Europe*, *The First Book of Urizen*, *The Ghost of Abel*, *The Marriage of Heaven and Hell*, *The Song of Los*, *Songs of Innocence and of Experience*, *Tiriel* and *Visions of the Daughters of Albion*. There are extensive passages from *Poetical Sketches*, Blake's Notebook, *Vala* or *The Four Zoa's*, *Milton*, *Jerusalem*, The Ballads Manuscript, and *For the Sexes: The Gates of Paradise*.

The chief omissions for reasons of space are *The Book of Los* (1795), *The Book of Ahania* (1795) and some manuscript poems, including drafts of poems in *Songs of Experience*.

Of course the illustrations that accompanied most of these poems are missing, though some of the more important ones are described in the Notes.

The chief anomaly in the selection of Blake's poetry, aside from the absence of the intrinsic designs, is the inclusion of *The Marriage of Heaven and Hell* ([1790]) which is in prose except for brief poems at the beginning and end. *The Marriage* is included here because it is central to Blake's thought and because it demonstrates the consistency and longevity of his ideas – and also because it is witty and wonderfully impudent. Many of the same ideas and occasionally the same words of *The Marriage* are repeated, for instance, in 'The Everlasting Gospel' ([?1826]). Further, part of its proverbial form, as in its 'Proverbs of Hell', is prevalent elsewhere, for example in 'An Ancient Proverb' in his Notebook. *The Marriage of Heaven and Hell* is not poetic in form, but it is wonderfully helpful in understanding Blake's formal poetry – and its conception is certainly poetic.

My work on this volume is dedicated to BBB Invicta.

NOTES

1. Robert Hunt, review of 'Mr. Blake's Exhibition', *The Examiner*, 17 September 1809. See G. E. Bentley, Jr, *Blake Records* (second edition, New Haven and London: Yale University Press, 2004), p. 283, the source of the biographical facts here.
2. Allan Cunningham, *Lives of the Most Eminent British Painters, Sculptors, and Architects* (1830). See *Blake Records*, pp. 655, 656.
3. *Blake Records*, p. 310.
4. G. E. Bentley, Jr, *The Stranger from Paradise: A Biography of William Blake* (2001), p. 80.
5. A. C. Swinburne, *William Blake* (1868), p. 8.
6. *The Marriage of Heaven and Hell*, pl. 27, ¶92, *Visions*, pl. 11, l. 215, *America*, pl. 10, l. 71, *Vala*, pl. 34, l. 79. All quotations cited in this Introduction, if not appearing in the main text, are taken from *William Blake's Writings*, edited by G. E. Bentley, Jr (1978).
7. 'A Dream', 16; 'The Little Boy Found', 4; 'Night', 12–13; 'A Cradle Song', 24, 32.
8. 'Introduction' to *Songs of Experience*, 12, 8–9; 'Earth's Answer', 5, 14, 7, 11.
9. *The Stranger from Paradise*, pp. 132, 144–8.
10. *The Marriage of Heaven and Hell* (?1790), pl. 25; *America* (1793) pl. 8.
11. *The First Book of Urizen* (1794), pl. 10, l. 190; *Vala* ([?1796–?1807]), p. 54, l. 4; *Milton* (1804[–11]), pl. b, l. 6.
12. *The First Book of Urizen*, pl. 10, l. 184; *Vala*, p. 54, l. 1.
13. *Jerusalem*, pl. 10, l. 20.
14. J. T. Smith (1828) in *Blake Records*, pp. 606–7.
15. More recent plays include Elliot Hayes, *Blake's Innocence and Experience* (1983); Jack Shepherd, *In Lambeth* (1990), with the Blakes naked in a tree in their Lambeth garden; George Coates, *20/20* (1996), in which Urizen plays the bass guitar; and Thomas Kilroy, *Blake* (2001).
16. Letter of 1 September 1800.
17. *Blake Records*, p. 120; see p. 121.
18. J. T. Smith in *Blake Records*, p. 606.
19. George Richmond's letter of 15 August 1827, *Blake Records*, p. 464.
20. See Donald Fitch, *Blake Set to Music: A Bibliography of Musical Settings of the Poems and Prose of William Blake* (Berkeley, Los Angeles and Oxford: University of California Press, 1990).
21. Margaret La France, *An Island in the Moon* (1983) and *The Marriage of Heaven and Hell* (1983), and T. A. Smirnov, *Tiriel: Oper nach William Blake* (1989).
22. 'You say their Pictures', *William Blake's Writings*, edited by G. E.

Bentley, Jr (1978), p. 953; this text is the source of Blake's writings cited in this Introduction.

23. Vision of the Last Judgement in Notebook, p. 94; marginalia to Bishop Watson, *Apology for the Bible* (1797), p. 5; *Milton*, pl. c, l. 13 (*William Blake's Writings*, pp. 336, 1026, 1409).
24. Blake's marginalia (1798) to Watson's *Apology for the Bible* (1797), p. 23 and title-page verso (*William Blake's Writings*, p. 1420).
25. The doggerel 'a Petty sneaking Knave' is from Blake's Notebook, p. 29, in *William Blake's Writings*, p. 940; the letter is of 9 June 1818 in *William Blake's Writings*, p. 1648.
26. So Catherine Blake said about 1810 (*Blake Records*, p. 294). Blake wrote of himself: 'The artist is an inhabitant of that happy country', i.e. Eden (*Descriptive Catalogue*, ¶74).
27. 'Vision of the Last Judgment', Notebook, pp. 84, 94 (*William Blake's Writings*, pp. 1026, 1021).
28. *The Marriage of Heaven and Hell*, pl. 7.
29. 'Vision of the Last Judgment', Notebook, p. 95 (*William Blake's Writings*, p. 1027).
30. 'The Everlasting Gospel', part e, ll. 1–2, 13–14.
31. *Descriptive Catalogue* (1809), ¶68.
32. Blake believed that Isaac Newton's invariable laws of physical nature ignored or denied spiritual agency.
33. 'Laocoon', ¶26. 24–9 (*William Blake's Writings*, pp. 665, 666).
34. *Blake Records*, pp. 234, 631n, *The Marriage of Heaven and Hell*, pl. 12, ¶31.
35. 'I rose up at the dawn of day', 9–14 (*William Blake's Writings*, p. 965).
36. *Blake Records*, p. 404.
37. Alexander Gilchrist, *Life of William Blake, 'Pictor Ignotus'* (1863), p. 69 (*Blake Records*, p. 45).
38. For details of when he printed which copies, see Joseph Viscomi's magisterial *William Blake and the Idea of the Book* (1993).
39. *Vala*, p. 90, ll. 36–7.
40. Letter of 7 October 1803 (*William Blake's Writings*, p. 1582).
41. Letter of 19 December 1808 (*William Blake's Writings*, pp. 1644, 1645).
42. See G. E. Bentley, Jr, '"What Is the Price of Experience?" William Blake and the Economics of Illuminated Printing', *University of Toronto Quarterly*, LXVIII (1999), pp. 617–41.
43. The easiest ways to see coloured copies of Blake's works in Illuminated Printing are in *The Complete Illuminated Books*, ed. David Bindman (2000) and in the William Blake Archive online at <http.iath.virginia.edu/blake>
44. When Catherine Blake was on her deathbed on 18 October 1831, she 'passed the remaining time – about five hours – calmly and cheerfully; "repeating texts of scripture, and calling continually to her William,

as if he were only in the next room, to say she was coming to him, and would not be long now"' (*Blake Records*, pp. 545–6, quoting Gilchrist quoting Tatham).

45. *Jerusalem*, pl. 95, l. 20.
46. 'Auguries of Innocence', 1–4.

A Note on the Texts

SOURCES OF TEXTS

Blake's works printed here derive from three kinds of originals:

(1) Conventional typography: *Poetical Sketches*, *The French Revolution*, and 'To the Queen'. The first two were not published at all, and the third was not published by Blake.
(2) Unique manuscripts: 'An Island in the Moon', 'Songs by Shepherds', *Tiriel*, 'A Fairy Leapt', *Vala* or *The Four Zoa's*, letters, and the Ballads Manuscript; *Tiriel*, the Notebook and *Vala* are extensively illustrated.
(3) The unique method of etching, which Blake invented and called Illuminated Printing, in which designs and text are combined on the same page. This is the method in which virtually all his poetry was published, including *Songs of Innocence*, *The Book of Thel*, *The Marriage of Heaven and Hell*, *Visions of the Daughters of Albion*, *America*, *Songs of Experience*, *Europe*, *The First Book of Urizen*, *The Song of Los*, *Milton*, *Jerusalem*, *The Ghost of Abel*, and *For the Sexes: The Gates of Paradise*. Coloured copies of each of Blake's works in Illuminated Printing are reproduced in *The Complete Illuminated Books*, edited by David Bindman (2000) and online in the William Blake Archive (University of Virginia), the latter often with several copies reproduced.

The first two sources present relatively simple and familiar problems of transcription, except of course for the illustrations, particularly to *Tiriel* and *Vala*.

Illuminated Printing is very different, for the designs are intrinsic to the texts and often significantly affect the reader's understanding of the work. For instance, in 'The Tyger', the ferocious and voracious tiger of the text is depicted in the accompanying design as a smug creature looking much like a child's stuffed toy. In 'London', the narrator who 'mark[s] in every face I meet Marks of weakness, marks of woe' is depicted in the accompanying design as a blind old man being led through the streets by a child – he cannot see 'every face I meet' at all – and in *Jerusalem*, pl. 84, a remarkably similar design, reversed, is identified as 'London blind & age-bent begging thro the Streets of Babylon, led by a child; his tears running down his beard'. Any text of Blake's works in Illuminated Printing which omits the designs presents something very different from what Blake had intended.

Further, the colouring of the designs may make a significant difference in the interpretation of the poems. In general, Blake and his wife coloured the designs in early copies (before 1800) very lightly, while in late copies the colouring is heavy and includes the text as well as the design, sometimes making the text difficult to read. Clearly many of Blake's early readers were more interested in the designs than in the poems.

PUNCTUATION

Blake's punctuation is sparse and idiosyncratic. In particular, Blake rarely used quotation marks and frequently omitted apostrophes in possessives. I have silently added punctuation where there might otherwise be confusion: for instance, Blake's 'Ill' becomes 'I'll', 'well' becomes 'we'll, and 'wont' becomes 'won't'.

SPELLING

I have retained Blake's eighteenth-century and sometimes idiosyncratic spelling (e.g., 'Tyger', 'center', 'shew', 'recieve') but have silently corrected mere errors in transcription (e.g., 'the' for 'thee', 'here' for 'hear'). He regularly omitted the 'e' in verbs in the past tense, which can be a source of ambiguity, as in 'wood' for 'wooed', but I have not corrected this.

DESIGNS

The most important designs in the works in Illuminated Printing are briefly described in the Notes: *Songs of Innocence*, *The Book of Thel*, *The Marriage of Heaven and Hell*, *Visions of the Daughters of Albion*,

America, *Songs of Experience*, *Europe*, *The First Book of Urizen*, *The Song of Los*, *Milton*, *Jerusalem* and *For the Sexes: The Gates of Paradise*. The designs in the illustrated manuscripts (*Tiriel*, the Notebook and *Vala*) are largely ignored. Blake made no design for *Poetical Sketches*, 'An Island in the Moon', 'Songs by Shepherds', 'A Fairy leapt', 'I Asked a Thief', Letters, 'To the Queen', and the Ballads Manuscript.

SOURCES OF INFORMATION IN THE PRESENT EDITION

Facts about Blake's life here derive from G. E. Bentley, Jr, *Blake Records* (second edition, New Haven and London: Yale University Press for the Paul Mellon Centre for Studies in British Art, 2004). See also G. E. Bentley, Jr, *The Stranger from Paradise: A Biography of William Blake* (New Haven and London: Yale University Press for the Paul Mellon Centre for Studies in British Art, 2001).

Bibliographical information about Blake's books (such as copy and plate number) and manuscripts (such as page number and location), commercial books for which he made engravings, and writings about him comes chiefly from G. E. Bentley, Jr, *Blake Books* (Oxford: Clarendon Press, 1977) and *Blake Books Supplement* (Oxford: Clarendon Press, 1995).

Line numbers are identified and texts and notes are adapted from *William Blake's Writings*, edited by G. E. Bentley, Jr (1978), where the full texts and all significant designs to his works in Illuminated Printing may be found. These texts are based upon personal examination of all known copies of Blake's writings from Munich to Melbourne. The transcriptions of manuscripts here omit all but the most important deletions and corrections.

Dates given in the Contents and the text are dates of composition, and fuller information is provided in the Notes.

LAYOUT

Some of the longer poems in this selection are set as they appeared in manuscript or etched form, and an indication is given in square brackets in the margin where a new page or plate began. Each of these pages or plates is line-numbered separately and ellipses indicate where lines have been omitted. The poems to which this applies are *Vala*, *Milton* and *Jerusalem*. In addition, Blake wrote several versions of sections of *Vala* and reorganized the poem so that the page numbering is often out of sequence and jumps backwards and forwards, with the same page number occurring in different places.

SELECTED POEMS

Poetical Sketches by W. B.

(London: Printed in the Year MDCC LXXXIII [1783])

ADVERTISEMENT

The following Sketches were the production of untutored youth, commenced in his twelfth, and occasionally resumed by the author till his twentieth year; since which time, his talents having been wholly directed to the attainment of excellence in his profession, he has been deprived of the leisure requisite to such a revisal of these sheets, as might have rendered them less unfit to meet the public eye.

Conscious of the irregularities and defects to be found in almost every page, his friends have still believed that they possessed a poetical originality, which merited some respite from oblivion. These their opinions remain, however, to be now reproved or confirmed by a less partial public.

TO SPRING

O thou, with dewy locks, who lookest down
Thro' the clear windows of the morning; turn
Thine angel eyes upon our western isle,
Which in full choir hails thy approach, O Spring!

The hills tell each other, and the list'ning
Vallies hear; all our longing eyes are turned
Up to thy bright pavillions: issue forth,
And let thy holy feet visit our clime.

Come o'er the eastern hills, and let our winds
Kiss thy perfumed garments; let us taste
Thy morning and evening breath; scatter thy pearls
Upon our love-sick land that mourns for thee.

O deck her forth with thy fair fingers; pour
Thy soft kisses on her bosom; and put
Thy golden crown upon her languish'd head,
Whose modest tresses were bound up for thee!

TO SUMMER

O thou, who passest thro' our vallies in
Thy strength, curb thy fierce steeds, allay the heat
That flames from their large nostrils! thou, O Summer,
Oft pitched'st here thy golden tent, and oft,
Beneath our oaks hast slept, while we beheld
With joy, thy ruddy limbs and flourishing hair.

Beneath our thickest shades we oft have heard
Thy voice, when noon upon his fervid car
Rode o'er the deep of heaven; beside our springs
Sit down, and in our mossy vallies, on
Some bank beside a river clear, throw thy
Silk draperies off, and rush into the stream:
Our vallies love the Summer in his pride.

Our bards are fam'd who strike the silver wire:
Our youth are bolder than the southern swains:
Our maidens fairer in the sprightly dance:
We lack not songs, nor instruments of joy,
Nor echoes sweet, nor waters clear as heaven,
Nor laurel wreaths against the sultry heat.

TO AUTUMN

O autumn, laden with fruit, and stained
With the blood of the grape, pass not, but sit
Beneath my shady roof, there thou may'st rest,
And tune thy jolly voice to my fresh pipe;
And all the daughters of the year shall dance!
Sing now the lusty song of fruits and flowers.

'The narrow bud opens her beauties to
The sun, and love runs in her thrilling veins;
Blossoms hang round the brows of morning, and
Flourish down the bright cheek of modest eve
Till clust'ring Summer breaks forth into singing,
And feather'd clouds strew flowers round her head.

'The spirits of the air live on the smells
Of fruit; and joy, with pinions light, roves round
The garden, or sits singing in the trees.'
Thus sang the jolly Autumn as he sat,
Then rose, girded himself, and o'er the bleak
Hills fled from our sight; but left his golden load.

TO WINTER

O winter! Bar thine adamantine doors:
The north is thine; there hast thou built thy dark
Deep-founded habitation. Shake not thy roofs,
Nor bend thy pillars with thine iron car.

He hears me not, but o'er the yawning deep
Rides heavy; his storms are unchain'd; sheathed
In ribbed steel, I dare not lift mine eyes;
For he hath rear'd his sceptre o'er the world.

Lo! now the direful monster, whose skin clings
To his strong bones, strides o'er the groaning rocks:
He withers all in silence, and his hand
Unclothes the earth, and freezes up frail life.

He takes his seat upon the cliffs, the mariner
Cries in vain. Poor little wretch! That deal'st
With storms; till heaven smiles, and the monster
Is driv'n yelling to his caves beneath mount Hecla.

TO THE EVENING STAR

Thou fair-hair'd angel of the evening,
Now, whilst the sun rests on the mountains, light
Thy bright torch of love; thy radiant crown
Put on, and smile upon our evening bed!
Smile on our loves; and, while thou drawest the
Blue curtains of the sky, scatter thy silver dew
On every flower that shuts its sweet eyes
In timely sleep. Let thy west wind sleep on
The lake; speak silence with thy glimmering eyes,
And wash the dusk with silver. Soon, full soon,
Dost thou withdraw; then the wolf rages wide,
And the lion glares thro' the dun forest:
The fleeces of our flocks are cover'd with
Thy sacred dew; protect them with thine influence.

SONG

How sweet I roam'd from field to field,
  And tasted all the summer's pride,
'Till I the prince of love beheld,
  Who in the sunny beams did glide!

He shew'd me lilies for my hair,
  And blushing roses for my brow;
He led me through his gardens fair,
  Where all his golden pleasures grow.

With sweet May dews my wings were wet,
  And Phœbus fir'd my vocal rage;
He caught me in his silken net,
  And shut me in his golden cage.

He loves to sit and hear me sing,
  Then, laughing, sports and plays with me;
Then stretches out my golden wing,
  And mocks my loss of liberty.

SONG

My silks and fine array;
  My smiles and languish'd air,
By love are driv'n away;
  And mournful lean Despair
Brings me yew to deck my grave:
Such end true lovers have.

His face is fair as heav'n,
  When springing buds unfold;
O why to him was't giv'n,
  Whose heart is wintry cold?
His breast is love's all worship'd tomb,
Where all love's pilgrims come.

Bring me an axe and spade,
  Bring me a winding sheet;
When I my grave have made,
  Let winds and tempests beat:
Then down I'll lie, as cold as clay.
True love doth pass away!

MAD SONG

The wild winds weep,
  And the night is a-cold;
Come hither, Sleep,
  And my griefs infold:
But lo! The morning peeps
  Over the eastern steeps,
And the rustling birds of dawn
The earth do scorn.

Lo! To the vault
  Of paved heaven,
With sorrow fraught
  My notes are driven:

They strike the ear of night,
  Make weep the eyes of day;
They make mad the roaring winds,
  And with tempests play.

Like a fiend in a cloud
  With howling woe,
After night I do croud,
  And with night will go;
I turn my back to the east,
From whence comforts have increas'd;
For light doth seize my brain
With frantic pain.

TO THE MUSES

Whether on Ida's shady brow,
  Or in the chambers of the East,
The chambers of the sun, that now
  From antient melody have ceas'd;

Whether in Heav'n ye wander fair,
  Or the green corners of the earth,
Or the blue regions of the air,
  Where the melodious winds have birth;

Whether on crystal rocks ye rove,
  Beneath the bosom of the sea
Wand'ring in many a coral grove,
  Fair Nine, forsaking Poetry!

How have you left the antient love
  That bards of old enjoy'd in you!
The languid strings do scarcely move!
  The sound is forc'd, the notes are few!

An Island in the Moon
(Manuscript [c. 1784])

Quid— 'Oho' said Doctor Johnson
To Scipio Africanus
'If you don't own me a Philosopher
I'll kick your Roman Anus.'

Suction— 'A ha' To Doctor Johnson
Said Scipio Africanus,
'Lift up my Roman Petticoat
And kiss my Roman Anus.'

Songs by Shepherds
(Manuscript [?1787])

Song 1st by a Shepherd

1st

Welcome stranger to this place,
Where joy doth sit on Every bough,
Paleness flies from every face,
We reap not, what we do not sow.

2nd

Innocence doth like a Rose,
Bloom on every Maiden's cheek;
Honor twines around her brows,
The jewel Health adorns her neck.

Song 2d by a Young Shepherd

1st

'When the trees do laugh with our merry Wit,
And the green hill laughs with the noise of it,
When the meadows laugh with lively green
And the grasshopper laughs in the merry scene,

2d

'When the greenwood laughs with the voice of joy,
And the dimpling stream runs laughing by,
When Edessa, & Lyca, and Emilie,
With their sweet round mouths sing ha, ha, he,

3d

'When the painted Birds laugh in the shade,
Where our table with cherries & nuts is spread;
Come live & be merry & join with me
To sing the sweet chorus of ha, ha, he.'

Song 3d by an old Shepherd

1st

When silver snow decks Sylvio's cloaths
And jewel hangs at shepherd's nose,
We can abide life's pelting storm
That makes our limbs quake, if our hearts be warm.

2d

Whilst Virtue is our walking staff,
And truth a lantern to our path;
We can abide life's pelting storm
That makes our limbs quake, if our hearts be warm.

3d

Blow boisterous Wind, stern Winter frown,
Innocence is a winter's gown;
So clad, we'll abide life's pelting storm
That makes our limbs quake, if our hearts be warm.

Tiriel
(Manuscript [c. 1789])

I

And Aged Tiriel stood before the Gates of his beautiful palace
With Myratana, once the Queen of all the western plains,
But now his eyes were darkned, & his wife fading in death.
They stood before their once delightful palace, & thus the Voice
Of aged Tiriel arose, that his sons might hear in their gates:

'Accursed race of Tiriel, behold your father.
Come forth & look on her that bore you. Come you accursed sons.
In my weak arms I here have born your dying mother.
Come forth sons of the Curse, come forth, see the death of
Myratana.'

His sons ran from their gates & saw their aged parents stand
And thus the eldest son of Tiriel raisd his mighty voice:

'Old man, unworthy to be calld the father of Tiriel's race,
For every one of those thy wrinkles, each of those grey hairs
Are cruel as death & as obdurate as the devouring pit.
Why should thy sons care for thy curses, thou accursed man?
Were we not slaves till we rebeld? Who cares for Tiriel's curse?
His blessing was a cruel curse. His curse may be a blessing.'

He ceast; the aged man raisd up his right hand to the heavens;
His left supported Myratana shrinking in pangs of death.
The orbs of his large eyes he opend, & thus his voice went forth:

'Serpents, not sons, wreathing around the bones of Tiriel,
Ye worms of death feasting upon your aged parents' flesh,
Listen & hear your mother's groans. No more accursed Sons
She bears. She groans not at the birth of Heuxos or Yuva.
These are the groans of death, ye serpents, These are the groans of
death.
Nourishd with milk ye serpents, nourishd with mother's tears &
cares.
Look at my eyes blind as the orbless scull among the stones,
Look at my bald head. Hark, listen ye serpents, listen!

What Myratana? What my wife? O Soul! O Spirit! O Fire!
What Myratana? Art thou dead? Look here, ye serpents, look!
The serpents sprung from her own bowels have draind her dry as
this.
Curse on your ruthless heads, for I will bury her even here.'

So saying he began to dig a grave with his aged hands
But Heuxos calld a son of Zazel to dig their mother a grave.

'Old cruelty, desist & let us dig a grave for thee.
Thou hast refusd our charity, thou hast refusd our food,
Thou hast refusd our clothes, our beds, our houses for thy dwelling
Chusing to wander like a Son of Zazel in the rocks.
Why dost thou curse; is not the curse now come upon your head?
Was it not you enslavd the sons of Zazel, & they have cursd
And now you feel it. Dig a grave & let us bury our mother.'

'There take the body, cursed sons, & may the heavens rain wrath
As thick as northern fogs around your gates to choke you up
That you may lie as now your mother lies, like dogs cast out,
The stink of your dead carcases annoying man & beast
Till your white bones are bleached with age for a memorial.
No, your remembrance shall perish, for when your carcases
Lie stinking on the earth, the buriers shall arise from the east
And not a bone of all the sons of Tiriel remain.
Bury your mother but you cannot bury the curse of Tiriel.'

He ceast & darkling oer the mountains sought his pathless way.

2

He wandered day & night; to him both day & night were dark.
The sun he felt but the bright moon was now a useless globe.
Oer mountains & thro vales of woe, the blind & aged man
Wanderd till he that leadeth all led him to the vales of Har

And Har & Heva like two children sat beneath the Oak.
Mnetha now aged waited on them, & brought them food & clothing
But they were as the shadow of Har, & as the years forgotten,
Playing with flowers & running after birds they spent the day
And in the night like infants slept delighted with infant dreams.

Soon as the blind wanderer enterd the pleasant gardens of Har
They ran weeping like frighted infants for refuge in Mnetha's arms.
The blind man felt his way & cried 'Peace to these open doors.
Let no one fear, for poor blind Tiriel hurts none but himself.
Tell me O friends where I am now, & in what pleasant place.'

'This is the valley of Har,' said Mnetha '& this the tent of Har.
Who art thou poor blind man, that takest the name of Tiriel on thee?
Tiriel is king of all the west. Who art thou? I am Mnetha
And this is Har & Heva, trembling like infants by my side.'

'I know Tiriel is king of the west & there he lives in joy.
No matter who I am O Mnetha. If thou hast any food
Give it me, for I cannot stay; my journey is far from hence.'

Then Har said 'O my mother Mnetha, venture not so near him
For he is the king of rotten wood & of the bones of death.
He wanders without eyes & passes thro thick walls & doors.
Thou shalt not smite my mother Mnetha, O thou eyeless man.'

'A wanderer, I beg for food. You see I cannot weep.
I cast away my staff the kind companion of my travel
And I kneel down that you may see I am a harmless man.'

He kneeled down & Mnetha said, 'Come Har & Heva, rise.
He is an innocent old man & hungry with his travel.'

Then Har arose & laid his hand upon old Tiriel's head.

'God bless thy poor bald pate. God bless thy hollow winking eyes.
God bless thy shriveld beard. God bless thy many wrinkled forehead.
Thou hast no teeth old man & thus I kiss thy sleek bald head.
Heva, come kiss his bald head for he will not hurt us Heva.'

Then Heva came & took old Tiriel in her mother's arms.

'Bless thy poor eyes old man, & bless the old father of Tiriel.
Thou art my Tiriel's old father. I know thee thro thy wrinkles
Because thou smellest like the figtree, thou smellest like ripe figs.
How didst thou lose thy eyes old Tiriel? Bless thy wrinkled face.'

Mnetha said, 'come in, aged wanderer, tell us of thy name.
Why shouldest thou conceal thyself from those of thine own flesh?'

'I am not of this region', said Tiriel dissemblingly.
'I am an aged wanderer, once father of a race
Far in the north, but they were wicked & were all destroyd
And I their father sent an outcast. I have told you all.
Ask me no more I pray for grief hath seald my precious sight.'

'O Lord,' said Mnetha, 'how I tremble; are there then more people,
More human creatures on this earth beside the sons of Har?'

'No more,' said Tiriel 'but I remain on all this globe
And I remain an outcast. Hast thou any thing to drink?'

Then Mnetha gave him milk & fruits, & they sat down together.

3

They sat & eat & Har & Heva smild on Tiriel.

'Thou art a very old old man but I am older than thou.
How came thine hair to leave thy forehead? How came thy face so
brown?
My hair is very long, my beard doth cover all my breast.
God bless thy piteous face. To count the wrinkles in thy face
Would puzzle Mnetha. Bless thy face for thou art Tiriel.'

'Tiriel I never saw but once. I sat with him & eat.
He was as cheerful as a prince & gave me entertainment
But long I staid not at his palace for I am forcd to wander.'

'What wilt thou leave us too?' said Heva, 'thou shalt not leave us
too
For we have many sports to shew thee & many songs to sing
And after dinner we will walk into the cage of Har
And thou shalt help us to catch birds & gather them ripe cherries.
Then let thy name be Tiriel & never leave us more.'

'If thou dost go,' said Har 'I wish thine eyes may see thy folly.
My sons have left me; did thine leave thee? O twas very cruel!'

'No venerable man,' said Tiriel 'ask me not such things
For thou dost make my heart to bleed; my sons were not like thine
but worse. O never ask me more or I must flee away.'

'Thou shalt not go,' said Heva 'till thou hast seen our singing birds
And heard Har sing in the great cage & slept upon our fleeces.
Go not for thou art so like Tiriel, that I love thine head
Tho it is wrinkled like the earth parchd with the summer heat.'

Then Tiriel rose up from the seat & said 'god bless these tents.
My Journey is oer rocks & mountains, not in pleasant vales.
I must not sleep nor rest because of madness & dismay.'

And Mnetha said, 'Thou must not go to wander dark alone
But dwell with us & let us be to thee instead of eyes
And I will bring thee food old man, till death shall call thee hence.'

Then Tiriel frownd & answered: 'Did I not command you saying
"Madness & deep dismay possess the heart of the blind man
The wanderer who seeks the woods leaning upon his staff?"'

Then Mnetha trembling at his frowns led him to the tent door
And gave to him his staff & blest him. He went on his way

But Har & Heva stood & watchd him till he enterd the wood
And then they went & wept to Mnetha, but they soon forgot their
tears.

4

Over the weary hills the blind man took his lonely way.
To him the day & night alike was dark & desolate
But far he had not gone when Ijim from his woods come down
Met him at entrance of the forest in a dark & lonely way.

'Who art thou Eyeless wretch that thus obstructs the lion's path?
Ijim shall rend thy feeble joints thou tempter of dark Ijim.
Thou hast the form of Tiriel but I know thee well enough.
Stand from my path foul fiend; is this the last of thy deceits
To be a hypocrite & stand in shape of a blind beggar?'

The blind man heard his brother's voice & kneeld down on his knee.

'O brother Ijim if it is thy voice that speaks to me
Smite not thy brother Tiriel tho weary of his life.
My sons have smitten me already, and if thou smitest me
The curse that rolls over their heads will rest itself on thine.
'Tis now seven years since in my palace I beheld thy face.'

'Come thou dark fiend, I dare thy cunning; know that Ijim scorns
To smite thee in the form of helpless age & eyeless policy.
Rise up for I discern thee & I dare thy eloquent tongue.
Come, I will lead thee on thy way & use thee as a scoff.'

'O Brother Ijim thou beholdest wretched Tiriel.
Kiss me my brother & then leave me to wander desolate.'

'No artful fiend, but I will lead thee; dost thou want to go?
Reply not lest I bind thee with green flags of the brook.
Ay now thou art discovered I will use thee like a slave.'

When Tiriel heard the words of Ijim he sought not to reply.
He knew twas vain for Ijim's words were as the voice of Fate.

And they went on together over hills thro woody dales
Blind to the pleasures of the sight & deaf to warbling birds.
All day they walked & all the night beneath the pleasant Moon
Westwardly journeying till Tiriel grew weary with his travel.

'O Ijim I am faint & weary for my knees forbid
To bear me further. Urge me not lest I should die with travel.
A little rest I crave, a little water from a brook
Or I shall soon discover that I am a mortal man
And you will lose your once lovd Tiriel; alas how faint I am!'

'Impudent fiend,' said Ijim, 'hold thy glib & eloquent tongue.
Tiriel is a king & thou the tempter of dark Ijim.
Drink of this running brook, & I will bear thee on my shoulders.'

He drank & Ijim raisd him up & bore him on his shoulders.
All day he bore him & when evening drew her solemn curtain
Enterd the gates of Tiriel's palace, & stood & calld aloud:

'Heuxos come forth; I here have brought the fiend that troubles Ijim!
Look, knowst thou ought of this grey beard, or of these blinded eyes?'

Heuxos & Lotho ran forth at the sound of Ijim's voice
And saw their aged father borne upon his mighty shoulders.
Their eloquent tongues were dumb & sweat stood on their trembling limbs.
They knew twas vain to strive with Ijim; they bowd & silent stood.

'What Heuxos, call thy father for I mean to sport to night.
This is the hypocrite that sometimes roars a dreadful lion.
Then I have rent his limbs & left him rotting in the forest
For birds to eat but I have scarce departed from the place
But like a tyger he would come & so I rent him too.
Then like a river he would seek to drown me in his waves
But soon I buffetted the torrent; anon like to a cloud
Fraught with the swords of lightning, but I braved the vengeance too.
Then he would creep like a bright serpent till around my neck
While I was Sleeping he would twine; I squeezd his poisnous soul.
Then like a toad or like a newt would whisper in my ears
Or like a rock stood in my way, or like a poisnous shrub.
At last I caught him in the form of Tiriel blind & old
And so I'll keep him; fetch your father, fetch forth Myratana.'

They stood confounded, and Thus Tiriel raised his silver voice:

'Serpents, not sons, why do you stand? Fetch hither Tiriel!
Fetch hither Myratana & delight yourselves with scoffs
For poor blind Tiriel is returnd & this much injurd head
Is ready for your bitter taunts. Come forth, sons of the curse!'

Mean time the other sons of Tiriel ran around their father.
Confounded at the terrible strength of Ijim they knew twas vain;
Both spear & shield were useless & the coat of iron mail
When Ijim stretchd his mighty arm. The arrow from his limbs
Rebounded & the piercing sword broke on his naked flesh.
'Then is it true Heuxos that thou hast turnd thy aged parent
To be the sport of wintry winds?' (said Ijim) 'is this true?
It is a lie & I am like the tree torn by the wind.

Thou eyeless fiend & you dissemblers. Is this Tiriel's house?
It is as false as Matha & as dark as vacant Orcus.
Escape ye fiends for Ijim will not lift his hand against ye.'

So saying, Ijim gloomy turnd his back & silent sought
The secret forests & all night wandered in desolate ways.

5

And aged Tiriel stood & said 'where does the thunder sleep?
Where doth he hide his terrible head & his swift & fiery daughters?
Where do they shroud their fiery wings & the terrors of their hair?
Earth thus I stamp thy bosom; rouse the earthquake from his den
To raise his dark & burning visage thro the cleaving ground
To thrust these towers with his shoulders. Let his fiery dogs
Rise from the center belching flames & roarings, dark smoke.
Where art thou Pestilence that bathest in fogs & standing lakes?
Rise up thy sluggish limbs, & let the loathsomest of poisons
Drop from thy garments as thou walkest wrapt in yellow clouds.
Here take thy seat in this wide court. Let it be strown with dead
And sit & smile upon these cursed sons of Tiriel.
Thunder & fire & pestilence, hear you not Tiriel's curse?'

He ceast; the heaving clouds confusd rolld round the lofty towers
Discharging their enormous voices. At the father's curse
The earth trembled, fires belched from the yawning clefts
And when the shaking ceast a fog possesst the accursed clime.

The cry was great in Tiriel's palace; his five daughters ran
And caught him by the garments weeping with cries of bitter woe.

'Aye now you feel the curse, you cry, but may all ears be deaf
As Tiriel's and all eyes as blind as Tiriel's to your woes.
May never stars shine on your roofs; may never sun nor moon
Visit you but eternal fogs hover around your walls.
Hela, my youngest daughter, you shall lead me from this place
And let the curse fall on the rest & wrap them up together.'

He ceast & Hela led her father from the noisom place.
In haste they fled while all the sons & daughters of Tiriel
Chaind in thick darkness utterd cries of mourning all the night
And in the morning Lo an hundred men in ghastly death.

The four daughters stretchd on the marble pavement silent all
Falln by the pestilence, the rest moped round in guilty fears.

And all the children in their beds were cut off in one night.
Thirty of Tiriel's sons remained, to wither in the palace
Desolate, Loathed, Dumb, Astonishd waiting for black death.

6

And Hela led her father thro the silent of the night
Astonishd silent, till the morning beams began to spring.

'Now Hela I can go with pleasure & dwell with Har & Heva.
Now that the curse shall clean devour all those guilty sons.
This is the right & ready way, I know it by the sound
That our feet make. Remember Hela I have savd thee from death.
Then be obedient to thy father for the curse is taken off thee.
I dwelt with Myratana five years in the desolate rock
And all that time we waited for the fire to fall from heaven
Or for the torrents of the sea to overwhelm you all
But now my wife is dead & all the time of grace is past
You see the parent's curse. Now lead me where I have commanded.'

'O Leagued with evil spirits thou accursed man of sin!
True, I was born thy slave; who askd thee to save me from death?
Twas for thy self thou cruel man because thou wantest eyes.'

'True Hela this is the desert of all those cruel ones.
Is Tiriel cruel? Look. His daughter & his youngest daughter
Laughs at affection, glories in rebellion, scoffs at Love!
I have not eat these two days; lead me to Har & Heva's tent
Or I will wrap thee up in such a terrible father's curse
That thou shalt feel worms in thy marrow creeping thro thy bones
Yet thou shalt lead me. Lead me I command to Har & Heva.'

'O cruel! O destroyer! O consumer! O avenger!
To Har & Heva will I lead thee; then would that they would curse.
Then would they curse as thou hast cursed but they are not like thee.
O they are holy & forgiving filld with loving mercy
Forgetting the offences of their most rebellious children
Or else thou wouldest not have livd to curse thy helpless children.'

'Look on my eyes Hela & see for thou hast eyes to see
The tears swell from my stony fountains. Wherefore do I weep?
Wherefore from my blind orbs art thou not siezd with poisnous
stings?
Laugh serpent youngest venomous reptile of the flesh of Tiriel.
Laugh, for thy father Tiriel shall give thee cause to laugh
Unless thou lead me to the tent of Har, child of the curse.'

'Silence thy evil tongue, thou murderer of thy helpless children.
I lead thee to the tent of Har, not that I mind thy curse
But that I feel they will curse thee & hang upon thy bones
Fell shaking agonies & in each wrinkle of that face
Plant worms of death to feast upon the tongue of terrible curses.'

'Hela, my daughter, listen. Thou art the daughter of Tiriel.
Thy father calls. Thy father lifts his hand into the heavens
For thou hast laughed at my tears & curst thy aged father.
Let snakes rise from thy bedded locks & laugh among thy curls.'

He ceast; her dark hair upright stood while snakes infolded round
Her madding brows. Her shrieks appalld the soul of Tiriel.

'What have I done, Hela my daughter? Fearst thou now the curse
Or wherefore dost thou cry? Ah wretch to curse thy aged father!
Lead me to Har & Heva & the curse of Tiriel
Shall fail. If thou refuse, howl in the desolate mountains.'

7

She howling led him over mountains & thro frighted vales
Till to the caves of Zazel they approached at even tide.

Forth from their caves Old Zazal & his sons ran when they saw
Their tyrant prince blind & his daughter howling & leading him.

They laughd & mocked; some threw dirt & stones as they passd by
But when Tiriel turnd around & raised his awful voice
Some fled away but Zazel stood still & thus begun:
'Bald tyrant. Wrinkled cunning, listen to Zazel's chains.
Twas thou that chaind thy brother Zazel. Where are now thine eyes?
Shout beautiful daughter of Tiriel. Thou singest a sweet song!
Where are you going? Come & eat some roots & drink some water.

Thy crown is bald, old man; the sun will dry thy brains away
And thou wilt be as foolish as thy foolish brother Zazel.'

The blind man heard & smote his breast & trembling passed on.
They threw dirt after them, till to the covert of a wood
The howling maiden led her father where wild beasts resort
Hoping to end her woes, but from her cries the tygers fled.
All night they wanderd thro the wood & when the sun arose
They enterd on the mountains of Har; at Noon the happy tents
Were frighted by the dismal cries of Hela on the mountains

But Har & Heva slept fearless as babes on loving breasts.
Mnetha awoke; she ran & stood at the tent door & saw
The aged wanderer led towards the tents; she took her bow
And chose her arrows, then advancd to meet the terrible pair.

8

And Mnetha hasted & met them at the gate of the lower garden.

'Stand still or from my bow receive a sharp & winged death.'

Then Tiriel stood, saying 'what soft voice threatens such bitter things?
Lead me to Har & Heva. I am Tiriel King of the west!'

And Mnetha led them to the tent of Har, and Har & Heva
Ran to the door. When Tiriel felt the ankles of aged Har
He said, 'O weak mistaken father of a lawless race,
Thy laws O Har & Tiriel's wisdom end together in a curse.
Why is one law given to the lion & the patient Ox?
And why men bound beneath the heavens in a reptile form
A worm of sixty winters creeping on the dusky ground?
The child springs from the womb. The father ready stands to form
The infant head while the mother idle plays with her dog on her couch.
The young bosom is cold for lack of mother's nourishment & milk
Is cut off from the weeping mouth with difficulty & pain.
The little lids are lifted & the little nostrils opend.
The father forms a whip to rouze the sluggish senses to act
And scourges off all youthful fancies from the newborn man.
Then walks the weak infant in sorrow compelld to number footsteps

And when the drone has reachd his crawling length
Black berries appear that poison all around him. Such was Tiriel,
Compelld to pray repugnant & to humble the immortal spirit
Till I am subtil as a serpent in a paradise
Consuming all both flowers & fruits, insects & warbling birds
And now my paradise is falln & a drear sandy plain
Returns my thirsty hissings in a curse on thee O Har
Mistaken father of a lawless race my voice is past.'

He ceast outstretchd at Har & Heva's feet in awful death.

Songs of Innocence

([London:] The Author & Printer W Blake, 1789)

Introduction

Piping down the valleys wild,
Piping songs of pleasant glee
On a cloud I saw a child,
And he laughing said to me:

'Pipe a song about a Lamb:'
So I piped with merry chear.
'Piper pipe that song again;'
So I piped, he wept to hear.

'Drop thy pipe, thy happy pipe;
Sing thy songs of happy chear.'
So I sung the same again,
While he wept with joy to hear.

'Piper, sit thee down and write
In a book that all may read.'
So he vanish'd from my sight
And I pluck'd a hollow reed

And I made a rural pen,
And I stain'd the water clear,
And I wrote my happy songs
Every child may joy to hear.

The Shepherd

How sweet is the Shepherd's sweet lot!
From the morn to the evening he strays;
He shall follow his sheep all the day
And his tongue shall be filled with praise.

For he hears the lamb's innocent call,
And he hears the ewe's tender reply.
He is watchful while they are in peace,
For they know when their Shepherd is nigh.

The Ecchoing Green

The Sun does arise,
And make happy the skies.
The merry bells ring
To welcome the Spring.
The sky-lark and thrush,
The birds of the bush,
Sing louder around,
To the bells' chearful sound,
While our sports shall be seen
On the Ecchoing Green.

Old John with white hair
Does laugh away care,
Sitting under the oak,
Among the old folk.
They laugh at our play,
And soon they all say:
'Such such were the joys
When we all girls & boys,
In our youth-time were seen
On the Ecchoing Green.'

Till the little ones weary
No more can be merry;
The sun does descend,
And our sports have an end:

Round the laps of their mothers
Many sisters and brothers,
Like birds in their nest,
Are ready for rest:
And sport no more seen,
On the darkening Green.

The Lamb

Little Lamb, who made thee?
Dost thou know who made thee?
Gave thee life & bid thee feed
By the stream & o'er the mead;
Gave thee clothing of delight,
Softest clothing wooly bright;
Gave thee such a tender voice,
Making all the vales rejoice;
Little Lamb, who made thee?
Dost thou know who made thee?

Little Lamb, I'll tell thee,
Little Lamb, I'll tell thee:
He is called by thy name,
For he calls himself a Lamb:
He is meek & he is mild,
He became a little child:
I a child & thou a lamb,
We are called by his name.
Little Lamb, God bless thee.
Little Lamb, God bless thee.

The Little Black Boy

My mother bore me in the southern wild,
And I am black, but O! my soul is white.
White as an angel is the English child:
But I am black as if bereav'd of light.

My mother taught me underneath a tree
And sitting down before the heat of day
She took me on her lap and kissed me
And pointing to the east began to say:

'Look on the rising sun! there God does live
And gives his light and gives his heat away;
And flowers and trees and beasts and men receive
Comfort in morning, joy in the noon day.

'And we are put on earth a little space,
That we may learn to bear the beams of love;
And these black bodies and this sun-burnt face
Is but a cloud, and like a shady grove.

'For when our souls have learn'd the heat to bear
The cloud will vanish; we shall hear his voice
Saying: "come out from the grove my love & care
And round my golden tent like lambs rejoice." '

Thus did my mother say and kissed me,
And thus I say to little English boy:
When I from black and he from white cloud free,
And round the tent of God like lambs we joy:

I'll shade him from the heat till he can bear
To lean in joy upon our father's knee
And then I'll stand and stroke his silver hair
And be like him and he will then love me.

The Blossom

Merry Merry Sparrow
Under leaves so green
A happy Blossom
Sees you swift as arrow
Seek your cradle narrow
Near my Bosom.

Pretty Pretty Robin
Under leaves so green
A happy Blossom
Hears you sobbing sobbing
Pretty Pretty Robin
Near my Bosom.

The Chimney Sweeper

When my mother died I was very young,
And my father sold me while yet my tongue
Could scarcely cry 'weep weep weep weep,'
So your chimneys I sweep & in soot I sleep.

There's little Tom Dacre, who cried when his head
That curl'd like a lamb's back was shav'd, so I said:
'Hush Tom, never mind it, for when your head's bare,
You know that the soot cannot spoil your white hair.'

And so he was quiet, & that very night,
As Tom was asleeping he had such a sight,
That thousands of sweepers, Dick, Joe, Ned & Jack
Were all of them lock'd up in coffins of black,

And by came an Angel who had a bright key,
And he open'd the coffins & set them all free.
Then down a green plain leaping laughing they run
And wash in a river and shine in the Sun.

Then naked & white, all their bags left behind,
They rise upon clouds, and sport in the wind.
And the Angel told Tom if he'd be a good boy,
He'd have God for his father & never want joy.

And so Tom awoke and we rose in the dark
And got with our bags & our brushes to work.
Tho' the morning was cold, Tom was happy & warm.
So if all do their duty, they need not fear harm.

The Little Boy lost

'Father, father, where are you going?
O do not walk so fast.
Speak, father, speak to your little boy
Or else I shall be lost.'

The night was dark, no father was there;
The child was wet with dew.
The mire was deep, & the child did weep
And away the vapour flew.

The Little Boy found

The little boy lost in the lonely fen,
Led by the wand'ring light,
Began to cry, but God ever nigh,
Appeard like his father in white.

He kissed the child & by the hand led
And to his mother brought,
Who in sorrow pale thro' the lonely dale
Her little boy weeping sought.

Laughing Song

When the green woods laugh with the voice of joy
And the dimpling stream runs laughing by,
When the air does laugh with our merry wit,
And the green hill laughs with the noise of it,

When the meadows laugh with lively green
And the grasshopper laughs in the merry scene,
When Mary and Susan and Emily
With their sweet round mouths sing 'Ha, Ha, He,'

When the painted birds laugh in the shade
Where our table with cherries and nuts is spread,
Come live & be merry and join with me,
To sing the sweet chorus of 'Ha, Ha, He.'

A CRADLE SONG

Sweet dreams form a shade
O'er my lovely infant's head.
Sweet dreams of pleasant streams,
By happy silent moony beams.

Sweet sleep with soft down
Weave thy brows an infant crown.
Sweet sleep Angel mild,
Hover o'er my happy child.

Sweet smiles in the night,
Hover over my delight
Sweet smiles, Mother's smiles
All the livelong night beguiles.

Sweet moans, dovelike sighs,
Chase not slumber from thy eyes.
Sweet moans, sweeter smiles,
All the dovelike moans beguiles.

Sleep, sleep, happy child.
All creation slept and smil'd.
Sleep, sleep, happy sleep,
While o'er thee thy mother weep.

Sweet babe, in thy face,
Holy image I can trace.
Sweet babe, once like thee
Thy maker lay and wept for me,

Wept for me, for thee, for all,
When he was an infant small.
Thou his image ever see,
Heavenly face that smiles on thee,

Smiles on thee, on me, on all,
Who became an infant small.
Infant smiles are his own smiles;
Heaven & earth to peace beguiles.

The Divine Image

To Mercy, Pity, Peace and Love
All pray in their distress:
And to these virtues of delight
Return their thankfulness.

For Mercy, Pity, Peace and Love
Is God our father dear:
And Mercy, Pity, Peace and Love
Is Man his child and care.

For Mercy has a human heart,
Pity a human face:
And Love, the human form divine,
And Peace, the human dress.

Then every man of every clime,
That prays in his distress,
Prays to the human form divine
Love, Mercy, Pity, Peace.

And all must love the human form,
In heathen, turk or jew.
Where Mercy, Love & Pity dwell
There God is dwelling too.

HOLY THURSDAY

Twas on a Holy Thursday, their innocent faces clean,
The children walking two & two in red & blue & green;
Grey headed beadles walkd before with wands as white as snow
Till into the high dome of Paul's they like Thames waters flow.

O what a multitude they seemd these flowers of London town!
Seated in companies they sit, with radiance all their own.
The hum of multitudes was there but multitudes of lambs,
Thousands of little boys & girls raising their innocent hands.

Now like a mighty wind they raise to heaven the voice of song,
Or like harmonious thunderings the seats of heaven among.
Beneath them sit the aged men, wise guardians of the poor;
Then cherish pity, lest you drive an angel from your door.

Night

The sun descending in the west,
The evening star does shine.
The birds are silent in their nest,
And I must seek for mine,
The moon like a flower
In heaven's high bower;
With silent delight
Sits and smiles on the night.

Farewell green fields and happy groves,
Where flocks have took delight;
Where lambs have nibbled, silent moves
The feet of angels bright;
Unseen they pour blessing,
And joy without ceasing,
On each bud and blossom,
And each sleeping bosom.

They look in every thoughtless nest,
Where birds are coverd warm;
They visit caves of every beast
To keep them all from harm:
If they see any weeping
That should have been sleeping
They pour sleep on their head
And sit down by their bed.

When wolves and tygers howl for prey
They pitying stand and weep;
Seeking to drive their thirst away,
And keep them from the sheep.
But if they rush dreadful,
The angels most heedful
Recieve each mild spirit
New worlds to inherit.

And there the lion's ruddy eyes
Shall flow with tears of gold:
And pitying the tender cries,
And walking round the fold:
Saying: 'Wrath by his meekness
And by his health sickness,
Is driven away
From our immortal day.

'And now beside thee, bleating lamb,
I can lie down and sleep;
Or think on him who bore thy name,
Graze after thee and weep.
For wash'd in life's river,
My bright mane for ever
Shall shine like the gold,
As I guard o'er the fold.'

Spring

Sound the Flute!
Now it's mute.
Birds delight
Day and Night.
Nightingale
In the dale,
Lark in Sky
Merrily
Merrily Merrily to welcome in the Year.

Little Boy
Full of joy;
Little Girl
Sweet and small;
Cock does crow,
So do you.
Merry voice,
Infant noise,
Merrily Merrily to welcome in the Year.

Little Lamb,
Here I am;
Come and lick
My white neck.
Let me pull
Your soft Wool.
Let me kiss
Your soft face,
Merrily Merrily we welcome in the Year.

Nurse's Song

When the voices of children are heard on the green
And laughing is heard on the hill,
My heart is at rest within my breast
And everything else is still.

'Then come home my children, the sun is gone down
And the dews of night arise;
Come, come, leave off play and let us away
Till the morning appears in the skies.'

'No no, let us play, for it is yet day
And we cannot go to sleep;
Besides in the sky, the little birds fly
And the hills are all coverd with sheep.'

'Well well go & play till the light fades away
And then go home to bed.'
The little ones leaped & shouted & laugh'd
And all the hills ecchoed.

Infant Joy

'I have no name;
I am but two days old.'
What shall I call thee?
'I happy am,
Joy is my name,'
Sweet joy befall thee!

Pretty joy!
Sweet joy but two days old,
Sweet joy I call thee;
Thou dost smile,
I sing the while,
Sweet joy befall thee.

A Dream

Once a dream did weave a shade
O'er my Angel-guarded bed,
That an Emmet lost its way
Where on grass methought I lay.

Troubled, wilderd and forlorn,
Dark benighted, travel-worn,
Over many a tangled spray
All heart-broke I heard her say:

'O my children! do they cry?
Do they hear their father sigh?
Now they look abroad to see,
Now return and weep for me.'

Pitying I drop'd a tear:
But I saw a glow-worm near
Who replied: 'What wailing wight
Calls the watchman of the night?

'I am set to light the ground,
While the beetle goes his round:
Follow now the beetle's hum.
Little wanderer, hie thee home.'

On Another's Sorrow

Can I see another's woe,
And not be in sorrow too?
Can I see another's grief
And not seek for kind relief?

Can I see a falling tear,
And not feel my sorrow's share,
Can a father see his child
Weep, nor be with sorrow filld?

Can a mother sit and hear
An infant groan, an infant fear?
No, no, never can it be.
Never never can it be.

And can he who smiles on all
Hear the wren with sorrows small,
Hear the small birds grief & care,
Hear the woes that infants bear

And not sit beside the nest
Pouring pity in their breast;
And not sit the cradle near
Weeping tear on infant's tear;

And not sit both night & day,
Wiping all our tears away?
O! no never can it be.
Never never can it be.

He doth give his joy to all.
He becomes an infant small.
He becomes a man of woe;
He doth feel the sorrow too.

Think not thou canst sigh a sigh,
And thy maker is not by.
Think not thou canst weep a tear
And thy maker is not near.

O! he gives to us his joy,
That our grief he may destroy;
Till our grief is fled & gone
He doth sit by us and moan.

The Little Girl Lost

In futurity
I prophetic see,
That the earth from sleep
(Grave the sentence deep)

Shall arise and seek
For her maker meek:
And the desart wild
Become a garden mild.

In the southern clime,
Where the summer's prime
Never fades away,
Lovely Lyca lay.

Seven summers old
Lovely Lyca told,
She had wanderd long
Hearing wild birds' song.

'Sweet sleep come to me
Underneath this tree;
Do father, mother weep?
Where can Lyca sleep?

'Lost in desart wild
Is your little child,
How can Lyca sleep,
If her mother weep:

'If her heart does ake,
Then let Lyca wake:
If my mother sleep,
Lyca shall not weep.

'Frowning frowning night,
O'er this desart bright,
Let thy moon arise
While I close my eyes.'

Sleeping Lyca lay;
While the beasts of prey,
Come from caverns deep,
View'd the maid asleep.

The kingly lion stood
And the virgin view'd,
Then he gambold round
O'er the hallowd ground:

Leopards, tygers play,
Round her as she lay;
While the lion old
Bow'd his mane of gold,

And her bosom lick,
And upon her neck,
From his eyes of flame,
Ruby tears there came;

While the lioness
Loos'd her slender dress,
And naked they convey'd
To caves the sleeping maid.

The Little Girl Found

All the night in woe,
Lyca's parents go:
Over vallies deep
While the desarts weep.

Tired and woe-begone,
Hoarse with making moan:
Arm in arm seven days
They trac'd the desart ways.

Seven nights they sleep
Among shadows deep
And dream they see their child
Starv'd in desart wild.

Pale thro' pathless ways
The fancied image strays,
Famish'd, weeping, weak
With hollow piteous shriek.

Rising from unrest,
The trembling woman prest,
With feet of weary woe;
She could no further go.

In his arms he bore
Her arm'd with sorrow sore:
Till before their way
A couching lion lay.

Turning back was vain.
Soon his heavy mane
Bore them to the ground;
Then he stalk'd around

And smelling to his prey,
But their fears allay,
When he licks their hands:
And silent by them stands.

They look upon his eyes
Fill'd with deep surprise:
And wondering behold
A spirit arm'd in gold.

On his head a crown,
On his shoulders down
Flow'd his golden hair.
Gone was all their care.

'Follow me' he said,
'Weep not for the maid;
In my palace deep,
Lyca lies asleep.'

Then they followed
Where the vision led;
And saw their sleeping child,
Among tygers wild.

To this day they dwell
In a lonely dell
Nor fear the wolvish howl,
Nor the lions growl.

The School Boy

I love to rise in a summer morn,
When the birds sing on every tree;
The distant huntsman winds his horn,
And the sky-lark sings with me.
O! what sweet company.

But to go to school in a summer morn,
O! it drives all joy away:
Under a cruel eye outworn,
The little ones spend the day
In sighing and dismay.

Ah! then at times I drooping sit,
And spend many an anxious hour,
Nor in my book can I take delight,
Nor sit in learning's bower,
Worn thro' with the dreary shower.

How can the bird that is born for joy
Sit in a cage and sing?
How can a child when fears annoy
But droop his tender wing
And forget his youthful spring?

O! father & mother, if buds are nip'd,
And blossoms blown away,
And if the tender plants are strip'd
Of their joy in the springing day,
By sorrow and cares dismay,

How shall the summer arise in joy,
Or the summer fruits appear?
Or how shall we gather what griefs destroy
Or bless the mellowing year,
When the blasts of winter appear?

The Voice of the Ancient Bard

Youth of delight, come hither
And see the opening morn,
Image of truth new-born.
Doubt is fled & clouds of reason
Dark disputes & artful teazing.
Folly is an endless maze,
Tangled roots perplex her ways.
How many have fallen there!
They stumble all night over bones of the dead:
And feel they know not what but care;
And wish to lead others when they should be led.

The Book of Thel

([London:] The Author & Printer Will[m] Blake, 1789)

THEL

THEL'S Motto

Does the Eagle know what is in the pit?
Or wilt thou go ask the Mole;
Can Wisdom be put in a silver rod?
Or Love in a golden bowl?

I

The daughters of Mne Seraphim led round their sunny flocks,
All but the youngest. She in paleness sought the secret air,
To fade away like morning beauty from her mortal day:
Down by the river of Adona her soft voice is heard:
And thus her gentle lamentation falls like morning dew.

'O life of this our spring! why fades the lotus of the water?
Why fade these children of the spring? born but to smile & fall.
Ah! Thel is like a watry bow and like a parting cloud,
Like a reflection in a glass, like shadows in the water,
Like dreams of infants, like a smile upon an infant's face,
Like the dove's voice, like transient day, like music in the air:
Ah! gentle may I lay me down and gentle rest my head,
And gentle sleep the sleep of death and gentle hear the voice
Of him that walketh in the garden in the evening time.'

The Lilly of the valley breathing in the humble grass
Answerd the lovely maid and said, 'I am a watry weed,
And I am very small, and love to dwell in lowly vales:
So weak the gilded butterfly scarce perches on my head
Yet I am visited from heaven and he that smiles on all
Walks in the valley and each morn over me spreads his hand
Saying, "rejoice thou humble grass, thou new-born lilly flower,
Thou gentle maid of silent valleys and of modest brooks:
For thou shalt be clothed in light, and fed with morning manna;

Till summer's heat melts thee beside the fountains and the springs
To flourish in eternal vales:" then why should Thel complain?

'Why should the mistress of the vales of Har, utter a sigh?'

She ceasd & smild in tears, then sat down in her silver shrine.

Thel answerd, 'O thou little virgin of the peaceful valley,
Giving to those that cannot crave, the voiceless, the o'erfired,
Thy breath doth nourish the innocent lamb, he smells thy milky garments,
He crops thy flowers while thou sittest smiling in his face,
Wiping his mild and meekin mouth from all contagious taints.
Thy wine doth purify the golden honey, thy perfume,
Which thou dost scatter on every little blade of grass that springs
Revives the milked cow, & tames the fire-breathing steed.
But Thel is like a faint cloud kindled at the rising sun;
I vanish from my pearly throne, and who shall find my place?'

'Queen of the vales' the Lilly answerd, 'ask the tender cloud,
And it shall tell thee why it glitters in the morning sky,
And why it scatters its bright beauty thro' the humid air.
Descend O little Cloud & hover before the eyes of Thel.'

The Cloud descended, and the Lilly bowed her modest head:
And went to mind her numerous charge among the verdant grass.

II

'O little Cloud' the virgin said, 'I charge thee tell to me
Why thou complainest not when in one hour thou fade away:
Then we shall seek thee but not find: ah Thel is like to thee,
I pass away, yet I complain, and no one hears my voice.'

The cloud then shew'd his golden head & his bright form emerg'd,
Hovering and glittering on the air before the face of Thel.

'O virgin know'st thou not our steeds drink of the golden springs
Where Luvah doth renew his horses: Look'st thou on my youth,
And fearest thou because I vanish and am seen no more
Nothing remains; O maid, I tell thee when I pass away,

It is to tenfold life, to love, to peace and raptures holy:
Unseen descending weigh my light wings upon balmy flowers:
And court the fair eyed dew to take me to her shining tent:
The weeping virgin trembling kneels before the risen sun,
Till we arise link'd in a golden band and never part:
But walk united, bearing food to all our tender flowers.'

'Dost thou O little Cloud? I fear that I am not like thee:
For I walk through the vales of Har, and smell the sweetest flowers;
But I feed not the little flowers: I hear the warbling birds,
But I feed not the warbling birds; they fly and seek their food;
But Thel delights in these no more, because I fade away
And all shall say, "without a use this shining woman liv'd,
Or did she only live to be at death the food of worms?"'

The cloud reclined upon his airy throne and answer'd thus:

'Then if thou art the food of worms, O virgin of the skies,
How great thy use, how great thy blessing; every thing that lives,
Lives not alone, nor for itself: fear not and I will call
The weak worm from its lowly bed, and thou shalt hear its voice.
Come forth worm of the silent valley, to thy pensive queen.'

The helpless worm arose, and sat upon the Lilly's leaf,
And the bright Cloud saild on, to find his partner in the vale.

III

Then Thel astonish'd view'd the Worm upon its dewy bed.

'Art thou a Worm? Image of weakness, art thou but a Worm?
I see thee like an infant wrapped in the Lilly's leaf:
Ah weep not little voice, thou can'st not speak, but thou can'st weep;
Is this a Worm? I see thee lay helpless & naked: weeping,
And none to answer, none to cherish thee with mother's smiles.'

The Clod of Clay heard the Worm's voice, & raised her pitying head;
She bowd over the weeping infant, and her life exhal'd
In milky fondness; then on Thel she fix'd her humble eyes.

'O beauty of the vales of Har, we live not for ourselves.
Thou seest me the meanest thing, and so I am indeed;
My bosom of itself is cold and of itself is dark,
But he that loves the lowly, pours his oil upon my head
And kisses me, and binds his nuptial bands around my breast,
And says; "Thou mother of my children, I have loved thee,
And I have given thee a crown that none can take away"
But how this is sweet maid, I know not, and I cannot know,
I ponder and I cannot ponder; yet I live and love.'

The daughter of beauty wip'd her pitying tears with her white veil,
And said: 'Alas! I knew not this, and therefore did I weep:
That God would love a Worm I knew, and punish the evil foot
That wilful, bruis'd its helpless form; but that he cherishd it
With milk and oil I never knew; and therefore did I weep
And I complained in the mild air, because I fade away,
And lay me down in thy cold bed, and leave my shining lot.'

'Queen of the vales,' the matron Clay answerd; 'I heard thy sighs,
And all thy moans flew o'er my roof, but I have call'd them down;
Wilt thou O Queen enter my house? tis given thee to enter
And to return; fear nothing; enter with thy virgin feet.'

IV

The eternal gates' terrific porter lifted the northern bar:
Thel enter'd in & saw the secrets of the land unknown:
She saw the couches of the dead, & where the fibrous roots
Of every heart on earth infixes deep its restless twists:
A land of sorrows & of tears where never smile was seen.

She wander'd in the land of clouds thro' valleys dark, listning
Dolours & lamentations: waiting oft beside a dewy grave
She stood in silence, listning to the voices of the ground,
Till to her own grave plot she came, & there she sat down,
And heard this voice of sorrow breathed from the hollow pit.

'Why cannot the Ear be closed to its own destruction?
Or the glistning Eye to the poison of a smile!
Why are Eyelids stord with arrows ready drawn,
Where a thousand fighting men in ambush lie?
Or an Eye of gifts & graces show'ring fruits & coined gold!
Why a Tongue impress'd with honey from every wind?
Why an Ear, a whirlpool fierce to draw creations in?
Why a Nostril wide inhaling terror trembling & affright?
Why a tender curb upon the youthful burning boy!
Why a little curtain of flesh on the bed of our desire?'

The Virgin started from her seat, & with a shriek
Fled back unhinderd till she came into the vales of Har.

The End

The Marriage of Heaven and Hell
([London, ?1790])

The Argument

Rintrah roars & shakes his fires in the burdend air;
Hungry clouds swag on the deep.

Once meek, and in a perilous path,
The just man kept his course along
The vale of death.
Roses are planted where thorns grow,
And on the barren heath
Sing the honey bees.
Then the perilous path was planted:
And a river, and a spring
On every cliff and tomb;
And on the bleached bones
Red clay brought forth.

Till the villain left the paths of ease,
To walk in perilous paths, and drive
The just man into barren climes.

Now the sneaking serpent walks
In mild humility,
And the just man rages in the wilds
Where lions roam.

Rintrah roars & shakes his fires in the burdend air;
Hungry clouds swag on the deep.

[¶1] As a new heaven is begun, and it is now thirty-three years since its advent: the Eternal Hell revives. And lo! Swedenborg is the Angel sitting at the tomb; his writings arc the linen clothes folded up. Now is the dominion of Edom, & the return of Adam into Paradise; see Isaiah XXXIV & XXXV Chap:
[¶2] Without contraries is no progression. Attraction and Repulsion, Reason and Energy, Love and Hate, are necessary to Human existence.
[¶3] From these contraries spring what the religious call Good &

Evil. Good is the passive that obeys Reason. Evil is the active springing from Energy.

[¶4] Good is Heaven. Evil is Hell.

The voice of the Devil

[¶5] All Bibles or sacred codes have been the causes of the following Errors.

[¶6] 1. That Man has two real existing principles Viz: a Body & a Soul.

[¶7] 2. That Energy, calld Evil, is alone from the Body, & that Reason, calld Good, is alone from the Soul.

[¶8] 3. That God will torment Man in Eternity for following his Energies.

[¶9] 4. But the following Contraries to these are True:

[¶10] 1. Man has no Body distinct from his Soul for that called Body is a portion of Soul discernd by the five Senses, the chief inlets of Soul in this age.

[¶11] 2. Energy is the only life and is from the Body and Reason is the bound or outward circumference of Energy.

[¶12] 3. Energy is Eternal Delight.

[¶13] Those who restrain desire, do so because theirs is weak enough to be restrained; and the restrainer or reason usurps its place & governs the unwilling.

[¶14] And being restrained it by degrees becomes passive till it is only the shadow of desire.

[¶15] The history of this is written in Paradise Lost, & the Governor or Reason is call'd Messiah.

[¶16] And the original Archangel or possessor of the command of the heavenly host, is called the Devil or Satan and his children are call'd Sin & Death.

[¶17] But in the Book of Job Milton's Messiah is call'd Satan.

[¶18] For this history has been adopted by both parties.

[¶19] It indeed appear'd to Reason as if Desire were cast out, but the Devil's account is, that the Messiah fell, & formed a heaven of what he stole from the Abyss.

[¶20] This is shewn in the Gospel, where he prays to the Father to send the comforter or Desire that Reason may have Ideas to build on, the Jehovah of the Bible being no other than he who dwells in flaming fire. Know that after Christ's death, he became Jehovah.

[¶21] But in Milton; the Father is Destiny, the Son, a Ratio of the five senses, & the Holy-ghost, Vacuum!

[¶22] Note. The Reason Milton wrote in fetters when he wrote of Angels & God, and at liberty when of Devils & Hell, is because he was a true Poet and of the Devil's party without knowing it.

A Memorable Fancy

[¶23] As I was walking among the fires of hell, delighted with the enjoyments of Genius; which to Angels look like torment and insanity, I collected some of their Proverbs: thinking that as the sayings used in a nation marks its character, so the Proverbs of Hell, shew the nature of Infernal wisdom better than any description of buildings or garments.

[¶24] When I came home; on the abyss of the five senses, where a flat sided steep frowns over the present world, I saw a mighty Devil folded in black clouds, hovering on the sides of the rock, with corroding fires; he wrote the following sentence now percieved by the minds of men, & read by them on earth.

How do you know but ev'ry Bird that cuts the airy way,
Is an immense world of delight, clos'd by your senses five?

Proverbs of Hell

In seed time learn, in harvest teach, in winter enjoy.
Drive your cart and your plow over the bones of the dead.
The road of excess leads to the palace of wisdom.
Prudence is a rich ugly old maid courted by Incapacity.
He who desires but acts not, breeds pestilence.
The cut worm forgives the plow.
Dip him in the river who loves water.
A fool sees not the same tree that a wise man sees.
He whose face gives no light, shall never become a star.
Eternity is in love with the productions of time.
The busy bee has no time for sorrow.
The hours of folly are measur'd by the clock, but of wisdom:
    no clock can measure.
All wholsom food is caught without a net or a trap.
Bring out number weight & measure in a year of dearth.
No bird soars too high if he soars with his own wings.

A dead body revenges not injuries.
The most sublime act is to set another before you.
If the fool would persist in his folly he would become wise.
Folly is the cloke of knavery.
Shame is Prides cloke.

Proverbs of Hell

Prisons are built with stones of Law, Brothels with bricks of Religion.
The pride of the peacock is the glory of God.
The lust of the goat is the bounty of God.
The wrath of the lion is the wisdom of God.
The nakedness of woman is the work of God.
Excess of sorrow laughs. Excess of joy weeps.
The roaring of lions, the howling of wolves, the raging of the stormy sea, and the destructive sword, are portions of eternity too great for the eye of man.
The fox condemns the trap, not himself.
Joys impregnate. Sorrows bring forth.
Let man wear the fell of the lion, woman the fleece of the sheep.
The bird a nest, the spider a web, man friendship.
The selfish smiling fool & the sullen frowning fool, shall be both thought wise, that they may be a rod.
What is now proved was once only imagin'd.
The rat, the mouse, the fox, the rabbet; watch the roots, the lion, the tyger, the horse, the elephant, watch the fruits.
The cistern contains: the fountain overflows.
One thought fills immensity.
Always be ready to speak your mind, and a base man will avoid you.
Every thing possible to be believ'd is an image of truth.
The eagle never lost so much time as when he submitted to learn of the crow.

Proverbs of Hell

The fox provides for himself, but God provides for the lion.
Think in the morning, Act in the noon, Eat in the evening, Sleep in the night.
He who has sufferd you to impose on him knows you.
As the plow follows words, so God rewards prayers.
The tygers of wrath are wiser than the horses of instruction.
Expect poison from the standing water.
You never know what is enough unless you know what is more than enough.
Listen to the fool's reproach! It is a kingly title!
The eyes of fire, the nostrils of air, the mouth of water, the beard of earth.
The weak in courage is strong in cunning,
The apple tree never asks the beech how he shall grow, nor the lion the horse, how he shall take his prey.
The thankful reciever bears a plentiful harvest.
If others had not been foolish, we should be so.
The soul of sweet delight, can never be defil'd,
When thou seest an Eagle, thou seest a portion of genius; lift up thy head!
As the catterpiller chooses the fairest leaves to lay her eggs on, so the priest lays his curse on the fairest joys.
To create a little flower is the labour of ages.
Damn braces: Bless relaxes.
The best wine is the oldest, best water the newest.
Prayers plow not! Praises reap not!
Joys laugh not! Sorrows weep not!

Proverbs of Hell

The head Sublime, the heart Pathos, the genitals Beauty, the hands & feet Proportion.
As the air to a bird or the sea to a fish, so is contempt to the contemptible.
The crow wish'd every thing was black, the owl, that every thing was white.
Exuberance is Beauty.
If the lion was advised by the fox, he would be cunning.

Improvent makes strait roads, but the crooked roads without
Improvement are the roads of Genius.
Sooner murder an infant in its cradle than nurse unacted desires.
Where man is not nature is barren.
Truth can never be told so as to be understood, and not be
believ'd.
Enough! Or Too much.

[¶25] The ancient Poets animated all sensible objects with God or Geniuses, calling them by the names and adorning them with the properties of woods, rivers, mountains, lakes, cities, nations, and whatever their enlarged & numerous senses could percieve.
[¶26] And particularly they studied the genius of each city & country, placing it under its mental deity.
[¶27] Till a system was formed, which some took advantage of & enslav'd the vulgar by attempting to realize or abstract the mental deities from their objects; thus began Priesthood:
[¶28] Choosing forms of worship from poetic tales.
[¶29] And at length they pronouncd that the Gods had orderd such things.
[¶30] Thus men forgot that All deities reside in the human breast.

A Memorable Fancy

[¶31] The Prophets Isaiah and Ezekiel dined with me, and I asked them how they dared so roundly to assert, that God spake to them; and whether they did not think at the time, that they would be misunderstood, & so be the cause of imposition.
[¶32] Isaiah answer'd: 'I saw no God, nor heard any, in a finite organical perception; but my senses discover'd the infinite in every thing, and as I was then perswaded, & remain confirm'd; that the voice of honest indignation is the voice of God, I cared not for the consequences but wrote.'
[¶33] Then I asked: 'does a firm perswasion that a thing is so, make it so?'
[¶34] He replied, 'All poets believe that it does, & in ages of imagination this firm perswasion removed mountains; but many are not capable of a firm perswasion of any thing.
[¶35] Then Ezekiel said: 'The philosophy of the east taught the first principles of human perception; some nations held one principle for the origin & some another, we of Israel taught that the Poetic Genius

(as you now call it) was the first principle and all the others merely derivative, which was the cause of our despising the Priests & Philosophers of other countries, and prophecying that all Gods would at last be proved to originate in ours & to be the tributaries of the Poetic Genius, it was this that our great poet King David desired so fervently & invokes so pathetically, saying that by this he conquers enemies & governs kingdoms; and we so loved our God, that we cursed in his name all the deities of surrounding nations, and asserted that they had rebelld; from these opinions the vulgar came to think that all nations would at last be subject to the jews.

[¶36] 'This' said he, 'like all firm perswasions, is come to pass, for all nations believe the jews' code and worship the jews' god, and what greater subjection can be?'

[¶37] I heard this with some wonder, & must confess my own conviction. After dinner I ask'd Isaiah to favour the world with his last works, he said none of equal value was lost. Ezekiel said the same of his.

[¶38] I also asked Isaiah what made him go naked and barefoot three years? He answerd, 'the same that made our friend Diogenes the Grecian.'

[¶39] I then asked Ezekiel, why he eat dung, & lay so long on his right & left side? He answerd, 'the desire of raising other men into a perception of the infinite; this the North American tribes practise, & is he honest who resists his genius or conscience, only for the sake of present ease or gratification?'

[¶40] The ancient tradition that the world will be consumed in fire at the end of six thousand years is true, as I have heard from Hell.

[¶41] For the cherub with his flaming sword is hereby commanded to leave his guard at tree of life, and when he does, the whole creation will be consumed, and appear infinite and holy whereas it now appears finite & corrupt.

[¶42] This will come to pass by an improvement of sensual enjoyment.

[¶43] But first the notion that man has a body distinct from his soul, is to be expunged; this I shall do, by printing in the infernal method, by corrosives, which in Hell are salutary and medicinal, melting apparent surfaces away, and displaying the infinite which was hid.

[¶44] If the doors of perception were cleansed everything would appear to man as it is, infinite.

[¶45] For man has closed himself up, till he sees all things thro' narrow chinks of his cavern.

A Memorable Fancy

[¶46] I was in a Printing house in Hell & saw the method in which knowledge is transmitted from generation to generation.

[¶47] In the first chamber was a Dragon-Man, clearing away the rubbish from a cave's mouth; within, a number of Dragons were hollowing the cave,

[¶48] In the second chamber was a Viper folding round the rock & the cave, and others adorning it with gold, silver and precious stones.

[¶49] In the third chamber was an Eagle with wings and feathers of air, he caused the inside of the cave to be infinite, around were numbers of Eagle men, who built palaces in the immense cliffs.

[¶50] In the fourth chamber were Lions of flaming fire raging around & melting the metals into living fluids.

[¶51] In the fifth chamber were Unnam'd forms, which cast the metals into the expense.

[¶52] There they were reciev'd by Men who occupied the sixth chamber, and took the forms of books & were arranged in libraries.

[¶53] The Giants who formed this world into its sensual existence and now seem to live in it in chains, are in truth the causes of its life & the sources of all activity, but the chains are, the cunning of weak and tame minds, which have power to resist energy, according to the proverb, the weak in courage is strong in cunning.

[¶54] Thus one portion of being, is the Prolific, the other, the Devouring; to the devourer it seems as if the producer was in his chains, but it is not so, he only takes portions of existence and fancies that the whole.

[¶55] But the Prolific would cease to be Prolific unless the devourer as a sea recieved the excess of his delights.

[¶56] Some will say, 'Is not God alone the Prolific?' I answer, 'God only Acts & Is in existing beings or Men.'

[¶57] These two classes of men are always upon earth, & they should be enemies; whoever tries to reconcile them seeks to destroy existence.

[¶58] Religion is an endeavour to reconcile the two.

[¶59] Note. Jesus Christ did not wish to unite but to separate them, as in the Parable of sheep and goats! & he says 'I came not to send Peace but a Sword.'

[¶60] Messiah or Satan or Tempter was formerly thought to be one of the Antediluvians who are our Energies.

A Memorable Fancy

[¶61] An Angel came to me and said 'O pitiable foolish young man! O horrible! O dreadful state! Consider the hot burning dungeons thou art preparing for thyself to all eternity, to which thou art going in such career.'

[¶62] I said, 'perhaps you will be willing to shew me my eternal lot & we will contemplate together upon it and see whether your lot or mine is most desirable.'

[¶63] So he took me thro' a stable & thro' a church & down into the church vault at the end of which was a mill; thro' the mill we went, and came to a cave; down the winding cavern we groped our tedious way till a void boundless as a nether sky appeard beneath us, & we held by the roots of trees and hung over this immensity, but I said, 'if you please we will commit ourselves to this void, and see whether providence is here also, if you will not I will?' but he answered, 'do not presume O young-man but as we here remain behold thy lot which will soon appear when the darkness passes away.'

[¶64] So I remained with him sitting in the twisted root of an oak. He was suspended in a fungus which hung with the head downward into the deep;

[¶65] By degrees we beheld the infinite Abyss, fiery as the smoke of a burning city; beneath us at an immense distance was the sun, black but shining; round it were fiery tracks on which revolv'd vast spiders, crawling after their prey; which flew or rather swum in the infinite deep, in the most terrific shapes of animals sprung from corruption, & the air was full of them, & seemd composed of them; these are Devils, and are called Powers of the air, I now asked my companion which was my eternal lot? He said, 'between the black & white spiders.'

[¶66] But now, from between the black & white spiders a cloud and fire burst and rolled thro the deep blackning all beneath, so that the nether deep grew black as a sea & rolled with a terrible noise: beneath was nothing now to be seen but a black tempest, till looking east between the clouds & the waves, we saw a cataract of blood mixed with fire and not many stones throw from us appeard and sunk again the scaly fold of a monstrous serpent; at last to the east, distant about three degrees appeard a fiery crest above the waves. Slowly it reared like a ridge of golden rocks till we discoverd two globes of crimson fire, from which the sea fled away in clouds of smoke, and now we saw, it was the head of Leviathan, his forehead was divided into streaks of green & purple like those on a tyger's forehead: soon we saw his mouth & red gills hang just above the raging foam tinging the black deep with beams of blood, advancing towards us with all the fury of a spiritual existence.

[¶67] My friend the Angel climb'd up from his station into the mill; I remain'd alone, & then this appearance was no more, but I found myself sitting on a pleasant bank beside a river by moon light hearing a harper who sung to the harp, & his theme was, 'The man who never alters his opinion is like standing water, & breeds reptiles of the mind.'

[¶68] But I arose, and sought for the mill & there I found my Angel, who surprised asked me, how I escaped?

[¶69] I answerd, 'All that we saw was owing to your metaphysics: for when you ran away, I found myself on a bank by moonlight hearing a harper, But now we have seen my eternal lot, shall I shew you yours?' He laughd at my proposal; but I by force suddenly caught him in my arms, & flew westerly thro' the night, till we were elevated above the earth's shadow: then I flung myself with him directly into the body of the sun, here I clothed myself in white, & taking in my hand Swedenborg's volumes sunk from the glorious clime, and passed all the planets till we came to saturn, here I staid to rest & then leap'd into the void, between saturn & the fixed stars.

[¶70] 'Here' said I! 'Is your lot, in this space, if space it may be calld,' Soon we saw the stable and the church, & I took him to the altar and open'd the Bible, and lo! It was a deep pit, into which I descended driving the Angel before me, soon we saw seven houses of brick, one we enterd; in it were a number of monkeys, baboons, & all of that species chaind by the middle, grinning and snatching at one another, but withheld by the shortness of their chains; however I saw that they sometimes grew numerous, and then the weak were caught by the strong and with a grinning aspect, first coupled with & then devourd, by plucking off first one limb and then another till the body was left a helpless trunk; this after grinning & kissing it with seeming fondness they devourd too; and here & there I saw one savourily picking the flesh off of his own tail; as the stench terribly annoyd us both we went into the mill, & I in my hand brought the skeleton of a body, which in the mill was Aristotle's Analytics.

[¶71] So the Angel said: 'thy phantasy has imposed upon me & thou oughtest to be ashamed.'

[¶72] I answerd: 'we impose on one another, & it is but lost time to converse with you whose works are only Analytics.'

[¶73] Opposition is True Friendship.

[¶74] I have always found that Angels have the vanity to speak of themselves as the only wise; this they do with a confident insolence sprouting from systematic reasoning;

[¶75] Thus Swedenborg boasts that what he writes is new; tho' it is only the Contents or Index of already publish'd books.

[¶76] A man carried a monkey about for a shew, & because he was a little wiser than the monkey, grew vain, and conciev'd himself as much wiser than seven men. It is so with Swedenborg; he shews the folly of churches & exposes hypocrites, till he imagines that all are religious, & himself the single one on earth that ever broke a net.

[¶77] Now hear a plain fact: Swedenborg has not written one new truth: Now hear another: he has written all the old falsehoods.

[¶78] And now hear the reason. He conversed with Angels who are all religious, & conversed not with Devils who all hate religion, for he was incapable thro' his conceited notions.

[¶79] Thus Swedenborg's writings are a recapitulation of all superficial opinions, and an analysis of the more sublime, but no further.

[¶80] Have now another plain fact: Any man of mechanical talents may from the writings of Paracelsus or Jacob Behmen, produce ten thousand volumes of equal value with Swedenborg's, and from those of Dante or Shakespear an infinite number.

[¶81] But when he has done this, let him not say that he knows better than his master, for he only holds a candle in sunshine.

A Memorable Fancy

[¶82] Once I saw a Devil in a flame of fire, who arose before an Angel that sat on a cloud, and the Devil utterd these words:

[¶83] 'The worship of God is, Honouring his gifts in other men each according to his genius, and loving the greatest men best, those who envy or calumniate great men hate God, for there is no other God.'

[¶84] The Angel hearing this became almost blue but mastering himself he grew yellow, & at last white pink & smiling, and then replied,

[¶85] 'Thou Idolater, is not God One? & is not he visible in Jesus Christ? And has not Jesus Christ given his sanction to the law of ten commandments? Are not all other men fools, sinners, & nothings?'

[¶86] The Devil answer'd: 'bray a fool in morter with wheat, yet shall not his folly be beaten out of him: if Jesus Christ is the greatest man, you ought to love him in the greatest degree; now hear how he has given his sanction to the law of ten commandments: did he not mock at the sabbath, and so mock the sabbath's God: murder those who were murdered because of him? turn away the law from the woman taken in adultery? steal the labor of others to support him? bear false witness when he omitted making a defence before Pilate? covet when he pray'd for his disciples, and when he bid them shake off the dust of their feet against such as refused to lodge them? I tell you, no virtue can exist without breaking these ten commandments: Jesus was all virtue, and acted from impulse, not from rules.'

[¶87] When he had so spoken: I beheld the Angel who stretched out his arms embracing the flame of fire & he was consumed and arose as Elijah.

[¶88] Note: This Angel, who is now become a Devil, is my particular friend: we often read the Bible together in its infernal or diabolical sense which the world shall have if they behave well.

[¶89] I have also: The Bible of Hell: which the world shall have whether they will or no.

[¶90] One Law for the Lion & Ox is Oppression.

A Song of Liberty

1. The Eternal Female groand! It was heard over all the Earth:
2. Albion's coast is sick silent; the American meadows faint!
3. Shadows of Prophecy shiver along by the lakes and the rivers and mutter across the ocean, France rend down thy dungeon,
4. Golden Spain burst the barriers of old Rome;
5. Cast thy keys O Rome into the deep down falling, even to eternity down falling,
6. And weep!
7. In her trembling hands she took the new born terror howling;
8. On these infinite mountains of light now barr'd out by the atlantic sea, the new born fire stood before the starry king!
9. Flag'd with grey brow'd snows and thunderous visages the jealous wings wav'd over the deep.
10. The speary hand burned aloft, unbuckled was the shield, forth went the hand of jealousy among the flaming hair and hurl'd the new born wonder thro' the starry night.
11. The fire, the fire, is falling!
12. Look up! Look up! O citizen of London enlarge thy countenance, O Jew, leave counting gold! Return to thy oil and wine; O African! Black African! (Go, winged thought, widen his forehead.)
13. The fiery limbs, the flaming hair shot like the sinking sun into the western sea.

14. Wak'd from his eternal sleep, the hoary element roaring fled away;
15. Down rushd beating his wings in vain the jealous king; his grey brow'd councellors, thunderous warriors, curl'd veterans among helms, and shields, and chariots, horses, elephants, banners, castles, slings and rocks,
16. Falling, rushing, ruining! Buried in the ruins, on Urthona's dens.
17. All night beneath the ruins, then their sullen flames faded emerge round the gloomy king,
18. With thunder and fire: leading his starry hosts thro' the waste wilderness he promulgates his ten commands, glancing his beamy eyelids over the deep in dark dismay,
19. Where the son of fire in his eastern cloud, while the morning plumes her golden breast,
20. Spurning the clouds written with curses, stamps the stony law to dust, loosing the eternal horses from the dens of night, crying Empire is no more! And now the lion & wolf shall cease.

Chorus

[¶91] Let the Priests of the Raven of dawn, no longer in deadly black, with hoarse note curse the sons of joy. Nor his accepted brethren whom, tyrant, he calls free: lay the bound or build the roof. Nor pale religious letchery call that virginity, that wishes but acts not!
[¶92] For every thing that lives is Holy.

'A Fairy leapt'
(Manuscript [?1793])

A Fairy leapt upon my knee
Singing & dancing merrily.
I said 'Thou thing of patches rings
Pins Necklaces & Suchlike things
Disguiser of the Female Form,
Thou paltry gilded poisnous worm!'
Weeping he fell upon my thigh
And thus in tears did soft reply:
'Knowest thou not O Fairies Lord
How much by us Contemnd Abhorrd
Whatever hides the Female form
That cannot bear the Mental Storm?
Therefore in Pity still we give
Our lives to make the Female live
And what would turn into disease
We turn to what will joy & please.'

VISIONS of the Daughters of Albion

The Eye sees more than the Heart knows
([Lambeth:] Printed by Willm Blake: 1793)

The Argument

I loved Theotormon
And I was not ashamed;
I trembled in my virgin fears
And I hid in Leutha's vale!

I plucked Leutha's flower,
And I rose up from the vale;
But the terrible thunders tore
My virgin mantle in twain.

Visions

Enslav'd, the Daughters of Albion weep: a trembling lamentation
Upon their mountains; in their valleys, sighs towards America.

For the soft soul of America, Oothoon wandered in woe,
Along the vales of Leutha seeking flowers to comfort her,
And thus she spoke to the bright Marygold of Leutha's vale:

'Art thou a flower! art thou a nymph! I see thee now a flower:
Now a nymph! I dare not pluck thee from thy dewy bed!'

The Golden nymph replied; 'Pluck thou my flower Oothoon the mild,
And another flower shall spring, because the soul of sweet delight
Can never pass away.' She ceas'd & closd her golden shrine.

Then Oothoon pluck'd the flower saying, 'I pluck thee from thy bed
Sweet flower, and put thee here to glow between my breasts
And thus I turn my face to where my whole soul seeks.'

Over the waves she went in wing'd exulting swift delight;
And over Theotormon's reign took her impetuous course.

Bromion rent her with his thunders, on his stormy bed
Lay the faint maid, and soon her woes appalld his thunders
hoarse.

Bromion spoke, 'behold this harlot here on Bromion's bed,
And let the jealous dolphins sport around the lovely maid:
Thy soft American plains are mine, and mine thy north & south:
Stampt with my signet are the swarthy children of the sun:
They are obedient, they resist not, they obey the scourge:
Their daughters worship terrors and obey the violent:
Now thou maist marry Bromion's harlot, and protect the child
Of Bromion's rage, that Oothoon shall bring forth in nine moons'
time.'

Then storms rent Theotormon's limbs; he rolld his waves around
And folded his black jealous waters round the adulterate pair.
Bound back to back in Bromion's caves terror & meekness dwell;

At entrance Theotormon sits wearing the threshold hard
With secret tears; beneath him sound like waves on a desart
shore
The voice of slaves beneath the sun, and children bought with
money,
That shiver in religious caves beneath the burning fires
Of lust, that belch incessant from the summits of the earth.

Oothoon weeps not: she cannot weep! Her tears are locked up;
But she can howl incessant writhing her soft snowy limbs
And calling Theotormon's Eagles to prey upon her flesh.

'I call with holy voice! King of the sounding air,
Rend away this defiled bosom that I may reflect
The image of Theotormon on my pure transparent breast.'

The Eagles at her call descend & rend their bleeding prey;
Theotormon severely smiles, her soul reflects the smile;
As the clear spring mudded with feet of beasts grows pure &
smiles.

The Daughters of Albion hear her woes & eccho back her sighs.

'Why does my Theotormon sit weeping upon the threshold:
And Oothoon hovers by his side, perswading him in vain:
I cry arise O Theotormon for the village dog
Barks at the breaking day; the nightingale has done lamenting,
The lark does rustle in the ripe corn, and the Eagle returns
From nightly prey, and lifts his golden beak to the pure east;
Shaking the dust from his immortal pinions to awake
The sun that sleeps too long. Arise my Theotormon I am pure
Because the night is gone that clos'd me in its deadly black.
They told me that the night & day were all that I could see;
They told me that I had five senses to inclose me up,
And they inclos'd my infinite brain into a narrow circle,
And sunk my heart into the Abyss, a red round globe hot burning
Till all from life I was obliterated and erased.
Instead of morning arises a bright shadow, like an eye
In the eastern cloud; instead of night a sickly charnel house
That Theotormon hears me not! to him the night and morn
Are both alike: a night of sighs, a morning of fresh tears;
And none but Bromion can hear my lamentations.

'With what sense is it that the chicken shuns the ravenous hawk?
With what sense does the tame pigeon measure out the expanse?
With what sense does the bee form cells? have not the mouse & frog
Eyes and ears and sense of touch? yet their habitations
And their pursuits, as different as their forms and as their joys;
Ask the wild ass why he refuses burdens: and the meek camel
Why he loves man; is it because of eye, ear, mouth or skin
Or breathing nostrils? No, for these the wolf and tyger have.
Ask the blind worm the secrets of the grave, and why her spires
Love to curl round the bones of death; and ask the rav'nous snake
Where she gets poison; and the wing'd eagle why he loves the sun
And then tell me the thoughts of man, that have been hid of old.

'Silent I hover all the night, and all day could be silent,
If Theotormon once would turn his loved eyes upon me;
How can I be defild when I reflect thy image pure?

Sweetest the fruit that the worm feeds on & the soul prey'd on by woe,
The new wash'd lamb ting'd with the village smoke & the bright swan
By the red earth of our immortal river: I bathe my wings,
And I am white and pure to hover round Theotormon's breast.'

Then Theotormon broke his silence, and he answered:

'Tell me what is the night or day to one o'erflow'd with woe?
Tell me what is a thought? & of what substance is it made?
Tell me what is a joy? & in what gardens do joys grow?
And in what rivers swim the sorrows? and upon what mountains
Wave shadows of discontent? and in what houses dwell the wretched
Drunken with woe forgotten and shut up from cold despair?

'Tell me where dwell the thoughts forgotten till thou call them forth,
Tell me where dwell the joys of old? & where the ancient loves?
And when will they renew again & the night of oblivion past?
That I might traverse times & spaces far remote and bring
Comforts into a present sorrow and a night of pain.
Where goest thou O thought! to what remote land is thy flight?
If thou returnest to the present moment of affliction
Wilt thou bring comforts on thy wings, and dews and honey and balm;
Or poison From the desart wilds, from the eyes of the envier?'

Then Bromion said; and shook the cavern with his lamentation:

'Thou knowest that the ancient trees seen by thine eyes have fruit
But knowest thou that trees and fruits flourish upon the earth
To gratify senses unknown? trees beasts and birds unknown:
Unknown, not unpercievd, spread in the infinite microscope,
In places yet unvisited by the voyager and in worlds
Over another kind of seas, and in atmospheres unknown.
Ah! are there other wars, besides the wars of sword and fire!
And are there other sorrows, beside the sorrows of poverty?
And are there other joys, beside the joys of riches and ease?

And is there not one law for both the lion and the ox?
And is there not eternal fire, and eternal chains?
To bind the phantoms of existence from eternal life?'

Then Oothoon waited silent all the day, and all the night,
But when the morn arose, her lamentation renewd,
The Daughters of Albion hear her woes, & eccho back her sighs.

'O Urizen! Creator of men! mistaken Demon of heaven;
Thy joys are tears! thy labour vain, to form men to thine image.
How can one joy absorb another? are not different joys
Holy, eternal, infinite! and each joy is a Love.

'Does not the great mouth laugh at a gift? And the narrow eyelids mock
At the labour that is above payment, and wilt thou take the ape
For thy councellor? or the dog for a schoolmaster to thy children?
Does he who contemns poverty, and he who turns with abhorrence
From usury: feel the same passion or are they moved alike?
How can the giver of gifts experience the delights of the merchant?
How can the industrious citizen the pains of the husbandman?
How different far the fat fed hireling with hollow drum
Who buys whole corn fields into wastes, and sings upon the heath:
How different their eye and ear! how different the world to them!
With what sense does the parson claim the labours of the farmer?
What are his nets & gins & traps, & how does he surround him
With cold floods of abstraction, and with forests of solitude,
To build him castles and high spires, where kings & priests may dwell,
Till she who burns with youth, and knows no fixed lot, is bound
In spells of law to one she loathes; and must she drag the chain
Of life in weary lust? must chilling murderous thoughts obscure
The clear heaven of her eternal spring? to bear the wintry rage
Of a harsh terror driv'n to madness, bound to hold a rod
Over her shrinking shoulders all the day; & all the night
To turn the wheel of false desire: and longings that wake her womb
To the abhorred birth of cherubs in the human form
That live a pestilence & die a meteor & are no more,

Till the child dwell with one he hates, and do the deed he loaths
And the impure scourge force his seed into its unripe birth
E'er yet his eyelids can behold the arrows of day.

'Does the whale worship at thy footsteps as the hungry dog?
Or does he scent the mountain prey, because his nostrils wide
Draw in the ocean? does his eye discern the flying cloud
As the raven's eye? or does he measure the expanse like the vulture?
Does the still spider view the cliffs where eagles hide their young?
Or does the fly rejoice, because the harvest is brought in?
Does not the eagle scorn the earth & despise the treasures beneath?
But the mole knoweth what is there, & the worm shall tell it thee.
Does the worm erect a pillar in the mouldering church yard?
And a palace of eternity in the jaws of the hungry grave?
Over his porch these words are written: "Take thy bliss O Man!
And sweet shall be thy taste & sweet thy infant joys renew!"

'Infancy, fearless, lustful, happy! nestling for delight
In laps of pleasure; Innocence! honest, open, seeking
The vigorous joys of morning light; open to virgin bliss.
Who taught thee modesty, subtil modesty! child of night & sleep?
When thou awakest, wilt thou dissemble all thy secret joys
Or wert thou not awake when all this mystery was disclos'd?
Then com'st thou forth a modest virgin knowing to dissemble
With nets found under thy night pillow, to catch virgin joy,
And brand it with the name of whore; & sell it in the night,
In silence, ev'n without a whisper, and in seeming sleep.
Religious dreams and holy vespers light thy smoky fires:
Once were thy fires lighted by the eyes of honest morn
And does my Theotormon seek this hypocrite modesty!
This knowing, artful, secret, fearful, cautious, trembling hypocrite?
Then is Oothoon a whore indeed! and all the virgin joys
Of life are harlots: and Theotormon is a sick man's dream
And Oothoon is the crafty slave of selfish holiness.

'But Oothoon is not so; a virgin fill'd with virgin fancies
Open to joy and to delight where ever beauty appears;
If in the morning sun I find it: there my eyes are fix'd
In happy copulation; if in evening mild, wearied with work,
Sit on a bank and draw the pleasures of this free born joy.

'The moment of desire! the moment of desire! The virgin
That pines for man shall awaken her womb to enormous joys
In the secret shadows of her chamber; the youth shut up from
The lustful joy shall forget to generate & create an amorous image
In the shadows of his curtains and in the folds of his silent pillow.
Are not these the places of religion? the rewards of continence?
The self enjoyings of self denial? Why dost thou seek religion?
Is it because acts are not lovely, that thou seekest solitude,
Where the horrible darkness is impressed with reflections of desire?

'Father of Jealousy, be thou accursed from the earth!
Why hast thou taught my Theotormon this accursed thing?
Till beauty fades from off my shoulders darken'd and cast out,
A solitary shadow wailing on the margin of non-entity.

'I cry, Love! Love! Love! happy happy Love! free as the mountain wind!
Can that be Love, that drinks another as a sponge drinks water?
That clouds with jealousy his nights, with weepings all the day:
To spin a web of age around him, grey and hoary! dark!
Till his eyes sicken at the fruit that hangs before his sight?
Such is self-love that envies all! a creeping skeleton
With lamplike eyes watching around the frozen marriage bed.

'But silken nets and traps of adamant will Oothoon spread,
And catch for thee girls of mild silver, or of furious gold;
I'll lie beside thee on a bank & view their wanton play
In lovely copulation bliss on bliss with Theotormon:
Red as the rosy morning, lustful as the first born beam,
Oothoon shall view his dear delight, nor e'er with jealous cloud
Come in the heaven of generous love; nor selfish blightings bring.

'Does the sun walk in glorious raiment on the secret floor
Where the cold miser spreads his gold? or does the bright cloud
drop
On his stone threshold? does his eye behold the beam that brings
Expansion to the eye of pity? or will he bind himself
Beside the ox to thy hard furrow? does not the mild beam blot
The bat, the owl, the glowing tyger, and the king of night?
The sea fowl takes the wintry blast for a cov'ring to her limbs:
And the wild snake the pestilence to adorn him with gems &
gold,
And trees & birds & beasts & men behold their eternal joy.
Arise you little glancing wings and sing your infant joy!
Arise and drink your bliss, for every thing that lives is holy!'

Thus every morning wails Oothoon, but Theotormon sits
Upon the margined ocean conversing with shadows dire.

The Daughters of Albion hear her woes, & eccho back her sighs.

The End

AMERICA *a Prophecy*

([Lambeth:] Printed by William Blake in the year 1793)

Preludium

The shadowy Daughter of Urthona stood before red Orc,
When fourteen suns had faintly journey'd o'er his dark abode;
His food she brought in iron baskets, his drink in cups of iron;
Crown'd with a helmet & dark hair the nameless female stood;
A quiver with its burning stores, a bow like that of night,
When pestilence is shot from heaven; no other arms she need:
Invulnerable tho' naked, save where clouds roll round her loins
Their awful folds in the dark air; silent she stood as night;
For never from her iron tongue could voice or sound arise;
But dumb till that dread day when Orc assay'd his fierce embrace.

'Dark Virgin,' said the hairy youth, 'thy father stern abhorr'd;
Rivets my tenfold chains while still on high my spirit soars;
Sometimes an eagle screaming in the sky, sometimes a lion
Stalking upon the mountains, & sometimes a whale I lash
The raging fathomless abyss, anon a serpent folding
Around the pillars of Urthona, and round thy dark limbs,
On the Canadian wilds I fold, feeble my spirit folds,
For chaind beneath I rend these caverns; when thou bringest food
I howl my joy; and my red eyes seek to behold thy face
In vain! these clouds roll to & fro, & hide thee from my sight.'

Silent as despairing love, and strong as jealousy,
The hairy shoulders rend the links, free are the wrists of fire;
Round the terrific lions he siez'd the panting struggling womb;
It joy'd: she put aside her clouds & smiled her first-born smile;
As when a black cloud shews its light'nings to the silent deep.

Soon as she saw the terrible boy then burst the virgin cry:

'I know thee, I have found thee, & I will not let thee go;
Thou art the image of God who dwells in darkness of Africa;
And thou art fall'n to give me life in regions of dark death.
On my American plains I feel the struggling afflictions
Endur'd by roots that writhe their arms into the nether deep:

I see a Serpent in Canada, who courts me to his love;
In Mexico an Eagle, and a Lion in Peru;
I see a Whale in the South-sea, drinking my soul away.
O what limb rending pains I feel, thy fire & my frost
Mingle in howling pains, in furrows by thy lightnings rent;
This is eternal death; and this the torment long foretold.'

The stern Bard ceas'd, asham'd of his own song; enrag'd he swung
His harp aloft sounding, then dash'd its shining frame against
A ruin'd pillar in glittring fragments; silent he turn'd away,
And wander'd down the vales of Kent in sick & drear lamentings.

A PROPHECY

The Guardian Prince of Albion burns in his nightly tent,
Sullen fires across the Atlantic glow to America's shore:
Piercing the souls of warlike men, who rise in silent night.
Washington, Franklin, Paine & Warren, Gates, Hancock & Green
Meet on the coast glowing with blood from Albion's fiery Prince.

Washington spoke; 'Friends of America, look over the Atlantic sea;
A bended bow is lifted in heaven, & a heavy iron chain
Descends link by link from Albion's cliffs across the sea to bind
Brothers & sons of America, till our faces pale and yellow;
Heads deprest, voices weak, eyes downcast, hands work-bruis'd,
Feet bleeding on the sultry sands, and the furrows of the whip
Descend to generations that in future times forget.'

The strong voice ceas'd; for a terrible blast swept over the heaving sea:
The eastern cloud rent; on his cliffs stood Albion's wrathful Prince,
A dragon form clashing his scales at midnight he arose,
And flam'd red meteors round the land of Albion beneath;
His voice, his locks, his awful shoulders, and his glowing eyes,
Appear to the Americans upon the cloudy night.

Solemn heave the Atlantic waves between the gloomy nations
Swelling belching from its deeps red clouds & raging fires,
Albion is sick. America faints! enrag'd the Zenith grew.
As human blood shooting in veins all round the orbed heaven
Red rose the clouds from the Atlantic in vast wheels of blood
And in the red clouds rose a wonder o'er the Atlantic sea;
Intense! naked! a Human fire fierce glowing, as the wedge
Of iron heated in the furnace; his terrible limbs were fire
With myriads of cloudy terrors banners dark & towers
Surrounded; heat but not light went thro' the murky atmosphere.

The King of England looking westward trembles at the vision.

Albion's Angel stood beside the Stone of night, and saw
The terror like a comet, or more like the planet red
That once inclos'd the terrible wandering comets in its sphere.
Then Mars thou wast our center, & the planets three flew round
Thy crimson disk; so e'er the Sun was rent from thy red sphere;
The Spectre glowd his horrid length staining the temple long
With beams of blood; & thus a voice came forth, and shook the
temple:

'The morning comes, the night decays, the watchmen leave their
stations;
The grave is burst, the spices shed, the linen wrapped up;
The bones of death, the cov'ring clay, the sinews shrunk & dry'd
Reviving shake, inspiring move, breathing! awakening!
Spring like redeemed captives when their bonds & bars are burst;
Let the slave grinding at the mill, run out into the field;
Let him look up into the heavens & laugh in the bright air;
Let the inchained soul shut up in darkness and in sighing,
Whose face has never seen a smile in thirty weary years;
Rise and look out, his chains are loose, his dungeon doors are
open
And let his wife and children return from the oppressor's scourge;
They look behind at every step & believe it is a dream,
Singing, "The Sun has left his blackness, & has found a fresher
morning
And the fair Moon rejoices in the clear & cloudless night;
For empire is no more, and now the Lion & Wolf shall cease."'

In thunders ends the voice. Then Albion's Angel wrathful burnt
Beside the Stone of Night; and like the Eternal Lion's howl
In famine & war reply'd: 'Art thou not Orc, who serpent-form'd
Stands at the gate of Enitharmon to devour her children?
Blasphemous demon, Antichrist, hater of Dignities:
Lover of wild rebellion, and transgresser of God's Law;
Why dost thou come to Angels' eyes in this terrific form?'

The Terror answerd: 'I am Orc, wreath'd round the accursed tree:
The times are ended; shadows pass, the morning gins to break;
The fiery joy, that Urizen perverted to ten commands,
What night he led the starry hosts thro' the wide wilderness;
That stony law I stamp to dust; and scatter religion abroad
To the four winds as a torn book, & none shall gather the leaves;
But they shall rot on desart sands, & consume in bottomless deeps,
To make the desarts blossom, & the deeps drink to their fountains,
And to renew the fiery joy, and burst the stony roof,
That pale religious letchery, seeking Virginity,
May find it in a harlot, and in coarse-clad honesty
The undefil'd tho' ravish'd in her cradle night and morn:
For every thing that lives is holy, life delights in life;
Because the soul of sweet delight can never be defil'd.
Fires inwrap the earthly globe, yet man is not consumd;
Amidst the lustful fires he walks; his feet become like brass,
His knees and thighs like silver, & his breast and head like gold.'

'Sound! sound! my loud war-trumpets & alarm my Thirteen Angels!
Loud howls the eternal Wolf! the eternal Lion lashes his tail!
America is darkned; and my punishing Demons terrified
Crouch howling before their caverns deep like skins dry'd in the wind.
They cannot smite the wheat, nor quench the fatness of the earth.
They cannot smite with sorrows, nor subdue the plow and spade.
They cannot wall the city, nor moat round the castle of princes.
They cannot bring the stubbed oak to overgrow the hills,
For terrible men stand on the shores, & in their robes I see
Children take shelter from the lightnings, there stands Washington

And Paine and Warren with their foreheads reard toward the east
But clouds obscure my aged sight. A vision from afar!
Sound! sound! my loud war-trumpets & alarm my thirteen Angels:
Ah vision from afar! Ah rebel form that rent the ancient
Heavens, Eternal Viper self-renew'd, rolling in clouds
I see thee in thick clouds and darkness on America's shore,
Writhing in pangs of abhorred birth; red flames the crest rebellious
And eyes of death; the harlot womb oft opened in vain
Heaves in enormous circles, now the times are return'd upon thee,
Devourer of thy parent, now thy unutterable torment renews.
Sound! sound! my loud war trumpets & alarm my thirteen Angels.

'Ah terrible birth! a young one bursting! where is the weeping mouth?
And where the mother's milk? instead those ever-hissing jaws
And parched lips drop with fresh gore; now roll thou in the clouds;
Thy mother lays her length outstretch'd upon the shore beneath
Sound! sound! my loud war-trumpets & alarm my thirteen Angels!
Loud howls the eternal Wolf: the eternal Lion lashes his tail!'

Thus wept the Angel voice & as he wept the terrible blasts
Of trumpets, blew a loud alarm across the Atlantic deep.
No trumpets answer; no reply of clarions or of fifes,
Silent the Colonies remain and refuse the loud alarm.

On those vast shady hills between America & Albion's shore
Now barr'd out by the Atlantic sea, call'd Atlantean hills
Because from their bright summits you may pass to the Golden world,
An ancient palace, archetype of might Emperies,
Rears its immortal pinnacle, built in the forest of God
By Ariston the king of beauty for his stolen bride.

Here on their magic seats the thirteen Angels sat perturb'd,
For clouds from the Atlantic hover o'er the solemn roof.

Fiery the Angels rose, & as they rose deep thunder roll'd
Around their shores; indignant burning with the fires of Orc
And Boston's Angel cried aloud as they flew thro' the dark night.

He cried: 'Why trembles honesty and like a murderer,
Why seeks he refuge from the frowns of his immortal station?
Must the generous tremble & leave his joy to the idle: to the pestilence!
That mock him? who commanded this, what God! what Angel!
To keep the gen'rous from experience till the ungenerous
Are unrestrained performers of the energies of nature;
Till pity is become a trade, and generosity a science,
That men get rich by, & the sandy desart is giv'n to the strong?
What God is he, writes laws of peace, & clothes him in a tempest?
What pitying Angel lusts for tears, and fans himself with sighs?
What crawling villain preaches abstinence & wraps himself
In fat of lambs? no more I follow, no more obedience pay.'

So cried he rending off his robe & throwing down his scepter
In sight of Albion's Guardian and all the thirteen Angels
Rent off their robes to the hungry wind, & threw their golden scepters
Down on the land of America, indignant they descended
Headlong from out their heav'nly heights, descending swift as fires
Over the land; naked & flaming are their lineaments seen
In the deep gloom, by Washington & Paine & Warren they stood
And the flame folded roaring fierce within the pitchy night
Before the Demon red, who burnt towards America,
In black smoke thunders and loud winds rejoicing in its terror
Breaking in smoky wreaths from the wild deep & gath'ring thick
In flames as of a furnace on the land from North to South
What time the thirteen Governors that England sent converse
In Bernard's house; the flames coverd the land, they rouze, they cry
Shaking their mental chains they rush in fury to the sea
To quench their anguish; at the feet of Washington down fall'n
They grovel on the sand and writhing lie, while all
The British soldiers thro' the thirteen states sent up a howl
Of anguish; threw their swords & muskets to the earth & ran

From their encampments and dark castles seeking where to hide
From the grim flames; and from the visions of Orc; in sight
Of Albion's Angel; who enrag'd his secret clouds open'd
From north to south, and burnt outstretchd on wings of wrath cov'ring
The eastern sky, spreading his awful wings across the heavens;
Beneath him rolld his num'rous hosts, all Albion's Angels camp'd
Darkend the Atlantic mountains & their trumpets shook the valleys,
Arm'd with diseases of the earth to cast upon the Abyss,
Their numbers forty millions, must'ring in the eastern sky.

In the flames stood & view'd the armies drawn out in the sky
Washington Franklin Paine & Warren Allen Gates & Lee:
And heard the voice of Albion's Angel give the thunderous command.
His plagues obedient to his voice flew forth out of their clouds
Falling upon America, as a storm to cut them off,
As a blight cuts the tender corn when it begins to appear.
Dark is the heaven above & cold & hard the earth beneath;
And as a plague wind fill'd with insects cuts off man & beast;
And as a sea o'erwhelms a land in the day of an earthquake;
Fury! rage! madness! in a wind swept through America
And the red flames of Orc that folded roaring fierce around
The angry shores, and the fierce rushing of th'inhabitants together:
The citizens of New-York close their books & lock their chests;
The mariners of Boston drop their anchors and unlade;
The scribe of Pennsylvania casts his pen upon the earth;
The builder of Virginia throws his hammer down in fear.

Then had America been lost, o'erwhelm'd by the Atlantic,
And Earth had lost another portion of the infinite,
But all rush together in the night in wrath and raging fire.
The red fires rag'd! the plagues recoil'd! then rolld they back with fury
On Albion's Angels: then the Pestilence began in streaks of red
Across the limbs of Albion's Guardian, the spotted plague smote Bristol's
And the Leprosy London's Spirit, sickening all their bands:
The millions sent up a howl of anguish and threw off their hammerd mail,

And cast their swords & spears to earth, & stood a naked multitude.
Albion's Guardian writhed in torment on the eastern sky
Pale quivring toward the brain his glimmering eyes, teeth chattering,
Howling & shuddering, his legs quivering; convuls'd each muscle & sinew.
Sick'ning lay London's Guardian, and the ancient miter'd York,
Their heads on snowy hills, their ensigns sick'ning in the sky.

The plagues creep on the burning winds driven by flames of Orc,
And by the fierce Americans rushing together in the night
Driven o'er the Guardians of Ireland and Scotland and Wales.
They spotted with plagues forsook the frontiers & their banners seard
With fires of hell, deform their ancient heavens with shame & woe.
Hid in his caves the Bard of Albion felt the enormous plagues,
And a cowl of flesh grew o'er his head & scales on his back & ribs;
And rough with black scales all his Angels fright their ancient heavens.
The doors of marriage are open, and the Priests in rustling scales
Rush into reptile coverts, hiding from the fires of Orc,
That play around the golden roofs in wreathes of fierce desire,
Leaving the females naked and glowing with the lusts of youth

For the female spirits of the dead pining in bonds of religion
Run from their fetters reddening, & in long drawn arches sitting:
They feel the nerves of youth renew, and desires of ancient times.
Over their pale limbs as a vine when the tender grape appears.
Over the hills, the vales, the cities rage the red flames fierce;
The Heavens melted from north to south; and Urizen who sat
Above all heavens in thunders wrap'd, emerg'd his leprous head
From out his holy shrine, his tears in deluge piteous
Falling into the deep sublime; flag'd with grey-brow'd snows
And thunderous visages, his jealous wings wav'd over the deep;
Weeping in dismal howling woe he dark descended howling
Around the smitten bands, clothed in tears & trembling shudd'ring cold
His stored snows he poured forth, and his icy magazines
He open'd on the deep and on the Atlantic sea white shiv'ring.

Leprous his limbs, all over white, and hoary was his visage,
Weeping in dismal howlings before the stern Americans,
Hiding the Demon red with clouds & cold mists from the earth:
Till Angels & weak men twelve years should govern o'er the strong;
And then their end should come, when France reciev'd the Demon's light.

Stiff shudderings shook the heav'nly thrones! France, Spain, & Italy,
In terror view'd the bands of Albion, and the ancient Guardians
Fainting upon the elements, smitten with their own plagues
They slow advance to shut the five gates of their law-built heaven
Filled with blasting fancies and with mildews of despair,
With fierce disease and lust, unable to stem the fires of Orc;
But the five gates were consum'd, & their bolts and hinges melted
And the fierce flames burnt round the heavens, & round the abodes of men.

FINIS

Notebook

(Manuscript [?1793–?1818])

'My Spectre around me'

1
My Spectre around me night & day
Like a Wild beast guards my way.
My Emanation far within
Weeps incessantly for my Sin.

2
A Fathomless & boundless deep,
There we wander, there we weep
On the hungry craving wind
My Spectre follows thee behind.

3
He scents thy footsteps in the snow
Wheresoever thou dost go
Thro the wintry hail & rain;
When wilt thou return again?

4
[Stanza 4 is deleted]

5
Seven of my sweet loves thy knife
Has bereaved of their life.
Their marble tombs I built with tears
And with cold & shuddering fears.

6

Seven more loves weep night & day
Round the tombs where my loves lay
And seven more loves attend each night
Around my couch with torches bright.

7

And Seven more Loves in my bed
Crown with wine my mournful head,
Pitying & forgiving all
Thy transgressions great & small.

8

When wilt thou return & view
My loves & them to life renew?
When wilt thou return & live?
When wilt thou pity as I forgive?

9

Never Never I return.
Still for Victory I burn.
Living thee alone I'll have
And when dead I'll be thy Grave.

10

Thro Heavn & Earth & Hell
Thou shalt never never quell.
I will fly & thou pursue,
Night & Morn the flight renew.

11

Till I turn from Female Love
And root up the Infernal Grove
I shall never worthy be
To Step into Eternity

12

And to end thy cruel mocks
Annihilate thee on the rocks
And another form create
To be subservient to my Fate.

13

Let us agree to give up Love
And root up the infernal grove.
Then shall we return & see
The worlds of happy Eternity

14

& Throughout all Eternity
I forgive you, you forgive me,
As our dear Redeemer said
This the Wine & this the Bread.

[15]

Oer my Sins Thou Sit & moan.
Hast thou no Sins of thy own?
Oer my Sins thou sit & weep
And lull thy own Sins fast asleep.

[16]

What Transgressions I commit
Are for thy Transgressions fit,
They thy Harlots, thou their Slave
And my Bed becomes their Grave.

[17]

Poor pale pitiable form
That I follow in a Storm,
Iron tears & groans of lead
Bind around my aking head

[18]

And let us go to the high downs
With many pleasing wiles.
The Woman that does not love your Frowns
Will never embrace your smiles.

'When a Man has Married a Wife'

When a Man has Married a Wife he finds out whether
Her knees & elbows are only glued together.

'When Klopstock England defied'

When Klopstock England defied
Uprose William Blake in his pride
For old Nobodaddy aloft
Farted & Belchd & coughd,
Then swore a great oath that made heaven quake
And calld aloud to English Blake.
Blake was giving his body ease
At Lambeth beneath the poplar trees.
From his seat then started he
And turned himself round three times three.
The Moon at that sight blushd scarlet red,
The stars threw down their cups & fled
And all the devils that were in hell
Answered with a ninefold yell.
Klopstock felt the intripled turn
And all his bowels began to churn
And his bowels turned round three times three
And Lockd in his soul with a ninefold key
That from his body it neer could be parted
Till to the last trumpet it was farted.
Then again old Nobodaddy swore
He neer had seen such a thing before
Since Noah was shut in the ark,
Since Eve first chose her hell fire Spark,
Since twas the fashion to go naked,
Since the old anything was created
And so feeling he begd him to turn again
And ease poor Klopstock's ninefold pain.
From pity then he returnd round
And the ninefold spell unwound.
If Blake could do this when he rose up from shite
What might he not do if he sat down to write?

On the Virginity of the Virgin Mary & Johanna Southcott

Whateer is done to her she cannot know
And if you'll ask her she will swear it so;
Whether tis good or evil none's to blame,
No one can take the pride, no one the shame.

'Mock on, Mock on Voltaire, Rousseau'

Mock on, Mock on Voltaire, Rousseau,
Mock on, Mock on: tis all in vain!
You throw the sand against the wind
And the wind blows it back again

And every sand becomes a Gem
Reflected in the beams divine;
Blown back they blind the mocking Eye
But still in Israel's paths they shine.

The Atoms of Democritus
And Newton's Particles of light
Are sands upon the Red sea shore
Where Israel's tents do shine so bright.

'I saw a Monk of Charlemaine'

1 I saw a Monk of Charlemaine
Arise before my sight.
I talkd to the Grey Monk where he stood
In beams of infernal light.

2 Gibbon arose with a lash of steel
And Voltaire with a wracking wheel.
The Schools in clouds of Learning rolld,
Arose with War in iron & gold.

Gibbon plied his lash of steel,
Voltaire turnd his wracking wheel,
Charlemaine & his barons bold
Stood by & mockd in iron & gold.

The Wheel of Voltaire whirld on high,
Gibbon aloud his lash does ply,
Charlemaine & his clouds of War
Muster around the Polar Star.

A Grecian Scoff is a wracking wheel,
The Roman pride is a sword of steel,
Glory & Victory a plaited Whip
3 'Thou Lazy Monk' they sound afar
'In vain condemning Glorious War
And in thy Cell thou shalt ever dwell.
Rise War & bind him in his Cell!'

4 The blood red ran from the Grey monk's side,
His hands & feet were wounded wide.
His body bent, his arms & knees
Like to the roots of ancient trees,

Until the Tyrant himself relent,
The Tyrant who first the black bow bent,
Slaughter shall heap the bloody plain,
Resistance & war is the Tyrant's gain

But The Tear of Love & forgiveness sweet
And submission to death beneath his feet,
The Tear shall melt the sword of steel
And every wound it has made shall heal.

5 When Satan first the black bow bent
And the Moral Law from the Gospel rent
He forg'd the Law into a Sword
And spilld the blood of Mercy's Lord.

6 Titus, Constantine, Charlemaine,
O Voltaire, Rousseau, Gibbon, vain
Your Grecian mocks & Roman Sword
Against this image of his Lord

7 For the tear is an intellectual thing
And a Sigh is the Sword of an Angel King
And the bitter groan of the Martyr's woe
Is an arrow from the Almightie's bow.

'"I die I die" the Mother said'

'I die I die' the Mother said,
'My Children will die for lack of bread!
What more has the merciless tyrant said?'
The Monk sat down on her stony bed.

His Eye was dry, no tear could flow.
A hollow groan first spoke his woe.
He trembled & shudderd upon the bed.
At length with a feeble cry he said

'When God commanded this hand to write
In the studious hours of deep midnight
He told me that All I wrote should prove
The bane of all that on Earth I love.

'My brother starvd between two walls,
His children's cry my soul appalls.
I mockd at the wrack & griding chain,
My bent body mocks at their torturing pain.

'Thy father drew his sword in the north,
With his thousands strong he is marched forth.
Thy brother has armed himself in steel
To revenge the wrongs thy Children feel.

'But vain the sword & vain the bow,
They never can work war's overthrow!
The Hermit's prayer & the widow's tear
Alone can free the world from fear.'

The hand of vengeance sought the bed
To which the purple tyrant fled.
The iron hand crushd the tyrant's head
And became a tyrant in his stead.

'Beneath the white thorn'

Beneath the white thorn lovely May,
'Alas for wo! alas for wo! alas for wo!'
They cry & tears for ever flow.
3 The one was clothd in flames of fire,
4 The other clothd in Iron wire,
5 The other clothd in tears & sighs
6 Dazzling bright before my Eyes
1 They bore a Net of Golden twine
2 To hang upon the branches fine
And in tears clothd night & day
Melted all my soul away.
When they saw my tears a smile
That did heaven itself beguile
Bore the Golden net aloft
And by downy pinions soft
Oer the morning of my day.
Underneath the net I stray
Now intreating flaming fire,
Now intreating iron wire,
Now intreating tears & sighs.
O when will the Morning rise?

The Birds

He. Where thou dwellest, in what grove,
Tell me Fair one, tell me love
Where thou thy charming Nest does build,
O thou pride of every field.

She. Yonder stands a lonely tree,
There I live & mourn for thee.
Morning drinks my Silent tear
And Evning winds my sorrows bear.

He. O thou Summer's harmony,
I have livd & mournd for thee.
Each day I mourn along the wood
And night hath heard my sorrows loud.

She. Dost thou truly long for me
And am I thus sweet to thee?
Sorrow now is at an End
O my Lover & my Friend.

He. Come, on wings of joy we'll fly
To where my Bower hangs on high.
Come & make thy calm retreat
Among green leaves & blossoms sweet.

'You don't believe'

You don't believe, I won't attempt to make ye.
You are asleep, I won't attempt to wake ye.
Sleep on, Sleep on while in your pleasant dreams
Of Reason you may drink of Life's clear streams.
Reason and Newton, they are quite two things
For so the Swallow & the Sparrow sings.
Reason Says Miracle, Newton Says Doubt.
Aye, that's the way to make all Nature out.
Doubt, Doubt & don't believe without experiment,
That is the very thing that Jesus meant
When he said 'Only Believe, Believe & try
Try, Try & never mind the Reason why.'

'Anger & wrath my bosom rends'

Anger & wrath my bosom rends;
I thought them the Errors of friends
But all my limbs with warmth glow;
I find them the Errors of the foe.

'Madman I have been calld'

Madman I have been calld, Fool they Call thee.
I wonder which they Envy, Thee or Me.

To F—

I mock thee not tho I by thee am Mocked.
Thou callst me Madman but I call thee Blockhead.

'He's a Blockhead'

He's a Blockhead who wants a proof of what he Can't Percieve
And he's a Fool who tries to make such a Blockhead believe.

'Cr— loves artists'

Cr— loves artists as he loves his Meat;
He loves the Art but tis the Art to Cheat.

'He has observd the Golden Rule'

He has observd the Golden Rule
Till he's become the Golden Fool.

'The Angel that presided oer my birth'

The Angel that presided oer my birth
Said 'Little creature formd of Joy & Mirth
Go live without the help of any King on Earth.'

On F— & S—

I found them blind, I taught them how to see
And now they know neither themselves nor me.

'P— lovd me not'

P— lovd me not as he lovd his Friends
For he lovd them for gain to serve his Ends.
He loved me and for no Gain at all
But to rejoice & triumph in my fall.

'Great things are done'

Great things are done when Men & Mountains meet.
This is not done by Jostling in the Street.

'The only Man that eer I knew'

The only Man that eer I knew
Who did not make me almost spew
Was Fuseli, he was both Turk & Jew
And so dear Christian Friends how do you do?

William Cowper Esqre

For this is being a Friend just in the nick
Not when he's well but waiting till he's Sick.
He calls you to his help, be you not movd
Untill by being Sick his wants are provd.

You see him spend his Soul in Prophecy,
Do you believe it a Confounded lie
Till some Bookseller & the Public Fame
Proves there is truth in his extravagant claim

For tis atrocious in a Friend you love
To tell you any thing that he can't prove
And tis most wicked in a Christian Nation
For any Man to pretend to Inspiration.

'Grown old in Love'

Grown old in Love from Seven till Seven times seven
I oft have wishd for Hell for Ease from Heaven.

'Great Men & Fools do often me Inspire'

Great Men & Fools do often me Inspire
But the Greater Fool the Greater Liar.

To God

If you have formd a Circle to go into
Go into it yourself & see how you would do.

'Since all the Riches of this World'

Since all the Riches of this World
May be gifts from the Devil & Earthly Kings
I should suspect that I worshipd the Devil
If I thankd my God for Worldly things.

'Now Art has lost its mental Charms'

'Now Art has lost its mental Charms
France shall subdue the World in arms.'
So spoke an Angel at my birth,
Then Said 'Descend thou upon Earth,
Renew the Arts on Britain's Shore
And France shall fall down & adore.
With works of Art their Armies meet
And War shall sink beneath thy feet
But if thy Nation Arts refuse
And if they Scorn the immortal Muse
France shall the arts of Peace restore
And save thee from the Ungrateful Shore.

Spirit who lovst Brittannia's Isle
Round which the Fiends of Commerce smile [. . .]

'The Caverns of the Grave I've seen'

The Caverns of the Grave I've seen
And these I shewd to England's Queen
But now the Caves of Hell I view:
Who shall I dare to shew them to?
What mighty Soul in Beauty's form
Shall dauntless View the Infernal Storm?
Egremont's Countess can Controll
The flames of Hell that round me roll.
If she refuse I still go on
Till the Heavens & Earth are gone
Still admird by Noble minds,
Followd by Envy on the winds.
Reengravd Time after Time,
Ever in their Youthful prime
My Designs unchangd remain.
Time may rage but rage in vain
For above Time's troubled Fountains
On the Great Atlantic Mountains
In my Golden House on high
There they Shine Eternally.

'I rose up at the dawn of day'

I rose up at the dawn of day:
'Get thee away, get thee away!
Prayst thou for Riches? away, away!
This is the Throne of Mammon grey.'

Said I 'this sure is very odd.
I took it to be the throne of God.
For every Thing besides I have,
It is only for Riches that I can crave.

'I have Mental Joy & Mental Health
And Mental Friends & Mental wealth,
I've a Wife I love & that loves me,
I've all But Riches Bodily.

'I am in God's presence night & day
And he never turns his face away.
The accuser of sins by my side does Stand
And he holds my money bag in his hand.

'For my worldly things God makes him pay
And he'd pay for more if to him I would pray
And so you may do the worst you can do
Be assurd Mr Devil I won't pray to you.

'Then If for Riches I must not Pray
God knows I little of Prayers need say
So as a Church is known by its Steeple
If I pray it must be for other People.

'He says if I do not worship him for a God
I shall eat coarser food & go worse shod
So as I don't value such things as these
You must do Mr Devil just as God please.'

Several Questions Answerd

What is it men in women do require?
The Lineaments of Gratifid Desire.
What is it women do in men require?
The lineaments of Gratifid desire.

2 The look of love alarms
Because tis filld with fire
But the look of soft deceit
Shall Win the lover's hire.

3 Soft deceit & Idleness,
These are Beauty's sweetest dress.

1 He who bends to himself a joy
Does the winged life destroy
But he who kisses the joy as it flies
Lives in Eternity's sun rise.

'Fayette'

Fayette beheld the King & Queen
In tears & iron bound
But meek Fayette wept tear for tear
And guarded them around.

Who will exchange his own fire side
For the steps of another's door?
Who will exchange his wheaten loaf
For the links of a dungeon floor?

Fayette, Fayette, thou'rt bought & sold
And sold is thy happy morrow.
Thou givest the tears of Pity away
In exchange for the tears of sorrow.

O who would smile on the wintry seas
& Pity the stormy roar
Or who will exchange his newborn child
For the dog at the wintry door?

'Let the Brothels of Paris be opend'

1 'Let the Brothels of Paris be opend
2 With many an alluring dance
3 To awake the Physicians thro the city,'
4 Said the beautiful Queen of France.

9 The King awoke on his couch of gold
10 As soon as he heard these tidings told.
11 'Arise & come, both fife & drum,
12 And the Famine shall eat both crust & crumb.'

Then old Nobodaddy aloft
Farted & belchd & coughd
7 And Said 'I love hanging & drawing & quartering
8 Every bit as well as war & slaughtering.'

5 Then he swore a great & solemn Oath:
6 'To kill the people I am loth
But if they rebel they must go to hell;
They shall have a Priest & a passing bell.'

The Queen of France just touchd this Globe
And the Pestilence darted from her robe
But our good Queen quite grows to the ground
And a great many suckers grow all around.

'O I cannot cannot find'

2 O I cannot cannot find
The undaunted courage of a Virgin Mind
For Early I in Love was crost
Before my flower of love was lost.

1 An Old man early eer I knew
Ought but the love that on me grew
And now I'm coverd oer & oer
And wish that I had been a Whore.

Motto to the Songs of Innocence & of Experience

The Good are attracted by Men's perceptions
And Think not for themselves
Till Experience teaches them to catch
And to Cage the Fairies & Elves

And then the Knave begins to snarl
And the Hypocrite to howl
And all his good Friends shew their private ends
And the Eagle is known from the Owl.

An answer to the parson

'Why of the sheep do you not learn peace?'
'Because I don't want you to shear my fleece!'

'Abstinence sows sand all over'

Abstinence sows sand all over
The ruddy limbs & flourishing hair
But desire Gratified
Plants fruits of life & beauty there.

'In a wife I would desire'

In a wife I would desire
What in whores is always found,
The lineaments of Gratified desire.

'Deceit to secresy confind'

Deceit to secresy confind,
Lawful cautious & refind,
To every thing but interest blind
And forges fetters for the mind.

Merlin's prophecy

The harvest shall flourish in wintry weather
When two virginities meet together.

The King & the Priest must be tied in a tether
Before two virgins can meet together.

How to know Love from Deceit

Love to faults is always blind,
Always is to joy inclind,
Lawless, wingd & unconfind
And breaks all chains from every mind.

Soft Snow

I walked abroad in a snowy day.
I askd the soft snow with me to play.
She playd & she melted in all her prime
And the winter calld it a dreadful crime.

An ancient Proverb

Remove away that blackning church,
Remove away that marriage hearse,
Remove away that man of blood,
You'll quite remove the ancient curse.

London

I wander thro each dirty street
Near where the dirty Thames does flow
And ~~see~~ mark in every face I meet
Marks of weakness, marks of woe.

In every cry of every man,
In ~~every voice of every child~~ every infant's cry of fear,
In every voice, in every ban
The ~~german~~ mind forgd ~~links I hear~~ manacles I hear,

~~But most~~ How the chimney sweeper's cry
~~Blackens oer the churches walls~~
Every blackning church appals
And the hapless soldier's sigh
Runs in blood down palace walls.

But most the midnight harlot's curse
From every dismal street I hear
Weaves around the marriage hearse
And blasts the new born infant's tear.

But most ~~from every~~ thro wintry streets I hear
How the midnight harlot's curse
Blasts the new born infant's tear
And ~~hangs~~ smites with plagues the marriage hearse
But most the shrieks of youth I hear
But most thro midnight &
How the youthful

'I slept in the dark'

I slept in the dark
In the silent night,
I murmurd my fears
And I felt delight.

In the morning I went
As rosy as morn
To seek for new joy
But I met with scorn.

To Nobodaddy

Why art thou silent & invisible
Father of Jealousy?
Why dost thou hide thyself in clouds
From every searching Eye?

Why darkness & obscurity
In all thy words & laws
That none dare eat the fruit but from
The wily serpent's jaws
Or is it because Secrecy
gains females' loud applause

The Tyger

1 Tyger Tyger burning bright
In the forests of the night,
What immortal hand ~~&~~ or eye
~~Could~~ ~~Dare~~ frame thy fearful symmetry?

2 ~~In what~~ ~~Burnt in~~ distant deeps or Skies
~~Burnt the~~ ~~The cruel~~ fire of thine eyes?
On what wings dare he aspire?
What the hand dare seize the fire?

3 And what shoulder & what art
Could twist the sinews of thy heart
And when thy heart began to beat
What dread hand & what dread feet

Could fetch it from the furnace deep
And in ~~the~~ thy horrid ribs dare steep
In the well of sanguine woe
In what clay & in what mould
Were thy eyes of fire rolld

4 ~~What~~ Where the hammer, ~~what~~ where the chain,
In what furnace was thy brain?
What the anvil? What ~~the arm~~ ~~arm~~ ~~grasp~~ ~~clasp~~ dread grasp
~~Could~~ Dare its deadly terrors ~~clasp~~ ~~grasp~~ clasp?

5 ~~3~~ And ~~is did he laugh~~ dare he ~~smile~~ ~~laugh~~ his work to see
What the ~~Shoulder~~ ankle, what the knee
4 ~~Did~~ Dare he who made the lamb make thee?
1 When the stars threw down their spears
2 And waterd heaven with their tears

6 Tyger Tyger burning bright
In the forests of the night,
What immortal hand & eye
Dare ~~form~~ frame thy fearful symmetry?

[*Revised version*]

Tyger Tyger burning bright
In the forests of the night,
What immortal hand & eye
Dare frame thy fearful symmetry?

Burnt in distant deeps or skies
The cruel fire of thine eyes?
Could heart descend or wings aspire?
What the hand dare seize the fire

And what shoulder & what art
Could twist the sinews of thy heart
And when thy heart began to beat
What dread hand & what dread feet?

When the stars threw down their spears
And waterd heaven with their tears,
Did he smile his work to see?
Did he who made the Lamb make thee?

Tyger Tyger burning bright
In the forests of the night,
What immortal hand & eye
Dare frame thy fearful symmetry?

'Are not the joys of morning'

Are not the joys of morning sweeter
Than the joys of night
And are the vigrous joys of youth
Ashamed of the light?

Let age & sickness silent rob
The vineyards in the night
But those who burn with vigrous youth
Pluck fruits before the light.

'Thou hast a lap full of seed'

'Thou hast a lap full of seed
And this is a fine country.
Why dost thou not cast thy seed
And live in it merrily?'

'Shall I cast it on the sand
And turn it into fruitful land
For on no other ground
Can I sow my seed
Without tearing up
Some stinking weed.'

in a mirtle shade

1 Why should I be bound to thee
O my lovely mirtle tree?
Love free love cannot be bound
To any tree that grows on ground.

2 O how sick & weary I
Underneath my mirtle lie
Like to dung upon the ground
Underneath my mirtle bound.

3 Oft my mirtle sighd in vain
To behold my heavy chain.
Oft my father saw us sigh
And laughd at our simplicity

So I smote him & his gore
Staind the roots my mirtle bore
But the time of youth is fled
And grey hairs are on my head.

'Why should I care for the men of Thames'

Why should I care for the men of Thames
Or the cheating waves of charterd streams
Or shrink at the little blasts of fear
That the hireling blows into my ear?

Tho born on the cheating banks of Thames,
Tho his waters bathed my infant limbs,
The Ohio shall wash his stains from me,
I was born a slave but I go to be free.

'I feard the fury of my wind'

I feard the fury of my wind
Would blight all blossoms fair & true
And my sun it shind & shind
And my wind it never blew

But a blossom fair or true
Was not found on any tree
For all blossoms grew & grew
Fruitless false tho fair to see.

Infant Sorrow

My mother groand, my father wept,
Into the dangerous world I leapt
Helpless naked piping loud
Like a fiend hid in a cloud.

Struggling in my father's hands
Striving against my swaddling bands
Bound & weary I thought best
To sulk upon my mother's breast.

When I saw that rage was vain
And to sulk would nothing gain
Turning many a trick & wile
I began to soothe & smile.

And I Soothd day after day
Till upon the ground I stray
And I smild night after night
Seeking only for delight

And I saw before me shine
Clusters of the wandring vine
And many a lovely flower & tree
Stretchd their blossoms out to me.

My father then with holy look
In his hands a holy book
Pronouncd curses on my head
And bound me in a mirtle shade.

I beheld the Priests by night,
They embraced the blossoms bright.
I beheld the Priests by day
Where underneath the vines they lay

3 Like to serpents in the night
4 He embracd my blossoms bright
1 Like to holy men by day
2 Underneath the vines they lay

So I smote them & their gore
Staind the roots my mirtle bore
But the time of youth is fled
And grey hairs are on my head.

'Silent Silent Night'

Silent Silent Night
Quench the holy light
Of thy torches bright

For possessd of Day
Thousand spirits stray
That sweet joys betray.

Why should joys be sweet
Used with deceit
Nor with sorrows meet?

But an honest joy
Does itself destroy
For a harlot coy.

'O lapwing thou fliest around the heath'

O lapwing thou fliest around the heath
Nor seest the net that is spread beneath.
Why dost thou not fly among the corn fields?
They cannot spread nets where a harvest yields.

'I laid me down upon a bank'

I laid me down upon a bank
Where love lay sleeping.
I heard among the rushes dank
Weeping, Weeping.

Then I went to the heath & the wild,
To the thistles & thorns of the waste
And they told me how they were beguild
Driven out & compeld to be chaste.

'I saw a chapel all of gold'

I saw a chapel all of gold
That none did dare to enter in
And many weeping stood without
Weeping, mourning, worshipping.

I saw a serpent rise between
The white pillars of the door
And he forcd & forcd & forcd
Down the golden hinges tore

And along the pavement sweet
Set with pearls & rubies bright
All his slimy length he drew
Till upon the altar white

Vomiting his poisons out
On the bread & on the wine.
So I turnd into a sty
And laid me down among the swine.

[The Everlasting Gospel]
(Manuscript, [?1826])

[*Part a*]

There is not one Moral Virtue that Jesus Inculcated but Plato & Cicero did Inculcate before him; what then did Christ Inculcate? Forgiveness of Sins! This alone is the Gospel & this is the Life & Immortality brought to light by Jesus, Even the Covenant of Jehovah which is This: If you forgive one another your Trespasses so shall Jehovah forgive you That he himself may dwell among you but if you Avenge you Murder the Divine Image & he cannot dwell among you: because you Murder him he arises Again & you deny that he is Arisen & are blind to Spirit.

[*Part b*]

2

What can this Gospel of Jesus be,
What Life & Immortality?
What was it that he brought to Light
That Plato & Cicero did not write?
The Heathen Deities wrote them all,
These Mortal Virtues great & small.
What is the Accusation of Sin
But Moral Virtues' deadly Gin?
The Moral Virtues in their Pride
Did oer the World triumphant ride
In Wars & Sacrifice for Sin
And Souls to Hell ran trooping in.
The Accuser Holy God of All
This Pharisaic Worldly Ball
Amidst them in his Glory Beams
Upon the Rivers & the Streams.
Then Jesus rose & said to Me
'Thy Sins are all forgiven thee.'
Loud Pilate Howld, loud Caiaphas yelld
When they the Gospel Light beheld.
It was when Jesus said to Me
'Thy Sins are all forgiven thee.'
The Christian trumpets loud proclaim
Thro all the World in Jesus name
Mutual forgiveness of each Vice
And oped the Gates of Paradise.
The Moral Virtues in great fear
Formed the Cross & Nails & Spear
And the Accuser standing by
Cried out 'Crucify! Crucify!
Our Moral Virtues neer can be
Nor Warlike pomp & Majesty
For Moral Virtues all begin
In the Accusations of Sin
And all the Heroic Virtues End
In destroying the Sinner's Friend.
Am I not Lucifer the Great
And you my daughters in Great State

The fruit of my Mysterious Tree
Of Good & Evil & Misery
And death & Hell which now begin
On every one who Forgives Sin?'

[*Part c*]

1 This to come first.
If Moral Virtue was Christianity
Christ's Pretensions were all Vanity
And Caiaphas & Pilate Men
Praise Worthy & the Lion's Den
And not the Sheepfold Allegories
Of God & Heaven & their Glories.
The Moral Christian is the Cause
Of the Unbeliever & his Laws.
The Roman Virtues, Warlike Fame,
Take Jesus & Jehovah's Name
For what is Antichrist but those
Who against Sinners Heaven close
With Iron bars in Virtuous State
And Rhadamanthus at the Gate?

[*Part d*]

Was Jesus Born of a Virgin Pure
With narrow Soul & looks demure?
If he intended to take on Sin
The Mother Should an Harlot been,
Just such a one as Magdalen
With Seven devils in her Pen
Or were Jew Virgins still more Curst
And more sucking devils nurst
Or what was it which he took on
That he might bring Salvation?
A Body subject to be Tempted
From neither pain nor grief Exempted
Or such a body as must not feel
The passions that with Sinners deal?

Yes but they say he never fell.
Ask Caiaphas for he can tell.
He mockd the Sabbath & he mockd
The Sabbath's God & he unlockd
The Evil spirits from their Shrines
And turnd Fishermen to Divines,
Oerturnd the Tent of Secret Sins
& its golden cords & Pins.
Tis the Bloody Shrine of War
Pinnd around from Star to Star,
Halls of Justice hating Vice
Where the devil Combs his Lice.
He turnd the Devils into Swine
That he might tempt the Jews to Dine
Since which a Pig has got a look
That for a Jew may be mistook.
'Obey your Parents!' What says he?
'Woman, what have I to do with thee?
No Earthly Parents I confess;
I am doing my Father's Business.'
He scornd Earth's Parents, Scornd Earth's God
And mockd the one & the other's Rod,
His Seventy Disciples sent
Against Religion & Government.
They by the Sword of Justice fell
And him their Cruel Murderer tell.
He left his Father's trade to roam
A wandering Vagrant without Home
And thus he others' labour stole
That he might live above controll.
The Publicans & Harlots he
Selected for his Company
And from the Adulteress turnd away
God's righteous Law that lost its Prey.

[*Part e*]

The Vision of Christ that thou dost See
Is my Vision's greatest Enemy.
Thine has a great hook nose like thine.
Mine has a snub nose like to mine.

Thine is the friend of All Mankind,
Mine speaks in Parables to the Blind.
Thine loves the same world that mine hates,
Thy Heaven doors are my Hell Gates.
Socrates taught what Meletus
Loathd as a Nation's bitterest Curse
And Caiaphas was in his own Mind
A benefactor to Mankind.
Both read the Bible day & night
But thou readst black where I read White.

[*Part f*]

Was Jesus Chaste or did he
Give any Lessons of Chastity?
The morning blushed fiery red,
Mary was found in Adulterous bed.
Earth groand beneath & Heavn above
Trembled at discovery of Love.
Jesus was sitting in Moses' Chair;
They brought the trembling Woman There.
Moses commands she be stoned to death;
What was the Sound of Jesus breath?
He laid his hand on Moses' Law,
The ancient Heavens in Silent awe
Writ with Curses from Pole to Pole
All away began to roll;
The Earth trembling & Naked lay
In secret bed of Mortal Clay
On Sinai felt the hand divine
Putting back the bloody shrine
And She heard the breath of God
As she heard by Eden's flood:
'Good & Evil are no more!
Sinai's trumpets cease to roar!
Cease finger of God to Write!
The Heavens are not clean in thy Sight.
Thou art Good & thou Alone
Nor may the sinner cast one Stone.
To be Good only is to be
A Devil or else a Pharisee.

Thou Angel of the Presence divine
That didst create this Body of Mine,
Wherefore hast thou writ these Laws
And Created Hell's dark Jaws?
My Presence I will take from thee,
A Cold Leper thou shalt be
Tho thou wast so pure & bright
That Heaven was Impure in thy Sight,
Tho thy Oath turnd Heaven Pale,
Tho thy Covenant built Hell's jail,
Tho thou didst all to Chaos roll
With the Serpent for its soul,
Still the breath divine does move
And the breath divine is Love.
Mary, Fear Not! Let me See
The Seven Devils that torment thee!
Hide not from my Sight thy Sin
That forgiveness thou maist win.
Has no Man Condemned thee?'
'No Man, Lord!' 'Then what is he
Who shall Accuse thee? Come Ye forth
Fallen Fiends of Heavnly birth
That have forgot our Ancient Love
And driven away my trembling Dove.
You Shall bow before her feet,
You shall lick the dust for Meat
And tho you cannot Love but Hate
Shall be beggars at Love's Gate!
What was thy love? Let me See it!
Was it Love or dark Deceit?'
'Love too long from Me has fled.
Twas dark deceit to Earn my bread.
Twas Covet or Twas Custom or
Some trifle not worth caring for
That they may call a shame & Sin
Love's Temple that God dwelleth in
And hide in Secret hidden Shrine
    The Naked Human form divine
And render that a Lawless thing
    On which the Soul Expands its wing
But this, O Lord, this was my Sin
When first I let these Devils in

In dark pretence to Chastity
Blaspheming Love, blaspheming thee.
Thence Rose Secret Adulteries
And thence did Covet also rise
My Sin thou hast forgiven me.
Canst thou forgive my Blasphemy?
Canst thou return to this dark Hell
And in my burning bosom dwell
And canst thou die that I may live
And canst thou Pity & forgive?'
Then Rolld the Shadowy Man away
From the Limbs of Jesus to make him prey
An Ever devouring appetite
Glittering with festering Venoms bright
Crying 'Crucify this cause of distress
Who don't keep the secrets of Holiness!
All Mental Powers by Diseases we bind
But he heals the Deaf & the Dumb & the Blind.
Whom God has afflicted for Secret Ends
He Comforts & Heals & calls them Friends.'
But when Jesus was Crucified
Then was perfected his glittring pride
In three Nights he devourd his prey
And still he devours the Body of Clay
For dust & Clay is the Serpent's meat
Which never was made for Man to Eat.

[*Part g*]

Seeing this False Christ In fury & Passion
I made my Voice heard all over the Nation:
'What are those' &c

[*Part h*]

This was Spoke by My Spectre to Voltaire, Bacon &c
Did Jesus teach doubt or did he
Give any lessons of Philosophy,
Charge Visionaries with decieving
Or call Men wise for not Believing?

[*Part i*]

Was Jesus gentle or did he
Give any marks of Gentility?
When twelve years old he ran away
And left his Parents in dismay.
When after three days sorrow found,
Loud as Sinai's trumpet sound:
'No Earthly Parents I confess –
My Heavenly Father's business.
Ye understand not what I say
And angry force me to obey.'
Obedience is a duty then
And favour gains with God & Men.
John from the Wilderness loud cried;
Satan gloried in his Pride.
'Come' Said Satan 'come away.
I'll soon see if you'll obey.
John for disobedience bled
But you can turn the stones to bread.
God's high King & God's high Priest
Shall Plant their Glories in your breast.
If Caiaphas you will obey,
If Herod you with bloody Prey
Feed with the Sacrifice & be
Obedient, fall down, worship me!'
Thunders & lightnings broke around
And Jesus voice in thunders sound:
'Thus I seize the Spiritual Prey!
Ye Smiters with disease, make way!
I come Your King & God to seize.
Is God a Smiter with disease?'
The God of this World raged in vain.
He bound Old Satan in his Chain
And bursting forth his furious ire
Became a Chariot of fire.
Throughout the land he took his course
And traced diseases to their Source.
He cursd the Scribe & Pharisee
Trampling down Hipocrisy.

Where eer his Chariot took its way,
There Gates of death let in the day,
Broke down from every Chain & Bar
And Satan in his Spiritual War
Dragd at his Chariot wheels; loud howld
The God of this World; louder rolld
The Chariot Wheels & louder Still
His voice was heard from Zion's hill
And in his hand the Scourge shone bright.
He Scourgd the Merchant Canaanite
From out the Temple of his Mind
And in his Body tight does bind
Satan & all his Hellish Crew
And thus with wrath he did subdue
The Serpent Bulk of Nature's dross
Till he had naild it to the Cross.
He took on Sin in the Virgin's Womb
And put it off on the Cross & Tomb
To be Worshipd by the Church of Rome

[*Part j*]

Was Jesus Humble or did he
Give any proofs of Humility?
When but a Child he ran away
And left his Parents in dismay.
When they had wanderd three days long
These were the words upon his Tongue:
'No Earthly Parents I confess.
I am doing my Father's business.'
When the rich learned Pharisee
1 Came to consult him, secretly
4 He was too Proud to take a bribe.
5 He spoke with authority, not like a Scribe.
2 Upon his heart with Iron pen
3 He wrote 'Ye must be born again!'
6 He says with most consummate Art
'Follow me, I am meek & lowly of heart'
As that is the only way to Escape
The Miser's net & the Glutton's trap.

He who loves his Enemies hates his Friends.
This is surely not what Jesus intends.
He must mean the meer love of Civility
And so he must mean concerning Humility
But he acts with triumphant honest pride
And this is the Reason Jesus died.
If he had been Antichrist Creeping Jesus
He'd have done any thing to please us,
Gone sneaking into the Synagogues
And not used the Elders & Priests like dogs
But humble as a Lamb or an Ass
Obey himself to Caiaphas.
God wants not Man to humble himself.
This is the Trick of the Ancient Elf.
Humble toward God, Haughty toward Man,
This is the Race that Jesus ran
And when he humbled himself to God
Then descended the Cruel Rod.
'If thou humblest thyself thou humblest me.
Thou also dwelst in Eternity.
Thou art a Man, God is no more!
Thine own Humanity learn to Adore
And thy Revenge Abroad display
In terrors at the Last Judgment day!
God's Mercy & Long Suffering
Are but the Sinner to Judgment to bring.
Thou on the Cross for them shalt pray
And take Revenge at the last Day.'

Do what you will, this Life's a Fiction
And is made up of Contradiction.

[*Part k*]
The Everlasting Gospel

Was Jesus Humble or did he
Give any Proofs of Humility,
Boast of high Things with Humble tone
And give with Charity a Stone?
When but a Child he ran away
And left his Parents in dismay.

When they had wanderd three days long
These were the words upon his tongue:
'No Earthly Parents I confess!
I am doing my Father's business!'
When the rich learned Pharisee
Came to consult him secretly
Upon his heart with Iron pen
He wrote 'Ye must be born again.'
He was too proud to take a bribe.
He spoke with authority, not like a Scribe.
He says with most consummate Art
'Follow me, I am meek & lowly of heart'
As that is the only way to escape
The Miser's net & the Glutton's trap.
What can be done with such desperate Fools
Who follow after the Heathen Schools?
I was standing by when Jesus died.
What I call'd Humility they calld Pride
He who loves his Enemies betrays his Friends;
This Surely is not what Jesus intends
But the Sneaking Pride of Heroic Schools
And the Scribes' & Pharisees' Virtuous Rules
For he acts with honest triumphant Pride
And this is the cause that Jesus died.
He did not die with Christian Ease
Asking Pardon of his Enemies.
If he had Caiaphas would forgive;
Sneaking submission can always live.
He had only to say that God was the devil
And the devil was God like a Christian Civil,
Mild Christian regrets to the devil Confess
a For affronting him thrice in the Wilderness
Like d^{r} Priestly & Bacon & Newton
1 Poor Spiritual Knowledge is not worth a button
b He had soon been bloody Caesar's Elf
c And at last he would have been Caesar himself
2 For thus the Gospel Sr Isaac confutes:
3 'God can only be known by his Attributes
And as for the indwelling of the Holy Ghost
Or of Christ & his Father it's all a boast
And Pride & Vanity of the imagination
That disdains to follow this World's Fashion.'

To teach doubt & Experiment
Certainly was not what Christ meant.
What was he doing all that time
From twelve years old to manly prime?
Was he then Idle or the Less
About his Father's business
Or was his wisdom held in Scorn
Before his wrath began to burn
In Miracles throughout the Land
That quite unnervd the Caiaphas band?
If he had been Antichrist Creeping Jesus
He'd have done any thing to please us,
Gone Sneaking into Synagogues
And not usd the Elders & Priests like dogs
But Humble as a Lamb or Ass
Obeyd himself to Caiaphas.
God wants not Man to Humble himself;
This is the trick of the ancient Elf.
This is the Race that Jesus ran:
Humble to God, Haughty to Man,
Cursing the Rulers before the People
Even to the temple's highest Steeple
And when he Humbled himself to God
Then descended the Cruel Rod.
'If thou humblest thyself thou humblest me!
Thou also dwellst in Eternity!
Thou art a Man, God is no more!
Thy own humanity learn to adore
For this is my Spirit of Life.
Awake, arise to Spiritual Strife
And thy Revenge abroad display
In terrors at the Last Judgment day!
God's Mercy & Long Suffering
Is but the Sinner to Judgment to bring.
Thou on the Cross for them shalt pray
And take Revenge at the last day.'
Jesus replied & thunders hurld:
'I never will Pray for the World!
Once I did so when I prayd in the Garden;
I wished to take with me a Bodily Pardon.'
Can that which was of woman born
In the absence of the Morn

When the Soul fell into Sleep
And Archangels round it weep
Shooting out against the Light
Fibres of a deadly night
Reasoning upon its own dark Fiction
In doubt which is Self Contradiction?
Humility is only doubt
And does the Sun & Moon blot out
Rooting over with thorns & stems
The buried Soul & all its Gems.
This Life's dim Windows of the Soul
Distorts the Heavns from Pole to Pole
And leads you to Believe a Lie
When you see with, not thro the Eye
That was born in a night to perish in a night
When the Soul Slept in the beams of light.
Was Jesus Chaste or did he &c

[*Part l*]

I'm Sure This Jesus will not do
Either for Englishman or Jew.

Songs Of Innocence and Of Experience

Shewing the Two Contrary States of the Human Soul

SONGS of EXPERIENCE

([Lambeth:] 1794 The Author & Printer W. Blake)

Introduction

Hear the voice of the Bard!
Who Present, Past, & Future sees;
Whose ears have heard
The Holy Word
That walk'd among the ancient trees,

Calling the lapsed Soul
And weeping in the evening dew:
That might controll
The starry pole;
And fallen fallen light renew!

'O Earth O Earth return
Arise from out the dewy grass;
Night is worn,
And the morn
Rises from the slumberous mass.

'Turn away no more:
Why wilt thou turn away?
The starry floor,
The watry shore
Is giv'n thee till the break of day.'

EARTH'S Answer

Earth raisd up her head
From the darkness dread & drear.
Her light fled:
Stony dread!
And her locks cover'd with grey despair.

'Prison'd on watry shore
Starry Jealousy does keep my den;
Cold and hoar
Weeping o'er
I hear the father of the ancient men.

'Selfish father of men!
Cruel jealous selfish fear!
Can delight
Chain'd in night
The virgins of youth and morning bear?

'Does spring hide its joy
When buds and blossoms grow?
Does the sower
Sow by night
Or the plowman in darkness plow?

'Break this heavy chain
That does freeze my bones around.
Selfish! vain!
Eternal bane!
That free Love with bondage bound.'

The CLOD & the PEBBLE

'Love seeketh not Itself to please,
Nor for itself hath any care;
But for another gives its ease,
And builds a Heaven in Hell's despair.'

So sang a little Clod of Clay,
Trodden with the cattle's feet:
But a Pebble of the brook
Warbled out these metres meet:

'Love seeketh only Self to please
To bind another to Its delight;
Joys in another's loss of ease,
And builds a Hell in Heaven's despite.'

HOLY THURSDAY

Is this a holy thing to see,
In a rich and fruitful land,
Babes reducd to misery,
Fed with cold and usurous hand?

Is that trembling cry a song?
Can it be a song of joy?
And so many children poor?
It is a land of poverty!

And their sun does never shine,
And their fields are bleak and bare,
And their ways are fill'd with thorns:
It is eternal winter there.

For where-e'er the sun does shine,
And where-e'er the rain does fall:
Babe can never hunger there,
Nor poverty the mind appall.

THE Chimney Sweeper

A little black thing among the snow:
Crying 'weep, weep,' in notes of woe!
'Where are thy father & mother? say?'
'They are both gone up to the church to pray.

'Because I was happy upon the heath,
And smil'd among the winter's snow:
They clothed me in the clothes of death,
And taught me to sing the notes of woe.

'And because I am happy & dance & sing,
They think they have done me no injury:
And are gone to praise God & his Priest & King
Who make up a heaven of our misery.'

NURSE'S Song

When the voices of children are heard on the green
And whisprings are in the dale:
The days of my youth rise fresh in my mind,
My face turns green and pale.

Then come home my children, the sun is gone down
And the dews of night arise;
Your spring & your day are wasted in play
And your winter and night in disguise.

The SICK ROSE

O Rose, thou art sick,
The invisible worm,
That flies in the night
In the howling storm:

Has found out thy bed
Of crimson joy:
And his dark secret love
Does thy life destroy.

THE FLY

Little Fly
Thy summer's play
My thoughtless hand
Has brush'd away.

Am not I
A fly like thee?
Or art not thou
A man like me?

For I dance
And drink & sing:
Till some blind hand
Shall brush my wing.

If thought is life
And strength & breath:
And the want
Of thought is death;

Then am I
A happy fly,
If I live,
Or if I die.

The Angel

I dreamt a Dream! what can it mean?
And that I was a maiden Queen:
Guarded by an Angel mild:
Witless woe was neer beguil'd!

And I wept both night and day
And he wip'd my tears away
And I wept both day and night
And hid from him my heart's delight

So he took his wings and fled:
Then the morn blush'd rosy red:
I dried my tears & armd my fears
With ten thousand shields and spears.

Soon my Angel came again;
I was arm'd, he came in vain:
For the time of youth was fled
And grey hairs were on my head.

The Tyger

Tyger, Tyger, burning bright,
In the forests of the night:
What immortal hand or eye
Could frame thy fearful symmetry?

In what distant deeps or skies
Burnt the fire of thine eyes?
On what wings dare he aspire?
What the hand dare seize the fire?

And what shoulder, & what art,
Could twist the sinews of thy heart?
And when thy heart began to beat,
What dread hand? & what dread feet?

What the hammer? what the chain,
In what furnace was thy brain?
What the anvil? what dread grasp
Dare its deadly terrors clasp!

When the stars threw down their spears
And waterd heaven with their tears:
Did he smile his work to see?
Did he who made the Lamb make thee?

Tyger, Tyger burning bright,
In the forests of the night:
What immortal hand or eye
Dare frame thy fearful symmetry?

My Pretty ROSE TREE

A flower was offerd to me;
Such a flower as May never bore,
But I said 'I've a Pretty Rose-tree,'
And I passed the sweet flower o'er.

Then I went to my Pretty Rose-tree
To tend her by day and by night,
But my Rose turnd away with jealousy
And her thorns were my only delight.

AH! SUN FLOWER

Ah Sun-flower! weary of time,
Who countest the steps of the Sun:
Seeking after that sweet golden clime
Where the traveller's journey is done;

Where the Youth pined away with desire,
And the pale Virgin shrouded in snow
Arise from their graves and aspire
Where my Sun-flower wishes to go.

THE LILLY

The modest Rose puts forth a thorn:
The humble Sheep a threatning horn:
While the Lilly white shall in Love delight,
Nor a thorn nor a threat stain her beauty bright.

The GARDEN of LOVE

I went to the Garden of Love,
And saw what I never had seen:
A Chapel was built in the midst,
Where I used to play on the green.

And the gates of this Chapel were shut,
And 'Thou shalt not' writ over the door;
So I turn'd to the Garden of Love,
That so many sweet flowers bore,

And I saw it was filled with graves,
And tomb-stones where flowers should be:
And Priests in black gowns were walking their rounds,
And binding with briars my joys & desires.

The Little Vagabond

Dear Mother, dear Mother, the Church is cold,
But the Ale-house is healthy & pleasant & warm:
Besides I can tell where I am used well,
Such usage in heaven will never do well.

But if at the Church they would give us some Ale,
And a pleasant fire our souls to regale:
We'd sing and we'd pray all the live-long day;
Nor ever once wish from the Church to stray.

Then the Parson might preach & drink & sing,
And we'd be as happy as birds in the spring:
And modest dame Lurch, who is always at Church
Would not have bandy children nor fasting nor birch.

And God like a father rejoicing to see
His children as pleasant and happy as he;
Would have no more quarrel with the Devil or the Barrel
But kiss him & give him both drink and apparel.

LONDON

I wander thro' each charter'd street,
Near where the charter'd Thames does flow
And mark in every face I meet
Marks of weakness, marks of woe.

In every cry of every Man,
In every Infant's cry of fear,
In every voice; in every ban,
The mind-forg'd manacles I hear.

How the Chimney-sweeper's cry
Every blackning Church appalls,
And the hapless Soldier's sigh
Runs in blood down Palace walls

But most thro' midnight streets I hear
How the youthful Harlot's curse
Blasts the new born Infant's tear
And blights with plagues the Marriage hearse.

The Human Abstract

Pity would be no more
If we did not make somebody Poor:
And Mercy no more could be
If all were as happy as we;

And mutual fear brings peace;
Till the selfish loves increase.
Then Cruelty knits a snare,
And spreads his baits with care.

He sits down with holy fears,
And waters the ground with tears;
Then Humility takes its root
Underneath his foot.

Soon spreads the dismal shade
Of Mystery over his head;
And the Catterpiller and Fly
Feed on the Mystery.

And it bears the fruit of Deceit,
Ruddy and sweet to eat;
And the Raven his nest has made
In its thickest shade.

The Gods of the earth and sea
Sought thro' Nature to find this Tree
But their search was all in vain:
There grows one in the Human Brain.

INFANT SORROW

My mother groand! My father wept.
Into the dangerous world I leapt:
Helpless, naked, piping loud:
Like a fiend hid in a cloud.

Struggling in my father's hands:
Striving against my swadling bands:
Bound and weary I thought best
To sulk upon my mother's breast.

A POISON TREE

I was angry with my friend:
I told my wrath, my wrath did end.
I was angry with my foe:
I told it not, my wrath did grow.

And I waterd it in fears,
Night & morning with my tears:
And I sunned it with smiles,
And with soft deceitful wiles.

And it grew both day and night,
Till it bore an apple bright,
And my foe beheld it shine,
And he knew that it was mine,

And into my garden stole,
When the night had veild the pole:
In the morning glad I see
My foe outstretchd beneath the tree.

A Little BOY Lost

'Nought loves another as itself
Nor venerates another so,
Nor is it possible to Thought
A greater than itself to know:

'And Father, how can I love you,
Or any of my brothers more?
I love you like the little bird
That picks up crumbs around the door.'

The Priest saw by and heard the child,
In trembling zeal he siez'd his hair:
He led him by his little coat;
And all admir'd the Priestly care.

And standing on the altar high,
'Lo what a fiend is here!' said he:
'One who sets reason up for judge
Of our most holy Mystery.'

The weeping child could not be heard.
The weeping parents wept in vain:
They strip'd him to his little shirt
And bound him in an iron chain,

And burn'd him in a holy place,
Where many had been burn'd before:
The weeping parents wept in vain.
Are such things done on Albion's shore?

A Little GIRL Lost

Children of the future Age,
Reading this indignant page;
Know that in a former time,
Love! sweet Love! was thought a crime.

In the Age of Gold,
Free from winter's cold
Youth and maiden bright
To the holy light,
Naked in the sunny beams delight.

Once a youthful pair
Fill'd with softest care
Met in garden bright,
Where the holy light
Had just removd the curtains of the night.

There in rising day
On the grass they play:
Parents were afar:
Strangers came not near:
And the maiden soon forgot her fear.

Tired with kisses sweet
They agree to meet,
When the silent sleep
Waves o'er heaven's deep:
And the weary tired wanderers weep.

To her father white
Came the maiden bright:
But his loving look,
Like the holy book,
All her tender limbs with terror shook.

'Ona! pale and weak!
To thy father speak:
O the trembling fear!
O the dismal care!
That shakes the blossoms of my hoary hair.'

To Tirzah

Whate'er is Born of Mortal Birth
Must be consumed with the Earth
To rise from Generation free:
Then what have I to do with thee?

The Sexes sprung from Shame & Pride,
Blowd in the morn; in evening died
But Mercy changd Death into Sleep;
The Sexes rose to work & weep.

Thou Mother of my Mortal part
With cruelty didst mould my Heart
And with false self-decieving tears
Didst bind my Nostrils, Eyes & Ears,

Didst close my Tongue in senseless clay
And me to Mortal Life betray:
The Death of Jesus set me free,
Then what have I to do with thee?

A DIVINE IMAGE

Cruelty has a Human Heart
And Jealousy a Human Face,
Terror the Human Form Divine
And Secrecy the Human Dress.

The Human Dress is forged Iron,
The Human Form a fiery Forge,
The Human Face a Furnace seal'd,
The Human Heart its hungry Gorge.

EUROPE a PROPHECY
(LAMBETH: Printed by Will: Blake: 1794)

'Five windows light the cavern'd Man: thro one he breathes the air:
Thro' one, hears music of the spheres: thro' one, the eternal vine
Flourishes, that he may recieve the grapes; thro one can look,
And see small portions of the eternal world that ever groweth;
Thro' one, himself pass out what time he please, but he will not;
For stolen joys are sweet, & bread eaten in secret pleasant.'

So sang a Fairy mocking as he sat on a streak'd Tulip,
Thinking none saw him: when he ceas'd I started from the trees:
And caught him in my hat as boys knock down a butterfly.
'How know you this' said I 'small Sir? Where did you learn this song?'
Seeing himself in my possession thus he answerd me:
'My master, I am yours; command me, for I must obey.'

'Then tell me, what is the material world, and is it dead?'
He laughing answer'd: 'I will write a book on leaves of flowers,
If you will feed me on love-thoughts, & give me now and then
A cup of sparkling poetic fancies: so when I am tipsie,
I'll sing to you to this soft lute; and shew you all alive
The world, where every particle of dust breathes forth its joy.'

I took him home in my warm bosom: as we went along
Wild flowers I gatherd, & he shew'd me each eternal flower:
He laugh'd aloud to see them whimper because they were pluck'd.
They hover'd round me like a cloud of incense: when I came
Into my parlour and sat down, and took my pen to write:
My Fairy sat upon the table, and dictated EUROPE.

PRELUDIUM

The nameless shadowy female rose from out the breast of Orc:
Her snaky hair brandishing in the winds of Enitharmon:
And thus her voice arose:

'O mother Enitharmon, wilt thou bring forth other sons?
To cause my name to vanish, that my place may not be found?
For I am faint with travel!
Like the dark cloud disburdend in the day of dismal thunder.

'My roots are brandish'd in the heavens, my fruits in earth beneath
Surge, foam, and labour into life, first born & first consum'd!
Consumed and consuming!
Then why shouldst thou accursed mother bring me into life?

'I wrap my turban of thick clouds around my lab'ring head:
And fold the sheety waters as a mantle round my limbs,
Yet the red sun and moon
And all the overflowing stars rain down prolific pains.

'Unwilling I look up to heaven! Unwilling count the stars!
Sitting in fathomless abyss of my immortal shrine,
I seize their burning power
And bring forth howling terrors, all devouring fiery kings,

'Devouring & devouréd roaming on dark and desolate mountains
In forests of eternal death, shrieking in hollow trees.
Ah mother Enitharmon!
Stamp not with solid form this vig'rous progeny of fires.

'I bring forth from my teeming bosom myriads of flames,
And thou dost stamp them with a signet, then they roam abroad
And leave me void as death;
Ah! I am drown'd in shady woe, and visionary joy.

'And who shall bind the infinite with an eternal band?
To compass it with swaddling bands? And who shall cherish it
With milk and honey?
I see it smile & I roll inward & my voice is past.'

She ceast & rolld her shady clouds
Into the secret place.

A PROPHECY

The deep of winter came:
What time the secret child
Descended thro' the orient gates of the eternal day:
War ceas'd, & all the troops like shadows fled to their abodes.

Then Enitharmon saw her sons & daughters rise around;
Like pearly clouds they meet together in the crystal house;
And Los, possessor of the moon, joy'd in the peaceful night:
Thus speaking while his num'rous sons shook their bright fiery
wings:

'Again the night is come
That strong Urthona takes his rest,
And Urizen unloos'd from chains
Glows like a meteor in the distant north.
Stretch forth your hands and strike the elemental strings!
Awake the thunders of the deep.

'The shrill winds wake!
Till all the sons of Urizen look out and envy Los:
Seize all the spirits of life and bind
Their warbling joys to our loud strings;
Bind all the nourishing sweets of earth
To give us bliss, that we may drink the sparkling wine of Los
And let us laugh at war,
Despising toil and care,
Because the days and nights of joy in lucky hours renew.

'Arise O Orc from thy deep den.
First born of Enitharmon, rise!
And we will crown thy head with garlands of the ruddy vine;
For now thou art bound;
And I may see thee in the hour of bliss, my eldest born.'

The horrent Demon rose, surrounded with red stars of fire,
Whirling about in furious circles round the immortal fiend.

Then Enitharmon down descended into his red light,
And thus her voice rose to her children; the distant heavens reply:

'Now comes the night of Enitharmon's joy.
Who shall I call? Who shall I send?
That Woman, lovely Woman! may have dominion?
Arise O Rintrah: thee I call! & Palamabron thee!
Go! tell the human race that Woman's love is Sin:
That an Eternal life awaits the worm of sixty winters
In an allegorical abode where existence hath never come:
Forbid all Joy, & from her childhood shall the little female
Spread nets in every secret path.

'My weary eyelids draw towards the evening, my bliss is yet but new.

'Arise O Rintrah eldest born: second to none but Orc:
O Lion Rintrah, raise thy fury from thy forests black;
Bring Palamabron horned priest, skipping upon the mountains;
And silent Elynittria the silver bowed queen:
Rintrah, where hast thou hid thy bride!
Weeps she in desart shades?
Alas my Rintrah! bring the lovely jealous Ocalythron.

'Arise my son! bring all thy brethren, O thou king of fire.
Prince of the sun I see thee with thy innumerable race:
Thick as the summer stars:
But each ramping his golden mane shakes,
And thine eyes rejoice because of strength, O Rintrah furious king.'

Enitharmon slept,
Eighteen hundred years: Man was a Dream!
The night of Nature and their harps unstrung.
She slept in middle of her nightly song.
Eighteen hundred years, a female dream.

Shadows of men in fleeting bands upon the winds
Divide the heavens of Europe:
Till Albion's Angel smitten with his own plagues fled with his bands.

The cloud bears hard on Albion's shore:
Fill'd with immortal demons of futurity:
In council gather the smitten Angels of Albion.
The cloud bears hard upon the council house; down rushing
On the heads of Albion's Angels.

One hour they lay buried beneath the ruins of that hall;
But as the stars rise from the salt lake they arise in pain,
In troubled mists o'erclouded by the terrors of the struggling
times.

In thoughts perturb'd they rose from the bright ruins silent
following
The fiery King, who sought his ancient temple serpent-form'd
That stretches out its shady length along the Island white.
Round him roll'd his clouds of war; silent the Angel went
Along the infinite shores of Thames to golden Verulam.
There stand the venerable porches that high-towering rear
Their oak-surrounded pillars, form'd of massy stones, uncut
With tool; stones precious; such eternal in the heavens,
Of colours twelve, few known on earth, give light in the opake,
Plac'd in the order of the stars, when the five senses whelm'd
In deluge o'er the earth-born man; then turn'd the fluxile eyes
Into two stationary orbs, concentrating all things.
The every-varying spiral ascents to the heavens of heavens
Were bended downward; and the nostrils' golden gates shut,
Turn'd outward, barr'd and petrify'd against the infinite.

Thought chang'd the infinite to a serpent, that which pitieth
To a devouring flame; and man fled from its face and hid
In forests of night; then all the eternal forests were divided
Into earths rolling in circles of space, that like an ocean rush'd
And overwhelmed all except this finite wall of flesh.
Then was the serpent temple form'd, image of infinite
Shut up in finite revolutions, and man became an Angel;
Heaven a mighty circle turning; God a tyrant crown'd.

Now arriv'd the ancient Guardians at the southern porch
That planted thick with trees of blackest leaf, & in a vale
Obscure, inclos'd the Stone of Night; oblique it stood, o'erhung
With purple flowers and berries red; image of that sweet south
Once open to the heavens and elevated on the human neck,

Now overgrown with hair and coverd with a stony roof,
Downward 'tis sunk beneath th'attractive north that round the feet
A raging whirlpool draws the dizzy enquirer to his grave.

Albion's Angel rose upon the Stone of Night.
He saw Urizen on the Atlantic:
And his brazen Book,
That Kings & Priests had copied on Earth
Expanded from North to South.

And the clouds & fires pale rolld round in the night of Enitharmon
Round Albion's cliffs & London's walls; still Enitharmon slept;
Rolling volumes of grey mist involve Churches, Palaces, Towers:
For Urizen unclaspd his Book! feeding his soul with pity.
The youth of England hid in gloom curse the paind heavens: compell'd
Into the deadly night to see the form of Albion's Angel.
Their parents brought them forth & aged ignorance preaches canting.
On a vast rock, perciev'd by those senses that are clos'd from thought:
Bleak, dark, abrupt, it stands & overshadows London city.
They saw his boney feet on the rock, the flesh consum'd in flames:
They saw the Serpent temple lifted above, shadowing the Island white:
They heard the voice of Albion's Angel howling in flames of Orc,
Seeking the trump of the last doom.

Above the rest the howl was heard from Westminster louder & louder;
The Guardian of the secret codes forsook his ancient mansion,
Driven out by the flames of Orc; his furr'd robes & false locks
Adhered and grew one with his flesh and nerves & veins shot thro' them
With dismal torment sick hanging upon the wind: he fled
Groveling along Great George Street thro' the Park gate; all the soldiers
Fled from his sight: he drag'd his torments to the wilderness.

Thus was the howl thro Europe!
For Orc rejoic'd to hear the howling shadows
But Palamabron shot his lightnings trenching down his wide back
And Rintrah hung with all his legions in the nether deep.

Enitharmon laugh'd in her sleep to see (O woman's triumph)
Every house a den, every man bound; the shadows are fill'd
With spectres, and the windows wove over with curses of iron;
Over the doors 'Thou shalt not' & over the chimneys 'Fear' is written:
With bands of iron round their necks, fastend into the walls
The citizens: in leaden gyves the inhabitants of suburbs
Walk heavy: soft and bent are the bones of villagers.

Between the clouds of Urizen the flames of Orc roll heavy
Around the limbs of Albion's Guardian, his flesh consuming.
Howlings & hissings, shrieks & groans, & voices of despair
Arise around him in the cloudy Heavens of Albion, Furious
The red limb'd Angel siez'd in horror and torment
The Trump of the last doom: but he could not blow the iron tube!
Thrice he assay'd presumptuous to awake the dead to Judgment.

A mighty Spirit leap'd from the land of Albion
Nam'd Newton: he siez'd the Trump, & blow'd the enormous blast!
Yellow as leaves of Autumn the myriads of Angelic hosts
Fell thro' the wintry skies seeking their graves:
Rattling their hollow bones in howling and lamentation.

Then Enitharmon woke nor knew that she had slept
And eighteen hundred years were fled
As if they had not been.
She calld her sons & daughters
To the sports of night,
Within her crystal house;
And thus her song proceeds:

'Arise Ethinthus! tho' the earth-worm call:
Let him call in vain:
Till the night of holy shadows
And human solitude is past!

'Ethinthus, queen of waters, how thou shinest in the sky:
My daughter, how do I rejoice! for thy children flock around
Like the gay fishes on the wave, where the cold moon drinks the
dew,
Ethinthus! thou art sweet as comforts to my fainting soul:
For now thy waters warble round the feet of Enitharmon.

'Manathu-Varcyon! I behold thee flaming in my halls,
Light of thy mother's soul! I see thy lovely eagles round:
Thy golden wings are my delight, & thy flames of soft delusion.

'Where is my lureing bird of Eden! Leutha, silent love!
Leutha, the many colourd bow delights upon thy wings:
Soft soul of Flowers, Leutha!
Sweet smiling pestilence! I see thy blushing light:
Thy daughters many changing,
Revolve like sweet perfumes ascending, O Leutha, silken queen!

'Where is the youthful Antamon, prince of the pearly dew?

'O Antamon, why wilt thou leave thy mother Enitharmon?
Alone I see thee crystal form,
Floating upon the bosomd air:
With lineaments of gratified desire.
My Antamon, the seven churches of Leutha seek thy love.

'I hear the soft Oothoon in Enitharmon's tents:

'Why wilt thou give up woman's secrecy, my melancholy child?
Between two moments bliss is ripe:
O Theotormon robb'd of joy, I see thy salt tears flow
Down the steps of my crystal house.

'Sotha & Thiralatha, secret dwellers of dreamful caves,
Arise and please the horrent fiend with your melodious songs.
Still all your thunders golden hoofd, & bind your horses black,
Orc! Smile upon my children!
Smile, son of my afflictions.
Arise, O Orc, and give our mountains joy of thy red light.'

She ceas'd, For All were forth at sport beneath the solemn moon
Waking the stars of Urizen with their immortal songs,
That nature felt thro' all her pores the enormous revelry,
Till morning ope'd the eastern gate.
Then every one fled to his station, & Enitharmon wept.

But terrible Orc, when he beheld the morning in the east,
Shot from the heights of Enitharmon,
And in the vineyards of red France appear'd the light of his fury.

The sun glow'd fiery red!
The furious terror flew around!
On golden chariots raging, with red wheels dropping with blood;
The Lions lash their wrathful tails!
The Tigers couch upon the prey & suck the ruddy tide;
And Enitharmon groans & cries in anguish and dismay.

Then Los arose; his head he reard in snaky thunders clad:
And with a cry that shook all nature to the utmost pole,
Call'd all his sons to the strife of blood.

FINIS

THE FIRST BOOK OF URIZEN

(Lambeth: Printed by Will Blake, 1794)

PRELUDIUM TO THE FIRST BOOK OF URIZEN

Of the primeval Priest's assum'd power
When Eternals spurnd back his religion:
And gave him a place in the north,
Obscure, shadowy, void, solitary.

Eternals, I hear your call gladly,
Dictate swift winged words, & fear not
To unfold your dark visions of torment.

Chap: I

1. Lo, a shadow of horror is risen
In Eternity! Unknown, unprolific?
Self-closd, all-repelling; what Demon
Hath form'd this abominable void,
This soul-shuddring vacuum? Some said
'It is Urizen', But unknown, abstracted
Brooding secret, the dark power hid.

2. Times on times he divided, & measur'd
Space by space in his ninefold darkness.
Unseen, unknown: changes appeard
Like desolate mountains rifted furious
By the black winds of perturbation

3. For he strove in battles dire
In unseen conflictions with shapes
Bred from his forsaken wilderness
Of beast, bird, fish, serpent & element,
Combustion, blast, vapour and cloud.

4. Dark revolving in silent activity:
Unseen in tormenting passions;
An activity unknown and horrible;
A self-contemplating shadow,
In enormous labours occupied

5. But Eternals beheld his vast forests.
Age on ages he lay, clos'd, unknown,
Brooding shut in the deep; all avoid
The petrific abominable chaos.

6. His cold horrors silent, dark Urizen
Prepar'd; his ten thousands of thunders
Rang'd in gloom'd array stretch out across
The dread world, & the rolling of wheels
As of swelling seas, sound in his clouds,
In his hills of stor'd snows, in his mountains
Of hail & ice; voices of terror
Are heard, like thunders of autumn
When the cloud blazes over the harvests.

Chap: II

1. Earth was not: nor globes of attraction.
The will of the Immortal expanded
Or contracted his all flexible senses.
Death was not, but eternal life sprung.

2. The sound of a trumpet the heavens
Awoke & vast clouds of blood roll'd
Round the dim rocks of Urizen, so nam'd
That solitary one in Immensity.

3. Shrill the trumpet: & myriads of Eternity
Muster around the bleak desarts
Now fill'd with clouds darkness & waters
That roll'd perplex'd labring & utter'd
Words articulate, bursting in thunders
That roll'd on the tops of his mountains.

4. 'From the depths of dark solitude, From
The eternal abode in my holiness
Hidden, set apart in my stern counsels
Reserv'd for the days of futurity
I have sought for a joy without pain,
For a solid without fluctuation.
Why will you die, O Eternals?
Why live in unquenchable burnings?

5. 'First I fought with fire; consum'd
Inwards, into a deep world within:
A void immense, wild dark & deep
Where nothing was: Nature's wide womb
And self balanc'd stretch'd o'er the void
I alone, even I! the winds merciless
Bound; but condensing, in torrents
They fell & fell; strong, I repell'd
The vast waves, & arose on the waters
A wide world of solid obstruction.

6. 'Here alone I in books formd of metals
Have written the secrets of wisdom,
The secrets of dark contemplation
By fightings and conflicts dire,
With terrible monsters Sin-bred:
Which the bosoms of all inhabit:
Seven deadly Sins of the soul.

7. 'Lo! I unfold my darkness; and on
This rock, place with strong hand the book
Of eternal brass, written in my solitude.

8. 'Laws of peace, of love, of unity;
Of pity, compassion, forgiveness.
Let each chuse one habitation:
His ancient infinite mansion:
One command, one joy, one desire,
One curse, one weight, one measure,
One King, one God, one Law.'

Chap: III

1. The voice ended, they saw his pale visage
Emerge from the darkness; his hand
On the rock of eternity unclasping
The Book of brass. Rage siez'd the strong,

2. Rage, fury, intense indignation
In cataracts of fire, blood & gall,
In whirlwinds of sulphurous smoke:
And enormous forms of energy;
All the seven deadly sins of the soul
In living creations appear'd
In the flames of eternal fury.

3. Sund'ring, darkn'ning, thund'ring!
Rent away with a terrible crash,
Eternity roll'd wide apart,
Wide asunder rolling,
Mountainous all around
Departing; departing: departing:
Leaving ruinous fragments of life
Hanging frowning cliffs & all between
An ocean of voidness unfathomable.

4. The roaring fires ran o'er the heav'ns
In whirlwinds & cataracts of blood
And o'er the dark desarts of Urizen
Fires pour thro' the void on all sides
On Urizen's self-begotten armies

5. But no light from the fires, all was darkness
In flames of Eternal fury.

6. In fierce anguish & quenchless flames
To the desarts and rocks he ran raging
To hide, but he could not; combining
He dug mountains & hills in vast strength.
He piled them in incessant labour,

In howlings & pangs & fierce madness,
Long periods in burning fires labouring
Till hoary and age-broke, and aged,
In despair and the shadows of death,

7. And a roof vast petrific around,
On all sides he fram'd, like a womb:
Where thousands of rivers in veins
Of blood pour down the mountains to cool
The eternal fires beating without
From Eternals; & like a black globe
View'd by sons of Eternity, standing
On the shore of the infinite ocean.
Like a human heart strugling & beating
The vast world of Urizen appear'd.

8. And Los round the dark globe of Urizen
Kept watch for Eternals to confine
The obscure separation alone;
For Eternity stood wide apart,
As the stars are apart from the earth.

9. Los wept howling around the dark Demon
And cursing his lot for in anguish
Urizen was rent from his side:
And a fathomless void for his feet:
And intense fires for his dwelling.

10. But Urizen laid in a stony sleep
Unorganizd, rent from Eternity.

11. The Eternals said: 'What is this? Death!
Urizen is a clod of clay.'

12. Los howld in a dismal stupor,
Groaning! gnashing! groaning!
Till the wrenching apart was healed

13. But the wrenching of Urizen heal'd not.
Cold, featureless, flesh or clay
Rifted with direful changes
He lay in a dreamless night

14. Till Los rouz'd his fires affrighted
At the formless unmeasurable death.

Chap: IV[a]

1. Los smitten with astonishment
Frightend at the hurtling bones

2. And at the surging sulphureous
Perturbed Immortal mad raging

3. In whirlwinds & pitch & nitre
Round the furious limbs of Los

4. And Los formed nets & gins
And threw the nets round about.

5. He watch'd in shuddring fear
The dark changes & bound every change
With rivets of iron and brass;

6. And these were the changes of Urizen:

Chap: IV[b]

1. Ages on ages roll'd over him!
In a stony sleep ages roll'd over him!
Like a dark waste stretching chang'able.
By earthquakes riv'n, belching sullen fires.
On ages roll'd ages in ghastly
Sick torment; around him in whirlwinds
Of darkness the eternal Prophet howl'd
Beating still on his rivets of iron,
Pouring sodor of iron: dividing
The horrible night into watches.

2. And Urizen (so his eternal name)
His prolific delight obscurd more & more
In dark secrecy, hiding in surgeing
Sulphureous fluid his phantasies.

The Eternal Prophet heavd the dark bellows,
And turn'd restless the tongs, and the hammer
Incessant beat; forging chains new & new,
Numb'ring with links, hours, days & years.

3. The eternal mind bounded began to roll
Eddies of wrath ceaseless round & round
And the sulphureous foam, surgeing thick
Settled, a lake, bright & shining clear:
White as the snow on the mountains cold.

4. Forgetfulness, dumbness, necessity!
In chains of the mind locked up,
Like fetters of ice shrinking together,
Disorganiz'd, rent from Eternity.
Los beat on his fetters of iron:
And heated his furnaces & pour'd
Iron sodor and sodor of brass.

5. Restless turnd the immortal inchain'd
Heaving dolorous! anguish'd! unbearable
Till a roof shaggy wild inclos'd
In an orb, his fountain of thought.

6. In a horrible dreamful slumber;
Like the linked infernal chain;
A vast Spine writh'd in torment
Upon the winds; shooting pain'd
Ribs, like a bending cavern
And bones of solidness Froze,
Over all his nerves of joy.
And a first Age passed over,
And a state of dismal woe.

7. From the caverns of his jointed Spine,
Down sunk with fright a red
Round globe hot burning deep
Deep down into the Abyss:
Panting: Conglobing, Trembling
Shooting out ten thousand branches

Around his solid bones
And a second Age passed over,
And a state of dismal woe.

8. In harrowing fear rolling round;
His nervous brain shot branches
Round the branches of his heart
On high into two little orbs
And fixed in two little caves
Hiding carefully from the wind.
His Eyes beheld the deep.
And a third Age passed over;
And a state of dismal woe.

9. The pangs of hope began.
In heavy pain striving, struggling:
Two Ears in close volutions,
From beneath his orbs of vision
Shot spiring out and petrified
As they grew. And a fourth Age passed
And a state of dismal woe.

10. In ghastly torment sick
Hanging upon the wind
Two Nostrils bent down to the deep.
And a fifth Age passed over;
And a state of dismal woe.

11. In ghastly torment sick;
Within his ribs bloated round
A craving Hungry Cavern:
Thence arose his channeld Throat,
And like a red flame a Tongue
Of thirst & of hunger appeard.
And a sixth Age passed over:
And a state of dismal woe.

12. Enraged & stifled with torment
He threw his right Arm to the north,
His left Arm to the south

Shooting out in anguish deep.
And his Feet stampd the nether Abyss
In trembling & howling & dismay.
And a seventh Age passed over:
And a state of dismal woe.

Chap: V

1. In terrors Los shrunk from his task:
His great hammer fell from his hand:
His fires beheld, and sickening,
Hid their strong limbs in smoke,
For with noises ruinous loud:
With hurtlings & clashings & groans
The Immortal endur'd his chains,
Tho' bound in a deadly sleep.

2. All the myriads of Eternity:
All the wisdom & joy of life:
Rolld like a sea around him,
Except when his little orbs
Of sight by degrees unfold.

3. And now his eternal life
Like a dream was obliterated.

4. Shudd'ring, the Eternal Prophet smote
With a stroke, from his north to south region.
The bellows & hammer are silent now;
A nerveless silence, his prophetic voice
Siez'd; a cold solitude & dark void
The Eternal Prophet & Urizen clos'd.

5. Ages on ages rolld over them
Cut off from life & light frozen
Into horrible forms of deformity.
Los suffer'd his fires to decay
Then he look'd back with anxious desire
But the space undivided by existence
Struck horror into his soul.

6. Los wept obscur'd with mourning;
His bosom earthquak'd with sighs;
He saw Urizen deadly black,
In his chains bound, & Pity began

7. In anguish dividing & dividing,
For pity divides the soul,
In pangs eternity on eternity
Life in cataracts pourd down his cliffs.
The void shrunk the lymph into Nerves
Wand'ring wide on the bosom of night
And left a round globe of blood

Trembling upon the Void.
Thus the Eternal Prophet was divided
Before the death image of Urizen
For in changeable clouds and darkness
In a winterly night beneath,
The Abyss of Los stretch'd immense:
And now seen, now obscur'd to the eyes
Of Eternals, the visions remote
Of the dark seperation appear'd.
As glasses discover Worlds
In the endless Abyss of space,
So the expanding eyes of Immortals
Beheld the dark visions of Los,
And the globe of life blood trembling.

8. The globe of life blood trembled
Branching out into roots:
Fib'rous, writhing upon the winds:
Fibres of blood, milk and tears:
In pangs, eternity on eternity.
At length in tears & cries imbodied
A female form trembling and pale
Waves before his deathy face.

9. All Eternity shuddred at sight
Of the first female now separate
Pale as a cloud of snow
Waving before the face of Los.

10. Wonder, awe, fear, astonishment
Petrify the eternal myriads
At the first female form now separate;
They call'd her Pity, and fled.

11. 'Spread a Tent, with strong curtains around them;
Let cords & stakes bind in the Void
That Eternals may no more behold them.'

12. They began to weave curtains of darkness.
They erected large pillars round the Void
With golden hooks fastend in the pillars;
With infinite labour the Eternals
A woof wove and called it Science

Chap: VI

1. But Los saw the Female & pitied.
He embrac'd her, she wept, she refus'd
In perverse and cruel delight;
She fled from his arms, yet he followd.

2. Eternity shudder'd when they saw
Man begetting his likeness
On his own divided image.

3. A time passed over, the Eternals
Began to erect the tent;
When Enitharmon sick,
Felt a Worm within her womb.

4. Yet helpless it lay like a Worm
In the trembling womb
To be moulded into existence.

5. All day the worm lay on her bosom,
All night within her womb
The worm lay till it grew to a serpent
With dolorous hissings & poisons
Round Enitharmon's loins folding.

6. Coild within Enitharmon's womb
The serpent grew, casting its scales.
With sharp pangs the hissings began
To change to a grating cry.
Many sorrows and dismal throes,
Many forms of fish, bird & beast
Brought forth an Infant form
Where was a worm before.

7. The Eternals their tent finished
Alarm'd with these gloomy visions,
When Enitharmon groaning
Produc'd a man Child to the light.

8. A shriek ran thro' Eternity:
And a paralytic stroke
At the birth of the Human shadow.

9. Delving earth in his resistless way:
Howling, the Child with fierce flames
Issu'd from Enitharmon.

10. The Eternals closed the tent.
They beat down the stakes, the cords
Stretch'd for a work of eternity:
No more Los beheld Eternity.

11. In his hands he siez'd the infant.
He bathed him in springs of sorrow.
He gave him to Enitharmon.

Chap. VII

1. They named the child Orc, he grew
Fed with milk of Enitharmon.

2. Los awoke her; O sorrow & pain!
A tight'ning girdle grew
Around his bosom. In sobbings
He burst the girdle in twain,
But still another girdle

Oppressd his bosom. In sobbings
Again he burst it. Again
Another girdle succeeds.
The girdle was form'd by day:
By night was burst in twain.

3. These falling down on the rock
Into an iron Chain
In each other link by link lock'd.

4. They took Orc to the top of a mountain.
O how Enitharmon wept!
They chain'd his young limbs to the rock
With the Chains of Jealousy
Beneath Urizen's deathful shadow.

5. The dead heard the voice of the child
And began to awake from sleep.
All things heard the voice of the child
And began to awake to life.

6. And Urizen craving with hunger
Stung with the odours of Nature
Explor'd his dens around.

7. He form'd a line & a plummet
To divide the Abyss beneath.
He form'd a dividing rule:

8. He formed scales to weigh:
He formed massy weights:
He formed a brazen quadrant:
He formed golden compasses
And began to explore the Abyss
And he planted a garden of fruits

9. But Los encircled Enitharmon
With fires of Prophecy
From the sight of Urizen & Orc.

10. And she bore an enormous race.

Chap. VIII

1. Urizen explor'd his dens,
Mountains, moor & wilderness
With a globe of fire lighting his journey,
A fearful journey, annoy'd
By cruel enormities: Forms
Of life on his forsaken mountains

2. And his world teemd vast enormities
Frightening: Faithless; fawning;
Portions of life: similitudes
Of a foot, or a hand, or a head
Or a heart, or an eye, they swam mischevous
Dread terrors! Delighting in blood.

3. Most Urizen sicken'd to see
His eternal creations appear,
Sons & daughters of sorrow on mountains
Weeping! wailing! first Thiriel appear'd
Astonish'd at his own existence
Like a man from a cloud born, & Utha
From the waters emerging laments!
Grodna rent the deep earth howling
Amaz'd! his heavens immense cracks
Like the ground parch'd with heat; then Fuzon
Flam'd out! first begotten, last born;
All his eternal sons in like manner:
His daughters from green herbs & cattle,
From monsters, & worms of the pit.

4. He in darkness clos'd, view'd all his race
And his soul sicken'd! he curs'd
Both sons & daughters: for he saw
That no flesh nor spirit could keep
His iron laws one moment.

5. For he saw that life liv'd upon death:
The Ox in the slaughter house moans,
The Dog at the wintry door
And he wept, & he called it Pity
And his tears flowed down on the winds.

6. Cold he wander'd on high, over their cities
In weeping & pain & woe!
And where-ever he wanderd in sorrows
Upon the aged heavens
A cold shadow follow'd behind him
Like a spider's web, moist, cold, & dim
Drawing out from his sorrowing soul,
The dungeon-like heavens dividing,
Where ever the footsteps of Urizen
Walk'd over the cities in sorrow.

7. Till a Web dark & cold, throughout all
The tormented element stretch'd
From the sorrows of Urizen's soul
And the Web is a Female in embrio.
None could break the Web, no wings of fire,

8. So twisted the cords, & so knotted
The meshes: twisted like to the human brain

9. And all calld it The Net of Religion.

Chap: IX

1. Then the Inhabitants of those Cities
Felt their Nerves change into Marrow
And hardening Bones began
In swift diseases and torments,
In throbbings & shootings & grindings
Thro' all the coasts: till weaken'd
The Senses inward rush'd shrinking,
Beneath the dark net of infection.

2. Till the shrunken eyes clouded over
Discernd not the woven hipocrisy
But the streaky slime in their heavens
Brought together by narrowing perceptions
Appeard transparent air: for their eyes
Grew small like the eyes of a man
And in reptile forms shrinking together
Of seven feet stature they remaind.

3. Six days they shrunk up from existence
And on the seventh day they rested
And they bless'd the seventh day, in sick hope:
And forgot their eternal life

4. And their thirty cities divided
In form of a human heart.
No more could they rise at will
In the infinite void, but bound down
To earth by their narrowing perceptions
They lived a period of years,
Then left a noisom body
To the jaws of devouring darkness

5. And their children wept, & built
Tombs in the desolate places,
And form'd laws of prudence, and call'd them
The eternal laws of God

6. And the thirty cities remaind
Surrounded by salt floods, now call'd
Africa: its name was then Egypt.

7. The remaining sons of Urizen
Beheld their brethren shrink together
Beneath the Net of Urizen:
Perswasion was in vain:
For the ears of the inhabitants
Were wither'd, & deafend, & cold:
And their eyes could not discern
Their brethren of other cities.

8. So Fuzon call'd all together
The remaining children of Urizen:
And they left the pendulous earth:
They called it Egypt, & left it.

9. And the salt ocean rolled englob'd.

The End of the first book of Urizen

THE SONG OF LOS

(Lambeth: Printed by W Blake 1795)

AFRICA

I will sing you a song of Los, the Eternal Prophet:
He sung it to four harps at the tables of Eternity,
  In heart-formed Africa.
Urizen faded! Ariston shudderd!
  And thus the Song began:

Adam stood in the garden of Eden:
And Noah on the mountains of Ararat:
They saw Urizen give his Laws to the Nations
By the hands of the children of Los.

Adam, shudderd! Noah faded! black grew the sunny African
When Rintrah gave Abstract Philosophy to Brama in the East.
  (Night spoke to the Cloud:
'Lo these Human form'd spirits in smiling hipocrisy, War
Against one another; so let them War on; slaves to the eternal
    Elements.')
Noah shrunk beneath the waters:
Abram fled in fires from Chaldea:
Moses beheld upon Mount Sinai forms of dark delusion:

  To Trismegistus Palamabron gave an abstract Law:
  To Pythagoras, Socrates & Plato.

Times rolled on o'er all the sons of Har, time after time
Orc on Mount Atlas howld, chain'd down with the Chain of
    Jealousy.
Then Oothoon hoverd over Judah & Jerusalem
And Jesus heard her voice; (a man of sorrows) he reciev'd
A Gospel from wretched Theotormon.

The human race began to wither, for the healthy built
Secluded places, fearing the joys of Love
And the diseased only propagated;
So Antamon call'd up Leutha from her valleys of delight:

And to Mahomet a loose Bible gave.
But in the North, to Odin, Sotha gave a Code of War,
Because of Diralada thinking to reclaim his joy.

These were the Churches, Hospitals: Castles; Palaces;
Like nets & gins & traps to catch the joys of Eternity
    And all the rest a desart;
Till like a dream Eternity was obliterated & erased.

Since that dread day when Har and Heva fled
Because their brethren & sisters liv'd in War & Lust;
And as they fled they shrunk
Into two narrow doleful forms:
Creeping in reptile flesh upon
The bosom of the ground:
And all the vast of Nature shrunk
Before their shrunken eyes.

Thus the terrible race of Los & Enitharmon gave
Laws & Religions to the sons of Har binding them more
And more to Earth: closing and restraining:

Till a Philosophy of Five Senses was complete.
Urizen wept & gave it into the hands of Newton & Locke.

    Clouds roll heavy upon the Alps round Rousseau &
        Voltaire
    And on the mountains of Lebanon round the deceased Gods
    Of Asia: & on the desarts of Africa round the Fallen Angels
    The Guardian Prince of Albion burns in his nightly tent.

ASIA

The Kings of Asia heard
The howl rise up from Europe!
And each ran out from his Web;
From his ancient woven Den;
For the darkness of Asia was startled
At the thick-flaming, thought-creating fires of
    Orc.

And the Kings of Asia stood
And cried in bitterness of soul.
'Shall not the King call for Famine from the heath?
Nor the Priest, for Pestilence from the fen?
To restrain! to dismay! to thin!
The inhabitants of mountain and plain;
In the day of full-feeding prosperity;
And the night of delicious songs.

'Shall not the Councellor throw his curb
Of Poverty on the laborious?
To fix the price of labour:
To invent allegoric riches:

'And the privy admonishers of men
Call for Fires in the City
For heaps of smoking ruins,
In the night of prosperity & wantonness

'To turn man From his path,
To restrain the child From the womb,
To cut off the bread from the city,
That the remnant may learn to obey,

'That the pride of the heart may Fail:
That the lust of the eyes may be quench'd:
That the delicate ear in its infancy
May be dull'd; and the nostrils clos'd up:
To teach mortal worms the path
That leads from the gates of the Grave.'

Urizen heard them cry;
And his shudd'ring waving wings
Went enormous above the red flames
Drawing clouds of despair thro' the heavens
Of Europe as he went:
And his Books of brass, iron & gold
Melted over the land as he flew,
Heavy-waving, howling, weeping

And he stood over Judea,
And stay'd in his ancient place:
And stretch'd his clouds over Jerusalem

For Adam, a mouldering skeleton
Lay bleach'd on the garden of Eden:
And Noah as white as snow
On the mountains of Ararat.

Then the thunders of Urizen bellow'd aloud
From his woven darkness above.

Orc raging in European darkness
Arose like a pillar of fire above the Alps
Like a serpent of fiery flame!
The sullen Earth
Shrunk!

Forth from the dead dust rattling bones to bones
Join; shaking convuls'd the shivring clay breathes
And all flesh naked stands; Fathers and Friends;
Mothers & Infants; Kings & Warriors:

The Grave shrieks with delight, & shakes
Her hollow womb, & clasps the solid stem:
Her bosom swells with wild desire;
And mild & glandous wine
In rivers rush & shout & dance,
On mountain, dale and plain.

The SONG of LOS is Ended
Urizen Wept.

I Asked a Thief
(Manuscript, 1796)

I asked a thief to steal me a peach;
He turned up his eyes.
I asked a lithe lady to lie her down;
Holy & meek she cries –

As soon as I went
An angel came.
He wink'd at the thief
And smil'd at the dame –

And without one word said
Had a peach from the tree
And still as a maid
Enjoy'd the lady.

W Blake
Lambeth
1796

VALA:

The Death and Judgement of the Eternal Man:
A Dream of Nine Nights
By William Blake 1797

[*Revised as:*]

The Four Zoa's:

The torments of Love & Jealousy in The Death and
Judgement of Albion the Ancient Man
By William Blake 1797

VALA

Night the First

The Song of the Aged Mother which shook the heavens with wrath [P. 3]
Hearing the march of long resounding strong heroic Verse
Marshalld in order for the day of Intellectual Battle
The heavens quake, the earth was moved & shudderd & the mountains
With all their woods, the streams & valleys: waild in dismal fear.

. . .

Four Mighty Ones are in every Man: A Perfect Unity
Cannot Exist but from the Universal Brotherhood of Eden
The Universal Man, To Whom be Glory Evermore Amen.

. . .

Los was the fourth immortal starry one, & in the Earth
Of a bright Universe Empery attended day & night,
Days & nights of revolving joy, Urthona was his name

In Eden; in the Auricular Nerves of Human Life [P. 4]
Which is the Earth of Eden, he his Emanations propagated,
Like Sons & Daughters, Daughter of Beulah Sing
His fall into Division & his Resurrection to Unity.
His fall into the Generation of Decay & Death & his
Regeneration by the Resurrection from the dead.
Begin with Tharmas Parent power darkening in the West.

'Lost! Lost! Lost! are my Emanations. Enion O Enion.'

. . .

Enion said – 'Thy fear has made me tremble; thy terrors have surrounded me
All Love is lost! Terror succeeds & Hatred instead of Love
And stern demands of Right & Duty instead of Liberty.
Once thou wast to Me the loveliest son of heaven – But now
Why art thou Terrible and yet I love thee in thy terror till
I am almost Extinct & soon shall be a shadow in Oblivion
Unless some way can be found that I may look upon thee & live.
Hide me some Shadowy semblance, secret whispring in my Ear
In secret of soft Wings, in mazes of delusive beauty.
I have lookd into the secret soul of him I lovd
And in the Dark recesses found Sin & cannot return.'

Trembling & pale sat Tharmas weeping in his clouds.

'Why wilt thou examine every little fibre of my soul,
Spreading them out before the Sun like Stalks of flax to dry?
The infant joy is beautiful but its anatomy
Horrible Ghast & Deadly! nought shalt thou find in it
But Death Despair & Everlasting brooding Melancholy!
Thou wilt go mad with horror if thou Dost Examine thus.
Every moment of my secret hours.'

. . .

Tharmas groand among his Clouds [P. 5]
Weeping, then bending down from his Clouds he stoopd his innocent head
And stretching out his holy hand in the vast deep sublime
Turnd round the circle of Destiny with tears & bitter sighs
And said: 'Return O Wanderer when the day of Clouds is oer.'

. . .

In torment he sunk down & flowd among her filmy Woof 14

. . .

In gnawing pain drawn out by her lovd fingers, every nerve 16
She counted, every vein & lacteal threading them among
Her woof of terror. Terrified & drinking tears of woe
Shuddring she wove nine days & nights Sleepless; her food was tears. 19

. . .

Nine days she labourd at her work & nine dark sleepless nights 23
But on the tenth trembling morn, the Circle of Destiny Complete,
Round rolld the Sea Englobing in a watry Globe self balancd. 25
A Frowning Continent appeard Where Enion in the desart
Terrified in her own Creation viewing her woven shadow
Saw in a dread intoxication of Repentance & Contrition. 28

. . .

Mingling his terrible brightness with her tender limbs; then high she soar'd [P. 7, l. 21]
Above the ocean; a bright wonder Nature shudderd at 22
Half Woman & half Spectre, all his lovely changing colours mix
With her fair crystal clearness; in her lips & cheeks his poisons rose
In blushes like the morning, and his scaly armour softening 25
A monster lovely in the heavens or wandering on the earth 26

Till with fierce pain she brought forth on the rocks her sorrow & woe; [P. 8]
Behold two little Infants wept upon the desolate wind. 2

. . .

Ingrate they wanderd scorning her, drawing her Spectrous Life, [P. 9, l. 4]
Repelling her away & away by a dread repulsive power 5
Into Non Entity revolving round in dark despair, 6

. . .

Nine Times they livd among the forests, feeding on sweet fruits 20
And nine bright Spaces wandered weaving mazes of delight.

Snaring the wild Goats for their milk, they eat the flesh of Lambs,
A male & female naked & ruddy as the pride of summer.

. . .

Alternate Love & Hate his breast; hers Scorn & Jealousy
25 In embryon passions; they kiss'd not nor embrac'd for shame & fear.
His head beamd light & in his vigorous voice was prophecy.
He could controll the times & seasons, & the days & years;
28 She could controll the spaces, regions, desart, flood & forest

But Enitharmon answered with a dropping tear & frowning. [P. 10]
Dark as a dewy morning when the crimson light appears:

'To make us happy let them weary their immortal powers
While we draw in their sweet delights, while we return them scorn
5 On scorn to feed our discontent for if we grateful prove
6 They will withhold sweet love, whose food is thorns & bitter roots

. . .

9 Hear! I will sing a Song of Death! it is a Song of Vala!

. . .

I heard the sounding sea: I heard the voice weaker and weaker: [P. 11]
2 The voice came & went like a dream, I awoke in my secret bliss.'

. . .

7 Seeking to comfort Vala, she will not be comforted.
She rises from his throne and seeks the shadows of her garden
Weeping for Luvah lost in the bloody beams of your false morning.
10 Sickning lies the Fallen Man, his head sick, his heart faint

. . .

Eternity groand & was troubled at the Image of Eternal Death. [P. 12, l. 4]
5 The Wandering Man bow'd his faint head and Urizen descended

. . .

Indignant muttering low thunders; Urizen descended.

. . .

Ten thousand thousand were his hosts of spirits on the wind:

Ten thousand thousand glittering Chariots shining in the sky:
They pour upon the golden shore beside the silent ocean,
Rejoicing in the Victory & the heavens were filld with blood.

The Earth spread forth her table wide; the Night a silver cup
Fill'd with the wine of anguish waited at the golden feast
But the bright Sun was not as yet; he filling all the expanse
Slept as a bird in the blue shell that soon shall burst away.

. . .

They listend to the Elemental Harps & Sphery Song; [P. 13]
They view'd the dancing Hours, quick sporting thro' the sky
With winged radiance scattering joys thro the ever changing light

. . .

But purple night and crimson morning & the golden day
descending
Thro' the clear changing atmosphere display'd green fields
among
The varying clouds, like paradises stretch'd in the expanse
With towns & villages and temples, tents, sheep-folds and
pastures
Where dwell the children of the elemental worlds in harmony.
Not long in harmony they dwell, their life is drawn away
And wintry woes succeed successive driven into the Void
Where Enion craves: successive drawn into the golden feast

But Los & Enitharmon sat in discontent & scorn.
The Nuptial Song arose from all the thousand thousand spirits
Over the joyful Earth & Sea, and ascended into the Heavens
For Elemental Gods their thunderous Organs blew; creating
Delicious Viands, Demons of Waves their watry Eccho's woke!
Bright Souls of vegetative life, budding and blossoming
There is no City nor Corn field nor Orchard! all is [P. 16, l. 5]
Rock & Sand.

There is no Sun nor Moon nor Star, but rugged wintry rocks
Justling together in the void suspended by inward fires.
Impatience now no longer can endure; distracted Luvah

'Bursting forth from the Loins of Enitharmon, Thou fierce Terror
Go howl in vain, Smite Smite his fetters! Smite O wintry hammers!
Smite Spectre of Urthona, mock the fiend who drew us down
From heavens of joy into this deep. Now rage but rage in vain!'

Thus Sang the demons of the deep; the Chariots of War blew loud.
The Feast redounds & Crownd with roses & the circling vine
The Enormous Bride & Bridegroom sat, beside them Urizen
With faded radiance sighd, forgetful of the flowing wine
And of Ahania his pure Bride but She was distant far

But Los & Enitharmon sat in discontent & scorn
Craving the more the more enjoying, drawing out sweet bliss
From all the turning wheels of heaven & the chariots of the Slain.

At distance Far in Night repelld, in direful hunger craving
Summers and Winters round revolving in the frightful deep

Enion blind & age-bent wept upon the desolate wind: [P. 17]

'Why does the Raven cry aloud and no eye pities her?
Why fall the Sparrow & the Robin in the foodless winter?
Faint shivering they sit on leafless bush, or frozen stone
Wearied with seeking food across the snowy waste; the little
Heart, cold; and the little tongue consum'd, that once in thoughtless joy
Gave songs of gratitude to waving corn fields round their nest.

'Why howl the Lion & the Wolf? Why do they roar abroad?
Deluded by summer's heat they sport in enormous love
And cast their young out to the hungry wilds & sandy desarts.
Why is the Sheep given to the knife? The Lamb plays in the Sun [P. 18]
He starts! He hears the foot of Man! he says, "take thou my wool
But spare my life," he knows not that winter cometh fast.

'The Spider sits in his labourd Web, eager watching for the Fly;
Presently comes a famishd Bird & takes away the Spider;
His Web is left all desolate, that his little anxious heart
So careful wove: & spread it out with sighs and weariness.'
This was the Lamentation of Enion round the golden Feast.

End of The First Night

VALA

Night the First

. . .

'Take thou possession! Take this Scepter! go forth in my might [P. 23, l. 5]
For I am weary, & must sleep in the dark sleep of Death.'

. . .

Urizen rose from the bright Feast like a star thro' the evening sky
Indignant at the voice that calld him from the Feast of love.
First he beheld the body of Man pale, cold, the horrors of death.
Beneath his feet shot thro' him as he stood in the Human Brain
And all its golden porches grew pale with his sickening light.

. . .

Pale he beheld futurity; pale he beheld the Abyss
Where Enion blind & age bent wept in direful hunger craving
All rav'ning like the hungry worm, & like the silent grave.

Mighty was the draught of Voidness to draw Existence in. [P. 14]

Terrific Urizen strode above, in fear & pale dismay
He saw the indefinite space beneath & his soul shrunk with horror,
His feet upon the verge of Non Existence; his voice went forth.

Luvah & Vala trembling & shrinking, beheld the great Work master.
And heard his word! 'Divide ye bands influence by influence.
Build we a Bower for heaven's darling in the grizly deep.'

. . .

The Bands of Heaven flew thro the air singing & shouting to Urizen.
Some fix'd the anvil, some the loom erected, some the plow
And harrow formd & framd the harness of silver & ivory,
The golden compasses, the quadrant & the rule & balance.
They erected the furnaces, they formd the anvils of gold beaten in mills
Where winter beats incessant, fixing them firm on their base.
The bellows began to blow & the Lions of Urizen stood round the anvil
And the leopards coverd with skins of beasts tended the roaring fires [P. 25, l. 1]

. . .

The tygers of wrath called the horses of instruction from their mangers.
They unloos'd them & put on the harness of gold & silver & ivory.
In human forms distinct they stood round Urizen prince of Light.

. . .

Luvah was cast into the Furnaces of affliction & sealed
And Vala fed in cruel delight the furnaces with fire.
Stern Urizen beheld urg'd by necessity to keep
The evil day afar, & if perchance with iron power
He might avert his own despair; in woe & fear he saw
Vala incircle round the furnaces where Luvah was clos'd. [P. 26]
In Joy she heard his howlings, & forgot he was her Luvah
With whom she walk'd in bliss, in times of innocence & youth!

Hear ye the voice of Luvah from the furnaces of Urizen:

'If I indeed am Vala's King & ye O sons of Men
The workmanship of Luvah's hands; in times of Everlasting
When I calld forth the Earth-worm from the cold & dark obscure
I nurturd her, I fed her with my rains & dews, she grew
A scaled Serpent, yet I fed her tho' she hated me;
Day after day she fed upon the mountains in Luvah's sight.
I brought her thro' the Wilderness, a dry & thirsty land
And I commanded springs to rise for her in the black desart

Till she became a Dragon winged bright & poisonous.
I opened all the floodgates of the heavens to quench her thirst
And I commanded the Great deep to hide her in his hand [P. 27]
Till she became a little weeping Infant a span long.
I carried her in my bosom as a man carries a lamb;
I loved her, I gave her all my soul & my delight;
I hid her in soft gardens & in secret bowers of Summer
Weaving mazes of delight along the sunny Paradise,
Inextricable labyrinths, She bore me sons & daughters
And they have taken her away hid her from my sight.
They have surrounded me with walls of iron & brass.
. . .

'O Urizen my enemy, I weep for thy stern ambition
But weep in vain. O when will you return: Vala the wanderer?'
These were the word of Luvah patient in afflictions [P. 28, l. 1]
. . .

And when Luvah age after age was quite melted with woe
The fires of Vala faded like a shadow cold & pale,
An evanescent shadow; last she fell a heap of Ashes
Beneath the furnaces, a woful heap in living death.

Then were the furnaces unseald with spades & pickaxes
Roaring let out the fluid, the molten metal ran in channels
Cut by the plow of ages held in Urizen's strong hand
In many a valley, for the Bulls of Luvah dragd the Plow.
. . .

Then siezd the Lions of Urizen their work, & heated in the forge
Roar the bright masses, thund'ring beat the hammers, many a
pyramid
Is form'd & thrown down thund'ring into the deeps of Non
Entity.
Heated red hot they hizzing rend their way down many a league
Till resting, each his basement finds; suspended there they stand
Casting their sparkles dire abroad into the dismal deep
For measurd out in orderd spaces the Sons of Urizen
With compasses divide the deep; they the strong scales erect

That Luvah rent from the faint Heart of the Fallen Man [P. 29]
And weigh the massy Cubes, then fix them in their awful stations

. . .

Then rose the Builders; First the Architect divine his plan [P. 30, l. 8]
9 Unfolds, The Wondrous scaffold reard all round the infinite.

. . .

12 Multitudes without number work incessant: the hewn stone
Is placd in beds of mortar mingled with the ashes of Vala.
14 Severe the labour, female slaves the mortar trod oppressed.

The King of Light beheld her mourning among the Brick kilns compelld [P. 31]
To labour night & day among the fires, her lamenting voice
Is heard when silent night returns & the labourers take their rest:

'O Lord wilt thou not look upon our sore afflictions
5 Among these flames incessant labouring, our hard masters laugh
At all our sorrow. We are made to turn the wheel for water,
To carry the heavy basket on our scorched shoulders, to sift
8 The sand & ashes, & to mix the clay with tears & repentance.'

. . .

17 Thus she lamented day & night, compelld to labour & sorrow.
Luvah in vain her lamentations heard; in vain his love
19 Brought him in various forms before her, still she knew him not,

Still she despisd him, calling on his name & knowing him not, [P. 32]
2 Still hating, still professing love, still labouring in the smoke

. . .

7 But infinitely beautiful the wondrous work arose
In sorrow & care, a Golden World whose porches round the heavens
And pillard halls & rooms recievd the eternal wandering stars,
10 A wondrous golden Building; many a window, many a door
And many a division let in & out into the vast unknown
12 Circled immoveable, within its walls & cielings.

. . .

Thus were the stars of heaven created like a golden chain [P. 33, l. 16]
To bind the Body of Man to heaven from falling into the Abyss.
Each took his station, & his course began with sorrow & care.

And Los & Enitharmon were drawn down by their desires [P. 34]
Descending sweet upon the wind among soft harps & voices.
. . .

Urizen saw & envied & his imagination was filled.
Repining he contemplated the past in his bright sphere
Terrified with his heart & spirit at the visions of futurity
That his dread fancy formd before him in the unformd void

For Los & Enitharmon walkd forth on the dewy Earth
Contracting or expanding their all flexible senses
At will to murmur in the flowers small as the honey bee,
At will to stretch across the heavens & step from star to star
Or standing on the Earth erect, or on the stormy waves
Driving the storms before them or delighting in sunny beams
While round their heads the Elemental Gods kept harmony.
. . .

Thus livd Los driving Enion far into the infinite
That he may also draw Ahania's spirit into her Vortex.
Ah happy blindness, Enion sees not the terrors of the uncertain
Thus Enion wails from the dark deep, the golden heavens tremble:

'I am made to sow the thistle for wheat; the nettle for a nourishing dainty. [P. 35]
I have planted a false oath in the earth, it has brought forth a poison tree.
I have chosen the serpent for a councellor & the dog
For a schoolmaster to my children.
I have blotted out from light & living the dove & nightingale
And I have caused the earth worm to beg from door to door.
I have taught the thief a secret path into the house of the just.
I have taught pale artifice to spread his nets upon the morning.

My heavens are brass, my earth is iron, my moon a clod of clay,
My sun a pestilence burning at noon & a vapour of death in night.

'What is the price of Experience? do men buy it for a song
Or wisdom for a dance in the street? No, it is bought with the price
Of all that a man hath, his house, his wife, his children.
Wisdom is sold in the desolate market where none come to buy
And in the witherd field where the farmer plows for bread in vain.

'It is an easy thing to triumph in the summer's sun
And in the vintage & to sing on the waggon loaded with corn.
It is an easy thing to talk of patience to the afflicted,
To speak the laws of prudence to the houseless wanderer,
To listen to the hungry ravens cry in wintry season [P. 36]
When the red blood is filld with wine & with the marrow of lambs.

'It is an easy thing to laugh at wrathful elements,
To hear the dog howl at the wintry door; the ox in the slaughter house moan,
To see a god on every wind & a blessing on every blast,
To hear sounds of love in the thunder storm that destroys our enemies house,
To rejoice in the blight that covers his field, & the sickness that cuts off his children
While our olive & vine sing & laugh round our door & our children bring fruits & flowers.

'Then the groan & the dolor are quite forgotten & the slave grinding at the mill
And the captive in chains & the poor in the prison, & the soldier in the field
When the shatterd bone hath laid him groaning among the happier dead.

'It is an easy thing to rejoice in the tents of prosperity.
Thus could I sing & thus rejoice, but it is not so with me.'

End of the Second Night

VALA

Night the Third

Now sat the King of Light on high upon his starry throne [P. 37]
And bright Ahania bow'd herself before his splendid feet.

'O Urizen look on Me; like a mournful stream
I Embrace round thy knees & wet My bright hair with my tears:

Why sighs my Lord! are not the morning stars thy obedient Sons?
Do they not bow their bright heads at thy voice? at thy command
Do they not fly into their stations & return their light to thee?
The immortal Atmospheres are thine, there thou art seen in glory
Surrounded by the ever changing Daughters of the Light.'
. . .

She ceas'd; the Prince his light obscurd & the splendors of his crown
Infolded in thick clouds, from whence his mighty voice burst forth: [P. 38]

'O bright Ahania, a Boy is born of the dark Ocean
Whom Urizen doth serve, with Light replenishing his darkness.
I am set here a King of trouble commanded here to serve
And do my ministry to those who eat of my wide table.
All this is mine yet I must serve & that Prophetic boy
Must grow up to command his Prince but hear my determind Decree:
But Vala shall become a Worm in Enitharmon's Womb
Laying her seed upon the fibres soon to issue forth
And Luvah in the loins of Los a dark & furious death.
Alas for me! what will become of me at that dread time?'

Ahania bow'd her head & wept seven days before the King
And on the eighth day when his clouds unfolded from his throne
She rais'd her bright head sweet perfumd & thus with heavenly voice:

'O Prince, the Eternal One hath set thee leader of his hosts.

. . .

Why didst thou listen to the voice of Luvah that dread morn [P. 39, l. 4]
To give the immortal steeds of light to his deceitful hands
No longer now obedient to thy will thou art compell'd
To forge the curbs of iron & brass, to build the iron mangers,
To feed them with intoxication from the wine presses of Luvah.

. . .

They call thy lions to the fields of blood, they rouze thy tygers
Out of the halls of justice, till these dens thy wisdom framd
Golden & beautiful but O how unlike those sweet fields of bliss
Where liberty was justice & eternal science was mercy.
Then O my dear lord listen to Ahania, listen to the vision,
The vision of Ahania in the slumbers of Urizen
When Urizen slept in the porch & the Ancient Man was smitten.

'The Darkning Man walkd on the steps of fire before his halls
And Vala walkd with him in dreams of soft deluding slumber.
He looked up & saw thee, Prince of Light, thy splendor faded.

. . .

Then Man ascended mourning into the splendors of his palace. [P. 40, l. 2]
Above him rose a Shadow from his wearied intellect
Of living gold, pure, perfect, holy; in white linen pure he hover'd,
A sweet entrancing self delusion, a watry vision of Man
Soft exulting in existence, all the Man absorbing!

'Man fell upon his face prostrate before the watry shadow
Saying "O Lord, whence is this change? thou knowest I am nothing."

. . .

'He ceasd: the shadowy voice was silent; but the cloud hoverd over their heads
In golden wreathes, the sorrow of Man & the balmy drops fell down [P. 41]
And Lo that Son of Man, that shadowy Spirit of Albion
Luvah, descended from the cloud; Albion rose.

'Indignant rose the Awful Man & turnd his back on Vala.
I heard the Voice of Albion starting from his sleep:

. . .

'"Whence is this voice crying Enion that soundeth in my ears?
O cruel pity! O dark deceit! can Love seek for dominion?"

'And Luvah strove to gain dominion over the Ancient Man.
They strove together above the Body where Vala was inclos'd
And the dark body of Albion left prostrate upon the crystal pavement
Coverd with boils from head to foot: the terrible smitings of Luvah.

'Then frownd Albion & put forth Luvah from his presence
Saying, "Go & die the Death of Man for Vala the sweet wanderer. [P. 42]
I will turn the volutions of your Ears outward; & bend your Nostrils
Downward: & your fluxile Eyes englob'd, roll round in fear;
Your withring Lips & Tongue shrink up into a narrow circle
Till into narrow forms you creep. Go take your fiery way
And learn what 'tis to absorb the Man, you Spirits of Pity & Love."

. . .

'They heard the Voice & fled swift as the winter's setting sun
And now the Human Blood foamd high, I saw that Luvah & Vala
Went down the Human Heart where Paradise & its joys abounded
In jealous fears, in fury & rage, & flames roll'd round their fervid feet
And the vast form of Nature like a Serpent play'd before them
And as they went in folding fires & thunders of the deep
Vala shrunk in like the dark sea that leaves its slimy banks
And from her bosom Luvah fell far as the east & west
And the vast form of Nature like a Serpent roll'd between.'

. . .

She ended, for the wrathful throne burst forth the black hail storm.

Then thunders rolld around & lightnings darted to & fro. [P. 43]
His visage changd to darkness & his strong right hand came forth
To cast Ahania to the Earth; he siezd her by the hair
And threw her from the steps of ice that froze around his throne

Saying 'Art thou also become like Vala? thus I cast thee out!'

. . .

Then fled the Sons of Urizen from his thunderous throne petrific.
They fled to East & West & left the North & South of Heaven.
A crash ran thro the immense. The bounds of Destiny were broken.
The bounds of Destiny Crashd direful & the swelling Sea
Burst from its bonds in whirlpools fierce roaring with Human voice
Triumphing even to the Stars of bright Ahania's fall.

Down from the dismal North the Prince in thunders & thick clouds
As when the thunder bolt down falleth on the appointed place [P. 44]
Fell down down rushing ruining thundering shuddering
Into the Caverns of the Grave & places of Human Seed
Where the impressions of Despair & Hope enroot forever,
A world of Darkness. Ahania fell far into Non Entity.

. . .

But from the Dolorous Groan one like a shadow of smoke appeard
And human bones rattling together in the smoke & stamping
The nether Abyss & gnashing in fierce despair, panting in sobs
Thick short incessant bursting sobbing, deep despairing stamping struggling,
Struggling to utter the voice of Man, struggling to take the features of Man, Struggling
To take the limbs of Man, at length emerging from the smoke
Of Urizen dashed in pieces from his precipitant fall
Tharmas reard up his hands & stood on the affrighted Ocean.
The dead reard up his Voice & stood on the resounding shore

Crying: 'fury in my limbs! destruction in my bones & marrow!
My skull riven into filaments, my eyes into sea jellies

Floating upon the tide wander bubbling & bubbling
Uttering my lamentations & begetting little monsters
Who sit mocking upon the little pebbles of the tide
In all my rivers & on dried shells that the fish
Have quite forsaken. O fool! fool! to lose my sweetest bliss. [P. 45]
Where art thou, Enion? ah too near to cunning, too far off
And yet too near. Dashd down I send thee into distant darkness.'

. . .

In terrors she witherd away to Entuthon Benithon.

. . .

'O Tharmas, do not thou destroy me quite but let
A little shadow, but a little showery form of Enion
Be near thee, loved Terror; let me still remain & then do thou
Thy righteous doom upon me, only let me hear thy voice.
Driven by thy rage I wander like a cloud into the deep
Where never yet Existence came, there losing all my life
I back return weaker & weaker, consume me not away
In thy great wrath; tho I have sinned, Tho I have rebelld
Make me not like the things forgotten as they had not been.
Make not the thing that loveth thee, a tear wiped away.'

Tharmas replied riding on storms, his voice of Thunder rolld:

'Image of grief, thy fading lineaments make my eyelids fail.
What have I done! both rage & mercy are alike to me.
Looking upon thee, Image of faint waters, I recoil
From my fierce rage into thy semblance. Enion return.
Why does thy piteous face Evanish like a rainy cloud
Melting, a shower of falling tears, nothing but tears! [P. 46]
Enion:
Substanceless, voiceless, weeping, vanishd, nothing but tears! Enion:
Art thou for ever vanishd from the watry eyes of Tharmas?
Rage Rage shall never from my bosom; winds & waters of woe
Consuming all, to the end consuming. Love & Hope are ended.'

For now no more remaind of Enion in the dismal air.

The End of the Third Night

VALA

Night The Fourth

But Tharmas rode on the dark Abyss; the voice of Tharmas rolld [P. 47]
Over the heaving deluge; he saw Los & Enitharmon Emerge
In strength & brightness from the Abyss; his bowels yearnd over them.
They rose in strength above the heaving deluge, in mighty scorn
Red as the Sun in the hot morning of the bloody day
Tharmas beheld them, his bowels yearnd over them.

'Deformd I see these lineaments of ungratified Desire. [P. 48]
The all powerful curse of an honest man be upon Urizen & Luvah
But thou My Son Glorious in brightness, comforter of Tharmas,
Go forth, Rebuild this Universe beneath my indignant power,
A Universe of Death & Decay . . .'

. . .

Los answerd in his furious pride sparks issuing from his hair:
'Hitherto shalt thou come, no further; here thy proud waves cease.
We have drunk up the Eternal Man by our unbounded power.
Beware lest we also drink up thee, rough demon of the waters.
Our God is Urizen the King, King of the Heavenly hosts.
We have no other God but he, thou father of worms & clay,
And he is fallen into the Deep, rough Demon of the waters,
And Los remains God over all, weak father of worms & clay.
I know I was Urthona, keeper of the gates of heaven,
But now I am all powerful Los & Urthona is but my shadow.'

'What Sovereign Architect' said Tharmas 'dare my will controll [P. 49]
For if I will I urge these waters. If I will they sleep
In peace beneath my awful frown; my will shall be my Law.'

So Saying in a Wave he rap'd bright Enitharmon far
Apart from Los, but coverd her with softest brooding care
On a broad wave in the warm west, balming her bleeding wound.

O how Los howld at the rending asunder, all the fibres rent
Where Enitharmon joind to his left side in griding pain.

. . .

Tharmas before Los stood & thus the Voice of Tharmas rolld: [P. 51, l. 11]

'Now all comes into the power of Tharmas. Urizen is falln
And Luvah hidden in the Elemental forms of Life & Death.
Urthona is My Son. O Los, thou art Urthona & Tharmas
Is God. The Eternal Man is sealed, never to be deliverd.

. . .

Is this to be A God? far rather would I be a Man
To know sweet Science & to do with simple companions
Sitting beneath a tent & viewing sheepfolds & soft pastures.
Take thou the hammer of Urthona, rebuild these furnaces.
Dost thou refuse? mind I the sparks that issue from thy hair?
I will compell thee to rebuild by these my furious waves. [P. 52]
Death choose or life; thou strugglest in my waters, now choose life
And all the Elements shall serve thee to their soothing flutes.
Their sweet inspiriting lyres thy labours shall administer
And they to thee; only remit not, faint not thou my Son.
Now thou dost know what tis to strive against the God of Waters.'

So saying Tharmas on his furious chariots of the Deep
Departed far into the Unknown & left a wondrous void
Round Los; afar his waters bore on all sides round with noise
Of wheels & horse's hoofs & Trumpets, Horns & Clarions.

Terrified Los beheld the ruins of Urizen beneath,
A horrible Chaos to his eyes, a formless unmeasurable Death
Whirling up broken rocks on high into the dismal air
And fluctuating all beneath in Eddies of molton fluid.

Then Los with terrible hands siezd on the Ruind Furnaces
Of Urizen. Enormous work: he builded them anew,
Labour of Ages in the Darkness & the war of Tharmas
And Los formd Anvils of Iron petrific, for his blows
Petrify with incessant beating many a rock, many a planet

But Urizen slept in a stoned stupor in the nether Abyss

. . .

And thus began the binding Of Urizen day & night in fear. [P. 53, l. 20]
Circling round the dark Demon with howlings, dismay & sharp blightings
The Prophet of Eternity beat on his iron links & links of brass
And as he beat round the hurtling Demon, terrified at the Shapes
Enslavd humanity put on, he became what he beheld.
Raging against Tharmas his God & uttering
Ambiguous words blasphemous filld with envy, firm resolvd
On hate Eternal, in his vast disdain he labourd beating
The Links of fate, link after link, an endless chain of sorrows.

The Eternal Mind bounded began to roll eddies of wrath ceaseless [P. 54]
Round & round & the sulphureous foam surging thick
Settled a Lake bright & shining clear: White as the snow.

Forgetfulness, dumbness, necessity in chains of the mind lockd up
In fetters of ice shrinking, disorganizd, rent from Eternity.
Los beat on his fetters & heated his furnaces
And pourd iron sodor & sodor of brass.

Restless the immortal inchaind heaving dolorous
Anguishd unbearable till a roof shaggy wild inclosd
In an orb his fountain of thought.

In a horrible dreamful slumber like the linked chain
A vast spine writhd in torment upon the wind
Shooting paind ribs like a bending Cavern
And bones of solidness froze over all his nerves of joy.
A first passed, a state of dismal woe.

From the Caverns of his jointed spine down sunk with fright
A red round globe, hot burning, deep deep down into the Abyss,
Panting, Conglobing, trembling, Shooting out ten thousand branches
Around his solid bones & a Second Age passed over.

In harrowing fear rolling his nervous brain shot branches

. . .

On high into two little orbs hiding in two little caves,
Hiding carefully from the wind his eyes beheld the deep
And a third age passed, a State of dismal woe.

The pangs of hope began in heavy pain, striving, struggling;
Two Ears in close volutions from beneath his orbs of vision
Shot spiring out & petrified as they grew. And a Fourth
Age passed over & a State of dismal woe.

In ghastly torment sick hanging upon the wind
Two nostrils bent down to the deeps –
And a fifth age passed & a state of dismal woe. [P. 55]

In ghastly torment sick, within his ribs bloated round
A craving hungry cavern. Thence arose his channeld
Throat; then like a red flame a tongue of hunger
And thirst appeard and a sixth age passed of dismal woe.

Enraged & stifled with torment he threw his right arm to the north,
His left arm to the south shooting out in anguish deep
And his feet stampd the nether abyss in trembling howling & dismay
And a seventh age passed over & a state of dismal woe.

. . .

The Saviour mild & gentle bent over the corse of Death [P. 56, l. 32]

. . .

And first he found the Limit of Opacity & namd it Satan

. . .

And next he found the Limit of Contraction & namd it Adam
While yet those beings were not born nor knew of good or Evil.

Then wondrously the Starry Wheels felt the divine hand. Limit
Was put to Eternal Death. Los felt the Limit & saw
The Finger of God touch the Seventh furnace in terror
And Los beheld the hand of God over his furnaces.

. . .

In terrors Los shrunk from his task; his great hammer [P. 55, l. 43]
Fell from his hand; his fires hid their strong limbs in smoke
For with noises ruinous, hurtlings & clashings & groans
The immortal endurd, tho bound in a deadly sleep.
Pale terror siezd the Eyes of Los as he beat round
The hurtling Demon; terrifid at the shapes
Enslavd humanity put on he became what he beheld;
He became what he was doing; he was himself transformd.

End of the Fourth Night

VALA

Night The Fifth

Infected Mad he dancd on his mountains high & dark as heaven. [P. 57]
Now fixd into one stedfast bulk his features stonify.
From his mouth curses & from his eyes sparks of blighting,
Beside the anvil cold he dancd with the hammer of Urthona
Terrific pale. Enitharmon stretchd on the dreary Earth
Felt her immortal limbs freeze stiffning pale inflexible.

. . .

Loud & more loud the living music floats upon the air, [P. 58, l. 6]
Faint & more faint the daylight wanes. The wheels of turning darkness
Began in solemn revolutions. Earth convulsd with rending pangs
Rockd to & fro & cried sore at the groans of Enitharmon.

. . .

The groans of Enitharmon shake the skies, the labring Earth,
Till from her heart rending his way a terrible Child sprang forth
In thunder, smoke & sullen flames & howlings & fury & blood.

Soon as his burning Eyes were opened on the Abyss
The horrid trumpets of the deep bellowd with bitter blasts.

. . .

'But now the times return upon thee. Enitharmon's womb [P. 59, l. 17]
Now holds thee soon to issue forth. Sound Clarions of War!
Call Vala from her close recess in all her dark deceit.
Then rage on rage shall fierce redound out of her crystal quiver.'

So Sung the Demons round red Orc & round faint Enitharmon 21

. . .

But when fourteen summers & winters had revolved over [P. 60, l. 6]
Their solemn habitation Los beheld the ruddy boy
Embracing his bright mother & beheld malignant fires
In his young eyes discerning plain that Orc plotted his death.
Grief rose upon his ruddy brows; a tightning girdle grew
Around his bosom like a bloody cord; in secret sobs
He burst it, but next morn another girdle suceeds
Around his bosom. Every day he viewd the fiery youth
With silent fear & his immortal cheeks grew deadly pale
Till many a morn & many a night passd over in dire woe
Forming a girdle in the day & bursting it at night.
The girdle was formd by day: by night was burst in twain
Falling down on the rock an iron chain link by link lockd.

Enitharmon beheld the bloody chain of nights & days
Depending from the bosom of Los & how with griding pain
He went each morning to his labours with the spectre dark,
Calld it the chain of Jealousy. Now Los began to speak
His woes aloud to Enitharmon, since he could not hide
His uncouth plague. He siezed the boy in his immortal hands
While Enitharmon followd him weeping in dismal woe
Up to the iron mountain's top & there the Jealous chain
Fell from his bosom on the mountain. The Spectre dark
Held the fierce boy, Los naild him down binding around his limbs
The accursed chain. O how bright Enitharmon howld & cried
Over her Son. Obdurate Los bound down her loved Joy.

. . .

His limbs bound down mock at his chains for over them a flame [P. 61, l. 11]
Of circling fire unceasing plays; to feed them with life & bring
The virtues of the Eternal worlds, ten thousand thousand spirits
Of life lament around the Demon going forth & returning.
At his enormous call they flee into the heavens of heavens
And back return with wine & food. Or dive into the deeps
To bring the thrilling joys of sense to quell his ceaseless rage.
His eyes the lights of his large soul contract or else expand:
Contracted they behold the secrets of the infinite mountains,
The veins of gold & silver & the hidden things of Vala,
Whatever grows from its pure bud or breathes a fragrant soul;
Expanded they behold the terrors of the Sun & Moon,
The Elemental Planets & the orbs of eccentric fire.
His nostrils breathe a fiery flame; his locks are like the forests
Of wild beasts; there the lion glares, the tyger & wolf howl there
And there the Eagle hides her young in cliffs & precipices.
His bosom is like starry heaven expanded; all the stars
Sing round; there waves the harvest & the vintage rejoices; the Springs
Flow into rivers of delight; there the spontaneous flowers
Drink, laugh & sing, the grasshopper, the Emmet & the Fly;
The golden Moth builds there a house & spreads her silken bed.

. . .

But when returnd to Golgonooza Los & Enitharmon [P. 62, l. 9]
Felt all the sorrow Parents feel, they wept toward one another
And Los repented that he had chaind Orc upon the mountain
And Enitharmon's tears prevaild; parental love returnd
Tho terrible his dread of that infernal chain. They rose
At midnight hasting to their much beloved care.
Nine days they traveld thro the Gloom of Entuthon Benithon.
Los taking Enitharmon by the hand led her along
The dismal vales & up to the iron mountain's top where Orc
Howld in the furious wind; he thought to give to Enitharmon
Her son in tenfold joy & to compensate for her tears
Even if his own death resulted, so much pity him paind

But when they came to the dark rock & to the spectrous cave,
Lo the young limbs had strucken root into the rock & strong
Fibres had from the Chain of Jealousy inwove themselves
In a swift vegetation round the rock & round the Cave

And over the immortal limbs of the terrible fiery boy.
In vain they strove now to unchain. In vain with bitter tears
To melt the chain of Jealousy; not Enitharmon's death
Nor the Consumation of Los could ever melt the chain
Nor unroot the infernal fibres from their rocky bed
Nor all Urthona's strength nor all the power of Luvah's Bulls
Tho they each morning drag the unwilling Sun out of the Deep
Could uproot the infernal chain, for it had taken root
Into the iron rock & grew a chain beneath the Earth [P. 63]
Even to the Center wrapping round the Center & the limbs
Of Orc entering with fibres became one with him a living Chain
Sustained by the Demon's life. Despair & Terror & Woe & Rage
Inwrap the Parents in cold clouds as they bend howling over
The terrible boy till fainting by his side the Parents fell.

. . .

When satiated with grief they returnd back to Golgonooza,
Enitharmon on the road of Dranthon felt the inmost gate
Of her bright heart burst open & again close with a deadly pain.
Within her heart Vala began to reanimate in bursting sobs
And when the Gate was open she beheld that dreary Deep
Where bright Ahania wept. She also saw the infernal roots
Of the chain of Jealousy & felt the rendings of fierce howling Orc.

. . .

The woes of Urizen shut up in the deep dens of Urthona:

'Ah how shall Urizen the King submit to this dark mansion?
Ah how is this! Once on the heights I stretchd my throne sublime;
The mountains of Urizen once of silver where the sons of wisdom dwelt
And on whose tops the Virgins sang are rocks of Desolation.

'My fountains once the haunt of Swans now breed the scaly tortoise;
The houses of my harpers are become a haunt of crows;
The gardens of wisdom are become a field of horrid graves
And on the bones I drop my tears & water them in vain.

Once how I walked from my palace in gardens of delight; [P. 64]
The sons of wisdom stood around; the harpers followd with harps;
Nine virgins clothd in light composd the song to their immortal voices

. . .

'I well remember for I heard the mild & holy voice
Saying "O light, spring up & shine" & I sprang up from the deep.
He gave to me a silver scepter & crownd me with a golden crown
& Said "Go forth & guide my Son who wanders on the ocean."

'I went not forth. I hid myself in black clouds of my wrath.
I calld the stars around my feet in the night of councils dark.
The stars threw down their spears & fled naked away.
We fell. I siezd thee dark Urthona. In my left hand falling

'I siezd thee beauteous Luvah; thou art faded like a flower
And like a lilly is thy wife Vala witherd by winds.

'Thy pure feet stepd on the steps divine, too pure for other feet [P. 65]
And thy fair locks shadowd thine eyes from the divine effulgence.
Then thou didst keep with Strong Urthona the living gates of heaven
But now thou art bound down with him even to the gates of hell.

'Because thou gavest Urizen the wine of the Almighty
For steeds of Light that they might run in thy golden chariot of pride
I gave to thee the Steeds, I pourd the stolen wine
And drunken with the immortal draught fell from my throne sublime.

'I will arise, Explore these dens & find that deep pulsation
That shakes my caverns with strong shudders; perhaps this is the night

Of Prophecy & Luvah hath burst his way from Enitharmon.
When Thought is closd in Caves, Then love shall shew its root in deepest Hell.'

End of the Fifth Night

VALA

Night the Sixth

So Urizen arose & leaning on his Spear explord his dens. [P. 67]
He threw his flight thro the dark air to where a river flowd
And taking off his silver helmet filled it & drank
But when unsatiated his thirst he assayd to gather more
Lo three terrific women at the verge of the bright flood
Who would not suffer him to approach, but drove him back with storms.

. . .

Then Urizen wept & thus his lamentation poured forth: [P. 68, l. 5]

'O horrible, O dreadful state! those whom I loved best,
On whom I pourd the beauties of my light adorning them
With jewels & precious ornament labourd with art divine,
Vests of the radiant colours of heaven & crowns of golden fire;
I gave sweet lillies to their breasts & roses to their hair,
I taught them songs of sweet delight. I gave their tender voices
Into the blue expanse & I invented with laborious art
Sweet instruments of sound; in pride encompassing my Knees
They pourd their radiance above all; the daughters of Luvah Envied
At their exceeding brightness & the sons of eternity sent them gifts.
Now I will pour my fury on them & I will reverse
The previous benediction; for their colours of loveliness
I will give blackness, for jewels hoary frost, for ornament deformity,
For crowns wreathd Serpents, for sweet odors stinking corruptibility,
For voices of delight hoarse croakings inarticulate thro frost,

For labourd fatherly care & sweet instruction, I will give
Chains of dark ignorance & cords of twisted self conceit
And whips of stern repentance & food of stubborn obstinacy
That they may curse Tharmas their God & Los his adopted son,
That they may curse & worship the obscure Demon of destruction,
That they may worship terrors & obey the violent.
Go forth, sons of my curse! Go forth daughters of my abhorrence!'

. . .

So Tharmas spoke but Urizen replied not. On his Way [P. 69, l. 23]
He took, high bounding over hills & desarts floods & horrible chasms.
Infinite was his labour, without end his travel; he strove
In vain for hideous monsters of the deeps annoyd him sore;
Scaled & finn'd with iron & brass they devourd the path before him.
Incessant was the conflict. On he bent his weary steps
Making a path toward the dark world of Urthona; he rose
With pain upon the dreary mountains & with pain descended
And saw their grizly fears & his eyes sickend at the Sight.

Los brooded on the darkness, nor saw Urizen with a Globe of fire [P. 70]
Lighting his dismal journey thro the pathless world of death
Writing in bitter tears & groans in books of iron & brass
The enormous wonders of the Abysses, once his brightest joy.

. . .

Urizen beheld the terrors of the Abyss wandring among
The horrid shapes & sights of torment in burning dungeons & in
Fetters of red hot iron; some with crowns of serpents & some
With monsters girding round their bosom; Some lying on beds of sulphur
On racks & wheels; he beheld women marching oer burning wastes
Of Sand in bands of hundreds & of fifties & of thousands strucken with
Lightnings which blazed after them upon their shoulders in their march.

. . .

Oft would he stand & question a fierce scorpion glowing with gold: [P. 71, l. 5]
In vain, the terror heard not; then a lion he would Seize
By the fierce mane staying his howling course; in vain the voice
Of Urizen; in vain the Eloquent tongue. A Rock a Cloud a Mountain
Were now not Vocal as in Climes of happy Eternity
Where the lamb replies to the infant voice & the lion to the man of years
Giving them sweet instructions; Where the Cloud, the River & the Field
Talk with the husbandman & shepherd. But these attacked him sore.

He could not take their fetters off for they grew from the soul [P. 71]
Nor could he quench the fires for they flamd out from the heart
Nor could he calm the Elements because himself was Subject
So he threw his flight in terror & pain & in repentant tears.

. . .

The ever pitying one who seeth all things saw his fall
And in the dark vacuity created a bosom of clay.
When wearied dead he fell his limbs reposd in the bosom of slime;
As the seed falls from the sower's hand so Urizen fell & death
Shut up his powers in oblivion; then as the seed shoots forth
In pain & sorrow, So the slimy bed his limbs renewd.

. . .

But Urizen said 'Can I not leave this world of Cumbrous wheels, [P. 72, l. 22]
Circle oer Circle, nor on high attain a void
Where self sustaining I may view all things beneath my feet?
Or sinking thro these Elemental wonders swift to fall
I thought perhaps to find an End, a world beneath of voidness
Whence I might travel round the outside of this Dark confusion.
When I bend downward, bending my head downward into the deep,
Tis upward all which way soever I my course begin

But when A Vortex formd on high by labour & sorrow & care
And weariness begins on all my limbs then sleep revives
My wearied spirits; waking then tis downward all which way
So ever I my spirits turn; no end I find of all.
O what a world is here, unlike those climes of bliss
Where my sons gatherd round my knees! O thou poor ruined world!
Thou horrible ruin! once like me thou wast all glorious
And now like me partaking desolate thy master's lot.
Art thou O ruin the once glorious heaven? are these thy rocks
Where joy sang in the trees & pleasant sported on the rivers
And laughter sat beneath the Oaks & innocence sported round [P. 73]
Upon the green plains & sweet friendship met in palaces
And books & instruments of song & pictures of delight?
Where are they, whelmed beneath these ruins in horrible destruction?'

. . .

So he began to dig of gold, silver & iron
And brass vast instruments to measure out the immense & fix
The whole into another world better suited to obey
His will where none should dare oppose his will, himself being King
Of All & all futurity he bound in his vast chain.

. . .

For Urizen lamented over them in a selfish lamentation;
Till a white woof coverd his cold limbs from head to feet,
Hair white as snow coverd him in flaky locks terrific
Overspreading his limbs; in pride he wanderd weeping
Clothed in aged venerableness, obstinately resolvd
Travelling thro darkness & wherever he traveld a dire Web
Followd behind him as the Web of a Spider dusky & cold
Shivering across from Vortex to Vortex drawn out from his mantle of years
And the Web of Urizen stretchd direful shivring in clouds
And uttering such woes, such bursts, such thunderings.
The eyelids expansive as morning & the Ears
As a golden ascent winding round to the heavens of heavens
Within the dark horrors of the Abysses, lion or tyger or scorpion.

. . .

Pangs smote thro the brain & a universal shriek [P. 74, l. 7]
Ran thro the Abysses rending the web torment on torment.

Thus Urizen in sorrows wanderd many a dreary way
Warring with monsters of the Deeps in his most hideous pilgrimage
Till his bright hair scatterd in snows, his skin barkd oer with wrinkles.

. . .

For Urizen fell as the Midday sun falls down into the West.
North stood Urthona's stedfast throne, a World of Solid darkness
Shut up in stifling obstruction rooted in dumb despair.
The East was Void. But Tharmas rolld his billows in ceaseless eddies,
Void, pathless, beat with Snows eternal & iron hail & rain
All thro the caverns of fire & air & Earth, Seeking
For Enion's limbs, nought finding but the black sea weed & sickning slime,
Flying away from Urizen that he might not give him food,
Above, beneath, on all sides round in the vast deep of immensity,
That he might starve the sons & daughters of Urizen on the winds
Making between horrible chasms into the vast unknown.
All these around the world of Los cast forth their monstrous births
But in Eternal times the Seat of Urizen is in the South,
Urthona in the North, Luvah in East, Tharmas in West

And now he came into the Abhorred world of Dark Urthona
By Providence divine conducted not bent from his own will
Lest death Eternal should be the result for the Will cannot be violated.
Into the doleful vales where no tree grew nor river flowd
Nor man nor beast nor creeping thing nor sun nor cloud nor star
Still he with his globe of fire immense in his venturous hand

Bore on thro the Affrighted vales ascending & descending,
Oerwearied or in cumbrous flight he venturd oer dark rifts
Or down dark precipices or climbd with pain & labour huge
Till he beheld the world of Los from the Peaked rock of Urthona
And heard the howlings of red Orc distincter & distincter.

. . .

Striding across the narrow vale the Shadow of Urthona [P. 75, l. 6]
A Spectre Vast appeard whose feet & legs with iron scaled
Stampd the hard rocks expectant of the unknown wanderer
Whom he had seen wandring his nether world when distant far
And watchd his swift approach; collected, dark the Spectre stood.

. . .

Four winged heralds mount the furious blasts & blow their trumps;
Gold, Silver, Brass & iron clangors clamoring rend the shores.
Like white clouds rising from the Vales his fifty two armies
From the four Cliffs of Urthona rise glowing around the Spectre.
Four sons of Urizen the Squadrons of Urthona led in arms
Of gold & silver, brass & iron; he knew his mighty sons.

Then Urizen arose upon the wind back many a mile
Retiring into his dire Web scattering fleecy snows,
As he ascended howling loud the Web vibrated strong
From heaven to heaven, from globe to globe. In vast excentric paths
Compulsive rolld the Comets at his dread command, the dreary way
Falling with wheel impetuous down among Urthona's vales
And round red Orc, returning back to Urizen gorgd with blood.

Slow roll the massy Globes at his command & slow oerwheel
The dismal squadrons of Urthona, weaving the dire Web
In their progressions & preparing Urizen's path before him.

End of The Sixth Night

VALA

Night the Seventh [a]

Then Urizen arose. The Spectre fled & Tharmas fled. [P. 77]
The darkning Spectre of Urthona hid beneath a rock.
Tharmas threw his impetuous flight thro the deeps of immensity
Revolving round in whirlpools fierce all round the cavernd worlds

But Urizen silent descended to the Caves of Orc & saw
A Cavernd Universe of flaming fire; the horses of Urizen
Here bound to fiery mangers furious dash their golden hoofs
Striking fierce sparkles from their brazen fetters; fierce his lions
Howl in the burning dens; his tygers roam in the redounding smoke
In forests of affliction; the adamantine scales of Justice
Consuming in the raging lamps of mercy pourd in rivers.

. . .

Howling & rending his dark caves the awful Demon lay.
Pulse after pulse beat on his fetters, pulse after pulse his spirit
Darted & darted higher & higher to the shrine of Enitharmon;
As when the thunder folds himself in thickest clouds
The watry nations couch & hide in the profoundest deeps

For Urizen fixed in Envy sat brooding & coverd with snow. [P. 78]
His book of iron on his knees he tracd the dreadful letters
While his snows fell & his storms beat to cool the flames of Orc
Age after Age till underneath his heel a deadly root
Struck thro the rock, the root of Mystery accursed shooting up
Branches into the heavens of Los, they pipe formd bending down
Take root again wherever they touch again branching forth
In intricate labyrinths oerspreading many a grizly deep.

Amazd started Urizen when he found himself compassd round
And high roofed over with trees, he arose but the stems
Stood so thick he with difficulty & great pain brought
His books out of the dismal shade, all but the book of iron.

. . .

And Urizen hung over Orc & viewd his terrible wrath;
Sitting upon an iron Crag at length his words broke forth:

. . .

'Pity for thee movd me to break my dark & long repose
And to reveal myself before thee in a form of wisdom.
Yet thou dost laugh at all these tortures & this horrible place,
Yet throw thy limbs these fires abroad that back return upon thee
While thou reposest throwing rage on rage, feeding thyself
With visions of sweet bliss far other than this burning clime.
Sure thou art bathd in rivers of delight, on verdant fields
Walking in joy, in bright Expanses sleeping on bright clouds
With visions of delight so lovely that they urge thy rage
Tenfold with fierce desire to rend thy chain & howl in fury
And dim oblivion of all woe & desperate repose
Or is thy joy founded on torment which others bear for thee?'

Orc answered: 'curse thy hoary brows. What dost thou in this deep?
Thy Pity I contemn! scatter thy snows elsewhere.
I rage in the deep for Lo my feet & hands are naild to the burning rock [P. 79]
Yet my fierce fires are better than thy snows. Shuddring thou sittest.
Thou art not chaind. Why shouldst thou sit, cold grovelling demon of woe,
In tortures of dire coldness? Now a Lake of waters deep
Sweeps over thee freezing to solid; still thou sitst closd up

. . .

. . . yet thou dost fixd obdurate brooding sit
Writing thy books. Anon a cloud filld with a waste of snows
Covers thee still obdurate, still resolvd & writing still
Tho rocks roll oer thee, tho floods pour, tho winds black as the Sea
Cut thee in gashes, tho the blood pours down around thy ankles
Freezing thy feet to the hard rock, still thy pen obdurate
Traces the wonders of Futurity in horrible fear of the future.
I rage furious in the deep for lo my feet & hands are naild
To the hard rock or thou shouldst feel my enmity & hate
In all the diseases of man falling upon thy grey accursed front.'

Urizen answerd 'Read my books, explore my Constellations,
Enquire of my Sons & they shall teach thee how to War.
Enquire of my Daughters who accursd in the dark depths
Kneed bread of Sorrow by my stern command for I am God
Of all this dreadful ruin. Rise O daughters at my Stern command!'

. . .

. . . they took the book of iron & placd above
On clouds of death & sang their songs Kneading the bread of Orc.

And Urizen Read in his book of brass in sounding tones: [P. 80, l. 1]

. . .

'Compell the poor to live upon a Crust of bread by soft mild arts:
Smile when they frown, frown when they smile & when a man looks pale
With labour & abstinence say he looks healthy & happy
And when his children sicken let them die; there are enough
Born, even too many & our Earth will be overrun
Without these arts. If you would make the poor live with temper,
With pomp give every crust of bread you give; with gracious cunning
Magnify small gifts; reduce the man to want a gift & then give with pomp.
Say he smiles if you hear him sigh; If pale say he is ruddy.
Preach temperance: say he is overgorgd & drowns his wit
In strong drink tho you know that bread & water are all
He can afford. Flatter his wife, pity his children till we can
Reduce all to our will as spaniels are taught with art.'

. . .

Then Orc cried 'Curse thy Cold hypocrisy! already round thy Tree
In scales that shine with gold & rubies thou beginnest to weaken
My divided Spirit. Like a worm I rise in peace unbound
From wrath. Now When I rage my fetters bind me more.'

. . .

And Orc began to Organize a Serpent body,
Despising Urizen's light & turning it into flaming fire,
Recieving as a poisond Cup Recieves the heavenly wine
And turning affection into fury & thought into abstraction,
A Self consuming dark devourer rising into the heavens.

Urizen envious brooding sat & saw the secret terror
Flame high in pride & laugh to scorn the source of his deceit
Nor knew the source of his own but thought himself the sole author
Of all his wandering Experiments in the horrible Abyss. [P. 81]
He knew that weakness stretches out in breadth & length, he knew
That wisdom reaches high & deep & therefore he made Orc,
In Serpent form compelld, stretch out & up the mysterious tree.
He sufferd him to Climb that he might draw all human forms
Into submission to his will nor knew the dread result.

Los sat in showers of Urizen watching cold Enitharmon.
. . .

Then Los mournd on the dismal wind in his jealous lamentation:

'Why can I not Enjoy thy beauty, Lovely Enitharmon?
When I return from clouds of Grief in the wandring Elements
Where thou in thrilling joy, in beaming summer loveliness
Delectable reposest ruddy in my absence flaming with beauty,
Cold, pale in sorrow at my approach trembling at my terrific
Forehead & eyes thy lips decay like roses in the spring.
How art thou Shrunk! thy grapes that burst in summer's vast Excess
Shut up in little purple covering faintly bud & die.
Thy olive trees that pourd down oil upon a thousand hills
Sickly look forth & scarcely stretch their branches to the plain.
Thy roses that expanded in the face of glowing morn
Hid in a little silken veil scarce breathe & faintly shine. [P. 82]
The lillies that gave light what time the morning looked forth
Hid in the Vales faintly lament & no one hears their voice.
All things beside the woful Los enjoy the delights of beauty!
Once how I sang & calld the beasts & birds to their delights
Nor knew that I alone exempted from the joys of love

Must war with secret monsters of the animating worlds.
O that I had not seen the day! then should I be at rest
Nor felt the stingings of desire nor longings after life.' 9

. . .

Thus Los lamented in the night unheard by Enitharmon 15
For the Shadow of Enitharmon descended down the tree of Mystery. 16

. . .

He turnd from side to side in tears; he wept & he embracd 26
The fleeting image & in whispers mild wood the faint shade:

'Loveliest delight of Men! Enitharmon, shady hiding
In secret places where no eye can trace thy watry way
Have I found thee? have I found thee? tremblest thou in fear 30
Because of Orc, because he rent his discordant way,
From thy sweet loins of bliss? red flowd thy blood.' 32

. . .

The Shadow of Enitharmon answerd: 'Art thou terrible Shade 37
Set over this sweet boy of mine to guard him lest he rend 38
His mother to the winds of heaven? Intoxicated with [P. 83]
The fruit of this delightful tree, I cannot flee away
From thy embrace, else be assurd so horrible a form
Should never in my arms repose . . . 4

. . .

'Vala was pregnant & brought forth Urizen Prince of Light, 12
First born of Generation. Then behold a wonder to the Eyes
Of the now fallen Man, a double form Vala appeard, A Male
And female; shuddering pale the Fallen Man recoild 15
From the Enormity & calld them Luvah & Vala, turning down
The vales to find his way back into Heaven but found none
For his frail eyes were faded & his ears heavy & dull.

'Urizen grew up in the plains of Beulah. Many Sons
And many daughters flourishd round the holy Tent of Man 20
Till he forgot Eternity, delighted in his sweet joy
Among his family, his flocks & herds & tents & pastures

'But Luvah close conferred with Urizen in darksom night
To bind the father & emulate the brethren. Nought he knew
Of sweet Eternity; the blood flowd round the holy tent & rivn
From its hinges, uttering its final groan, all Beulah fell
In dark confusion; mean time Los was born & Enitharmon
But how I know not; then forgetfulness quite wrapd me up
A period nor do I more remember till I stood
Beside Los in the Cavern dark enslavd to vegetative forms
According to the Will of Luvah who assumd the Place
Of the Eternal Man & smote him. But thou Spectre dark
Maist find a Way to punish Vala in thy fiery South,
To bring her down subjected to the rage of my fierce boy.'

The Spectre said: 'Thou lovely Vision this delightful Tree [P. 84]
Is given us for a Shelter from the tempests of Void & Solid
Till once again the morn of ages shall renew upon us.

. . .

. . . This thou well rememberest; listen, I will tell
What thou forgettest. They in us & we in them alternate Livd,
Drinking the joys of Universal Manhood. One dread morn,
Listen, O vision of delight, One dread morn of goary blood
The manhood was divided for the gentle passions making way
Thro the infinite labyrinths of the heart & thro the nostrils issuing
In odorous stupefaction stood before the Eyes of Man
A female bright. I stood beside my anvil dark, a mass
Of iron glowd bright prepard for spades & plowshares; sudden down
I sunk with cries of blood issuing downward in the veins
Which now my rivers were become, rolling in tubelike forms
Shut up within themselves descending down. I sunk along
The goary tide even to the place of seed & there dividing
I was divided in darkness & oblivion; thou an infant woe
And I an infant terror in the womb of Enion.
My masculine spirit scorning the frail body issud forth

From Enion's brain. In this deformed form leaving thee there

. . .

I view futurity in thee. I will bring down soft Vala
To the embraces of this terror & I will destroy

That body I created; then shall we unite again in bliss 35
For till these terrors planted round the Gates of Eternal life
Are driven away & annihilated we never can repass the Gates.' 37
. . .

Thus they conferrd among the intoxicating fumes of Mystery [P. 85, l. 5]
Till Enitharmon's shadow pregnant in the deeps beneath
Brought forth a wonder horrible . . . 7
. . .

The Spectre terrified gave her Charge over the howling Orc. 22
. . .

Los furious answerd: 'Spectre horrible, thy words astound my Ear [P. 86, l. 4]
With irresistible conviction. I feel I am not one of those 5
Who when convincd can still persist tho furious, controllable
By Reason's power. Even I already feel a World within
Opening its gates & in it all the real substances

'Of which these in the outward World are shadows which pass away.
Come then into my Bosom & in thy shadowy arms bring with thee 10
My lovely Enitharmon. I will quell my fury & teach
Peace to the Soul of dark revenge & repentance to Cruelty.' 12
But Enitharmon trembling fled & hid beneath Urizen's tree [P. 87]
But mingling together with his Spectre the Spectre of Urthona
Wondering beheld the Center opend; by Divine Mercy inspird 3
. . .

They Builded Golgonooza, Los labouring builded pillars high 7
And Domes terrific in the nether heavens for beneath
Was opend new heavens & a new Earth beneath & within,
Threefold within the brain, within the heart, within the loins, 10
A Threefold Atmosphere Sublime continuous from Urthona's world
But yet having a Limit Twofold named Satan & Adam. 12
. . .

The Spectre of Urthona wept before Los Saying 'I am the cause
That this dire state commences. I began the dreadful state
Of Separation & on my dark head the curse & punishment
Must fall unless a way be found to Ransom & Redeem.'

. . .

Los trembling answerd: 'Now I feel the weight of stern repentance.
Tremble not so my Enitharmon at the awful gates
Of thy poor broken Heart. I see thee like a shadow withering
As on the outside of Existence but look! behold! take comfort!
Turn inwardly thine Eyes & there behold the Lamb of God
Clothed in Luvah's robes of blood descending to redeem.'

. . .

Enitharmon answerd: 'I behold the Lamb of God descending
To Meet these Spectres of the Dead. I therefore fear that he
Will give us to Eternal Death, fit punishment for such
Hideous offenders, Uttermost extinction in eternal pain,
An ever dying life of stifling & obstruction shut out
Of existence to be a sign & terror to all who behold
Lest any should in futurity do as we have done in heaven.'

. . .

So Enitharmon spoke & Los his hands divine inspird began [P. 90, l. 25]
To modulate his fires; studious the loud roaring flames
He vanquishd with the strength of Art bending their iron points
And drawing them forth delighted upon the winds of Golgonooza
From out the ranks of Urizen's war & from the fiery lake
Of Orc bending down as the binder of the Sheaves follows
The reaper in both arms embracing the furious raging flames.
Los drew them forth out of the deeps planting his right foot firm
Upon the Iron crag of Urizen, thence springing up aloft
Into the heavens of Enitharmon in a mighty circle

And first he drew a line upon the walls of shining heaven
And Enitharmon tincturd it with beams of blushing love.
It remaind permanent, a lovely form inspird, divinely human.
Dividing into just proportions Los unwearied labourd
The immortal lines upon the heavens till with sighs of love
Sweet Enitharmon mild Entrancd breathd forth upon the wind

The Spectrous dead. Weeping the Spectres viewd the immortal works
Of Los Assimilating to those forms Embodied & Lovely
In youth & beauty in the arms of Enitharmon mild reposing.

First Rintrah & then Palamabron drawn from out the ranks of war
In infant innocence repos'd on Enitharmon's bosom.
. . .

But Los lovd them & refusd to sacrifice their infant limbs
And Enitharmon's smiles & tears prevaild over self protection.
They rather chose to meet Eternal death than to destroy
The offspring of their Care & Pity. Urthona's Spectre was comforted
But Tharmas most rejoicd in hope of Enion's return
For he beheld new Female forms born forth upon the air
Who wove soft silken veils of covering in sweet rapturd trance
Mortal & not as Enitharmon without a covering veil.

[The End of the Seventh Night]

VALA

Night the Seventh [b]

. . .

But in the Deeps beneath the Roots of Mystery in darkest night [P. 91, l. 15]
When Urizen sat on his rock the Shadow brooded
Urizen saw & triumphd & he cried to his warriors

'The time of Prophecy is now revolvd & all
This Universal Ornament is mine & in my hands
The ends of heaven like a Garment will I fold them round me
Consuming what must be consumd; then in power & majesty
I will walk forth thro those wide fields of endless Eternity,
A God & not a Man, a Conqueror in triumphant glory
And all the Sons of Everlasting shall bow down at my feet.'

And in the inner parts of the Temple, wondrous workmanship, [P. 96]
They formd the Secret place reversing all the order of delight
That whosoever enterd into the Temple might not behold
The hidden wonders allegoric of the Generations
Of secret lust when hid in chambers dark the nightly harlot
Plays in Disguise in whisperd hymn & mumbling prayer. The priests
He ordaind & Priestesses clothd in disguises beastial.

. . .

Los reard his mighty stature; on Earth stood his feet. Above
The moon his furious forehead circled with black bursting thunders,
His naked limbs glittring upon the dark blue sky, his knees
Bathed in bloody clouds, his lions in fires of war where spears
And swords rage, where the Eagles cry & Vultures laugh saying
'Now comes the night of Carnage, now the flesh of Kings & Princes
Pamperd in palaces for our food, the blood of Captains nurturd
With lust & murder for our drink; the drunken Raven Shall wander
All night among the slain & mock the wounded that groan in the field.'

Tharmas laughd furious among the Banners clothd in blood

Crying: 'As I will I rend the Nations all asunder, rending
The People, vain their combinations, I will scatter them
But thou, O Son whom I have crowned & inthrond, thee Strong
I will preserve tho Enemies arise around thee numberless.
I will command my winds & they shall scatter them or call
My Waters like a flood around thee; fear not, trust in me [P. 97]
And I will give thee all the ends of heaven for thy possession.
In war shalt thou bear rule, in blood shalt thou triumph for me
Because in times of Everlasting I was rent in sunder
And what I loved best was divided among my Enemies.
My little daughters were made captives & I saw them beaten
With whips along the sultry sands. I heard those whom I lovd
Crying in secret tents at night & in the morn compelld
To labour & behold my heart sunk down beneath
In sighs & sobbings all dividing till I was divided.'

. . .

So cried the Demon of the Waters in the Clouds of Los.
Outstretchd upon the hills lay Enitharmon; clouds & tempests
Beat round her head all night; all day she riots in Excess
But night or day Los follows War & the dismal moon rolls over her
That when Los warrd upon the South reflected the fierce fires
Of his immortal head into the North upon faint Enitharmon.
Red rage the furies of fierce Orc; black thunders roll round Los.

. . .

. . . The Serpent of the woods [P. 98, l. 20]
And of the waters & the scorpion of the desart irritate
With harsh songs every living soul. The Prester Serpent runs
Along the ranks crying: 'Listen to the Priest of God, ye warriors!
This Cowl upon my head he placd in times of Everlasting
And said "Go forth & guide my battles; like the jointed spine
Of Man I made thee when I blotted Man from life & light.
Take thou the seven Diseases of Man; store them for times to come
In store houses in secret places that I will tell thee of
To be my great & awful curses at the time appointed."'

The Prester serpent ceasd; the War song sounded loud & strong
Thro all the heavens. Urizen's Web vibrated torment on torment.

Now in the Caverns of the Grave & Places of human seed [P. 91]
The nameless shadowy Vortex stood before the face of Orc.
The Shadow reard her dismal head over the flaming youth
With sighs & howling & deep sobs; that he might lose his rage
And with it lose himself in meekness she embracd his fire;
As when the Earthquake rouzes from his den, his shoulders huge
Appear above the crumbling Mountains, Silence waits around him
A moment, then astounding horror belches from the Center,
The fiery dogs arise, the shoulders huge appear;
So Orc rolld round his clouds upon the deeps of dark Urthona

. . .

Silent as despairing love & strong as Jealousy

. . .

The hairy shoulders rend the links, free are the wrists of fire.
Red rage redounds; he rouzd his lions from his forests black;
They howl around the flaming youth rending the nameless shadow
And running their immortal course thro solid darkness borne.

Loud Sounds the war song round red Orc in his fury
And round the nameless shadowy Female in her howling terror
When all the Elemental Gods joind in the wondrous Song:

'Sound the War trumpet terrific, Souls clad in attractive steel!
Sound the shrill fife, serpents of war! I hear the northern drum.
Awake, I hear the flappings of the folding banners.
The dragons of the North put on their armour;
Upon the Eastern sea direct they take their course.
The glittring of their horses' trappings stains the vaults of night.

'Stop we the rising of the glorious King; spur, spur your clouds
Of death! O northern drum, awake! O hand of iron, sound [P. 92]
The northern drum! Now give the charge! bravely obscurd!
With darts of wintry hail. Again the black bow draw,
Again the Elemental Strings to your right breasts draw
And let the thundring drum speed on the arrows black.'

The arrows flew from cloudy bow all day, till blood
From east to west flowd like the human veins in rivers
Of life upon the plains of death & valleys of despair.

'Now sound the Clarions of Victory, now strip the slain;
Clothe yourselves in golden arms, brothers of war.'
They sound the clarions strong! they chain the howling captives;
They give the Oath of blood, They cast the lots into the helmet,
They vote the Death of Luvah & they naild him to the tree;
They piercd him with a spear & laid him in a sepulcher
To die a death of Six thousand years bound round with desolation.
The sun was black & the moon rolld a useless globe thro heaven.

Then left the Sons of Urizen the plow & harrow, the loom,
The hammer & the Chisel & the rule & compasses;

They forgd the sword, the chariot of war, the battle ax,
The trumpet fitted to the battle & the flute of summer
And all the arts of life they changd into the arts of death.
The hour glass contemnd because its simple workmanship
Was as the workmanship of the plowman & the water wheel
That raises water into Cisterns broken & burnd in fire
Because its workmanship was like the workmanship of the Shepherd
And in their stead intricate wheels invented, Wheel without wheel
To perplex youth in their outgoings & to bind to labours
Of day & night the myriads of Eternity, that they might file
And polish brass & iron hour after hour; laborious workmanship,
Kept ignorant of the use that they might spend the days of wisdom
In sorrowful drudgery to obtain a scanty pittance of bread,
In ignorance to view a small portion & think that All
And call it Demonstration, blind to all the simple rules of life.

Now, now the Battle rages round thy tender limbs, O Vala!
Now smile among thy bitter tears, now put on all thy beauty.
Is not the wound of the sword Sweet & the broken bone delightful?
Wilt thou now smile among the slain when the wounded groan in the field?
Lift up thy blue eyes, Vala, & put on thy sapphire shoes; [P. 93]
O Melancholy Magdalen behold the morning breaks;
Gird on thy flaming Zone, descend into the Sepulcher.
Scatter the blood from thy golden brow, the tears from thy silver locks;
Shake off the waters from thy wings & the dust from thy white garments.

'Remember all thy feigned terrors on the secret Couch
When the sun rose in glowing morn with arms of mighty hosts
Marching to battle who was wont to rise with Urizen's harps
Girt as a Sower with his seed to scatter life abroad.

'Arise, O Vala! bring the bow of Urizen, bring the swift arrows of light.
How ragd the golden horses of Urizen bound to the chariot of Love,

Compelld to leave the plow to the Ox, to snuff up the winds of desolation,
To trample the corn fields in boastful neighings; this is no gentle harp,
This is no warbling brook nor Shadow of a Myrtle tree

'But blood & wounds & dismal cries & clarions of war
And hearts laid open to the light by the broad grizly sword.'

. . .

So sung the demons of the deep; the Clarions of war blew loud.
Orc rent her & his human form consumd in his own fires.

. . .

And She said: 'Tharmas, I am Vala, bless thy innocent face!
Doth Enion avoid the sight of thy blue watry eyes?
Be not perswaded that the air knows this or the falling dew.'

Tharmas replid: 'O Vala, once I livd in a garden of delight;
I wakend Enion in the morning & she turnd away [P. 94]
Among the apple trees & all the gardens of delight
Swam like a Dream before my eyes. I went to seek the steps
Of Enion in the gardens & the shadows compassd me
And closd me in a watry world of woe where Enion stood
Trembling before me like a shadow, like a mist, like air
And she is gone & here alone I war with darkness & death.'

. . .

So Tharmas waild wrathful then rode upon the Stormy Deep
Cursing the Voice that mockd him with false hope, in furious mood.
Then She returns swift as a blight upon the infant bud
Howling in all the notes of woe to stay his furious rage,
Stamping the hills, wading or swimming, flying furious or falling
Or like an Earthquake rumbling in the bowels of the earth
Or like a cloud beneath & like a fire flaming on high,
Walking in pleasure of the hills or murmuring in the dales
Like to a rushing torrent beneath & a falling rock above,
A thunder cloud in the south & a lulling voice heard in the north

And she went forth & saw the forms of Life & of delight
Walking on Mountains or flying in the open expanse of heaven.

She heard sweet voices in the winds & in the voices of birds
That rose from waters for the waters were as the voice of Luvah.

For far & wide she stretchd thro all the worlds of Urizen's journey [P. 95]
And was Adjoind to Beulah as the Polypus to the Rock.
Mourning the daughters of Beulah saw nor could they have sustaind
The horrid sight of death & torment But the Eternal Promise
They wrote on all their tombs & pillars & on every Urn
These words: 'If ye will believe, your Brother shall rise again'
In golden letters ornamented with sweet labours of Love,
Waiting with Patience for the fulfilment of the Promise Divine

And all the Songs of Beulah sounded comfortable notes.

End of The Seventh Night

VALA

Night the Eighth

Then All in Great Eternity Met in the Council of God [P. 99]
As One Man, Even Jesus, upon Gilead & Hermon
Upon the Limit of Contraction to create the fallen Man.

. . .

The limit of Contraction now was fixd & Man began
To wake upon the Couch of Death; he sneezed Seven times;
A tear of blood dropped from either eye; again he reposd
In the saviour's arms, in the arms of tender mercy & loving kindness.

Then Los said 'I behold the Divine vision thro the broken Gates
Of thy poor broken heart, astonishd, melted into Compassion & Love'

And Enitharmon said, 'I see the Lamb of God upon Mount Zion.'
Wondring with love & Awe they felt the divine hand upon them.

. . .

. . . Then Enitharmon erected [P. 100, l. 2]
Looms in Luban's Gate
And calld the Looms Cathedron; in these Looms She wove the
Spectres
Bodies of Vegetation Singing lulling Cadences to drive away
Despair from the poor wondering spectres and Los loved them
With a parental love for the Divine hand was upon him
And upon Enitharmon & the Divine Countenance shone
In Golgonooza. Looking down the Daughters of Beulah saw
With joy the bright Life & in it a Human form
And knew he was the Saviour, Even Jesus, & they worshipped.
. . .

Astonishd Comforted Delighted in notes of Rapturous Extacy
All Beulah stood astonishd Looking down to Eternal Death.
They saw the Saviour beyond the Pit of death & destruction
For whether they lookd upward they saw the Divine Vision
Or whether they lookd downward still they saw the Divine Vision
Surrounding them on all sides beyond sin & death & hell.

Enitharmon wove in tears singing Songs of Lamentation
And pitying comfort as she sighd forth on the wind the Spectres.

When Urizen Saw the Lamb of God clothed in Luvah's [P. 101]
robes,
Perplexd & terrifid he Stood tho well he knew that Orc
Was Luvah But he now beheld a new Luvah, Or one
Who assumd Luvah's form & stood before him opposite
But he saw Orc a Serpent form augmenting times on times
In the fierce battle & he saw the Lamb of God & the World of
Los
Surrounded by his dark machines for Orc augmented swift
In fury, a Serpent wondrous among the Constellations of Urizen.
A crest of fire rose on his forehead red as the carbuncle,
Beneath down to his eyelids scales of pearl, then gold & silver
Immingled with the ruby overspread his Visage down
His furious neck; writhing contortive in dire budding pains
The scaly armour shot out. Stubborn down his back & bosom
The Emerald, Onyx, Sapphire, jasper, beryl, amethyst
Strove in terrific emulation which should gain a place
Upon the mighty Fiend, the fruit of the mysterious tree

. . .

But Urizen his mighty rage let loose in the mild deep. [P. 100]
Sparkles of Dire affliction issud round his frozen limbs.
Horrible hooks & nets he formd twisting the cords of iron
And brass & molton metals cast in hollow globes & bor'd
Tubes in petrific steel & rammd combustibles & wheels
And chains & pullies fabricated all round the heavens of Los,
Communing with the Serpent of Orc in dark dissimulation
And with the Synagogue of Satan in dark Sanhedrem
To undermine the World of Los & tear bright Enitharmon

. . .

To the four winds, hopeless of future. All futurity [P. 101, l. 39]
Seems teeming with Endless destruction never to be expelld;
Desperate remorse swallows the present in a quenchless rage.

. . .

Enormous Works Los Contemplated inspird by the holy Spirit.
Los builds the walls of Golgonooza against the stirring battle
That only thro the Gates of Death they can enter to Enitharmon.
Raging they take the human visage & the human form.

. . .

For the monsters of the Elements, lions or Tygers or Wolves, [P. 102, l. 3]
Sound loud the howling music, Inspird by Los & Enitharmon Sounding loud; terrific men
They seem to one another laughing terrible among the banners
And when the revolution of their day of battles over
Relapsing in dire torment they return to forms of woe,
To moping visages returning inanimate tho furious,
No more erect tho strong drawn out in length they ravin
For senseless gratification & their visages thrust forth
Flatten above & beneath & stretch out into beastial length.
Weakend they stretch beyond their power in dire droves till war begins
Or Secret religion in their temples before secret shrines

And Urizen gave life & sense by his immortal power
To all his Engines of deceit that linked chains might run
Thro ranks of war spontaneous & that hooks & boring screws

Might act according to their forms by innate cruelty.
He formed also harsh instruments of sound
To grate the soul into destruction or to inflame with fury
The spirits of life, to pervert all the faculties of sense
Into their own destruction if perhaps he might avert
His own despair even at the cost of every thing that breathes.

. . .

'I see the murderer of my Luvah clothd in robes of blood, [P. 103, l. 3]
He who assumd my Luvah's throne in times of Everlasting.
Where hast thou hid him whom I love? in what remote Abyss
Resides that God of my delight? O might my eyes behold
My Luvah, then could I deliver all the sons of God
From Bondage of these terrors & with influences sweet,
As once in those eternal fields in brotherhood & Love
United, we should live in bliss as those who sinned not.
The Eternal Man is seald by thee, never to be deliverd.
We are all servants to thy will. O King of Light, relent
Thy furious power; be our father & our loved King.'

. . .

Urizen heard the Voice and saw the shadow underneath
His woven darkness & in laws & deceitful religions
Beginning at the tree of Mystery circling its root
She spread herself thro all the branches in the power of Orc.

And Enitharmon namd the Female Jerusalem the holy. [P. 104]
Wondring she saw the Lamb of God within Jerusalem's Veil,
The divine Vision seen within the inmost deep recess
Of fair Jerusalem's bosom in a gently beaming fire.

Then sang the Sons of Eden round the Lamb of God & said:
'Glory! Glory! Glory! to the holy Lamb of God
Who now beginneth to put off the dark Satanic body.
Now we behold redemption. Now we know that life Eternal
Depends alone upon the Universal hand & not in us
Is aught but death In Individual weakness sorrow & pain.

. . .

. . . Rahab beholds the Lamb of God. [P. 113, l. 44]
She smites with her knife of flint, she destroys her own work
Times upon times thinking to destroy the Lamb blessed for Ever.
He puts off the clothing of blood, he redeems the spectres from their bonds.
He awakes the sleepers in Ulro; the daughters of Beulah praise him;
They anoint his feet with ointment, they wipe them with the hair of their head.

. . .

'We now behold the Ends of Beulah & we now behold [P. 104, l. 50]
Where Death Eternal is put off Eternally.
Assume the dark Satanic body in the Virgin's womb,
O Lamb divine! it cannot thee annoy. O pitying one,
Thy pity is from the foundation of the World & thy Redemption
Begun Already in Eternity. Come then, O Lamb of God,
Come, Lord Jesus, come quickly.'

. . .

Pitying the Lamb of God Descended thro Jerusalem's gates
To put off Mystery time after time & as a Man
Is born on Earth so was he born of Fair Jerusalem
In mystery's woven mantle & in the Robes of Luvah.

He stood in fair Jerusalem to awake up into Eden
The fallen Man but first to Give his vegetated body.

The Lamb of God stood before Satan opposite [P. 105]
In Entuthon Benithon in the shadows of torments & woe
Upon the heights of Amalek; taking refuge in his arms
The Victims fled from punishment for all his words were peace.

Urizen calld together the Synagogue of Satan in dire Sanhedrim
To Judge the Lamb of God to Death as a murderer & robber;
As it is written, he was numbered among the transgressors.

Cold, dark, opake, the Assembly met twelvefold in Amalek,
Twelve rocky unshapd forms terrific, forms of torture & woe,
Such seemd the Synagogue to distant view . . .

. . .

The Daughters of Amalek, Canaan & Moab, binding on the Stones
Their victims & with knives tormenting them, singing with tears
Over their victims. Hear ye the song of the Females of Amalek:

'O thou poor human form! O thou poor child of woe!
Why dost thou wander away from Tirzah? Why me compell to bind thee?
If thou dost go away from me I shall consume upon the rocks.
These fibres of thine eyes that used to wander in distant heavens
Away from me I have bound down with a hot iron.
These nostrils that Expanded with delight in morning skies
I have bent downward with lead molten in my roaring furnaces.
My soul is seven furnaces, incessant roars the bellows.

. . .

Epharim was a wilderness of joy where all my wild beasts ran.
The river Kanah wanderd by my sweet Manasseh's side.

. . .

Go Noah fetch the girdle of strong brass; heat it red hot;
Press it around the loins of this expanding cruelty.
Shriek not so my only love.
Bind him down, Sisters, bind him down on Ebal, mount of Cursing.
Mahlah come forth from Lebanon & Hoglah from Mount Sinai.
Come circumscribe this tongue of sweets & with a Screw of iron
Fasten this Ear into the Rock. Milcah the task is thine.
Weep not so, sisters, weep not so; our life depends on this
Or mercy & truth are fled away from Shechem & Mount Gilead
Unless my beloved is bound upon the Stems of Vegetation.'

Such are the songs of Tirzah, such the loves of Amalek.
The Lamb of God descended thro the twelve portions of Luvah
Bearing his sorrows & receiving all his cruel wounds.

Thus was the Lamb of God condemnd to Death. [P. 106]
They naild him upon the tree of Mystery weeping over him
And then mocking & then worshipping, calling him Lord & King.

. . .

Los wipd the sweat from his red brow & thus began: [P. 113, l. 25]

. . .

'I am that shadowy Prophet who six thousand years ago 27
Fell from my station in the Eternal bosom. I divided
To multitude & my multitudes are children of Care & Labour.
O Rahab, I behold thee. I was once like thee, a Son 30
Of Pride and I also have piercd the Lamb of God in pride & wrath. 31

. . .

But Satan accusd Palamabron before his brethren, also he maddend [P. 115, l. 12]
The horses of Palamabron's harrow, wherefore Rintrah & Palamabron
Cut him off from Golgonooza. But Enitharmon in tears
Wept over him, Created him a space closd with a tender moon 15
And he rolld down beneath the fires of Orc, a Globe immense. 16

. . .

'There is a State namd Satan; learn distinct to know, O Rahab 23
The Difference between States & Individuals of those States.
The State namd Satan never can be redeemd in all Eternity 25
But when Luvah in Orc became a Serpent he descended into
That State calld Satan. Enitharmon breathd forth on the Winds
Of Golgonooza her well beloved knowing he was Orc's human remains.
She tenderly lovd him above all his brethren; he grew up
In mother's tenderness. The Enormous worlds rolling in Urizen's power 30
Must have given Satan by these mild arts Dominion over all,
Wherefore Palamabron being accusd by Satan to Los
Calld down a Great Solemn assembly. Rintrah in fury & fire
Defended Palamabron & rage filld the Universal Tent.
Because Palamabron was good naturd Satan supposd he feard him 35
And Satan not having the Science of Wrath but only of Pity
Was soon condemnd & wrath was left to wrath & Pity to Pity. 37

. . .

. . . And those in Eden sent Lucifer for their Guard.
Lucifer refusd to die for Satan & in pride he forsook his charge.
Then they sent Moloch. Moloch was impatient. They Sent
Moloch impatient. They Sent Elohim who created Adam
To die for Satan. Adam refusd but was compelld to die
By Satan's arts. Then the Eternals Sent Shaddai.
Shaddai was angry. Pachad descended. Pachad was terrified
And then they sent Jehovah who leprous stretchd his hand to Eternity.
Then Jesus Came & Died willing beneath Tirzah & Rahab.

. . .

Darkness & sorrow coverd all flesh. Eternity was darkend. [P. 106, l. 33]
Urizen sitting in his web of decietful Religion
Felt the female death, a dull & numming stupor such as neer
Before assaulted the bright human form; he felt his pores
Drink in the deadly dull delusion; horrors of Eternal death
Shot thro him. Urizen sat Stonied upon his rock.
Forgetful of his own Laws, pitying he began to Embrace
The Shadowy Female; since life cannot be quenchd Life exuded.

. . .

No longer now Erect the King of Light outstretchd in fury
Lashes his tail in the wild deep; his Eyelids like the Sun
Arising in his pride enlighten all the Grizly deeps,
His scales transparent give forth light like windows of the morning,
His neck flames with wrath & majesty, he lashes the Abyss,
Beating the Desarts & the rocks; the desarts feel his power;
They shake their slumbers off. They wave in awful fear
Calling the Lion & the Tyger, the horse & the wild Stag,
The Elephant, the wolf, the Bear, the Lamia, the Satyr. [P. 107]
His Eyelids give their light around; his folding tail aspires
Among the stars; the Earth & all the Abysses feel his fury
When as the snow covers the mountain, oft petrific hardness
Covers the deeps, at his vast fury moving in his rock
Hardens the Lion & the Bear; trembling in the Solid mountain
They view the light & wonder; crying out in terrible existence
Up bound the wild stag & the horse; behold the King of Pride!

. . .

Los felt the stony stupor & his head rolld down beneath
Into the Abysses of his bosom; the vessels of his blood
Dart forth upon the wind in pipes writhing about in the Abÿss
And Enitharmon pale & cold in milky juices flowd
Into a form of Vegetation, living, having a voice,
Moving on rootlike fibres, trembling in fear upon the Earth

And Tharmas gave his Power to Los, Urthona gave his strength
Into the youthful prophet for the Love of Enitharmon
And of the nameless Shadowy female in the nether deep
And for the dread of the dark terrors of Orc & Urizen.

Thus in a living Death the nameless shadow all things bound,

. . .

And thus Ahania cries aloud to the Caverns of the Grave: [P. 108, l. 8]

'Will you keep a flock of wolves & lead them? will you take the wintry blast
For a covering to your limbs or the summer pestilence for a tent To abide in?
Will you erect a lasting habitation in the mouldering Church yard
Or a pillar & palace of Eternity in the jaws of the hungry grave?
Will you seek pleasure from the festering wound or marry for a Wife
The ancient Leprosy? that the King & Priest may still feast on your decay
And the grave mock & laugh at the plowd field saying
"I am the nourisher, thou the destroyer; in my bosom is milk & wine
And a fountain from my breasts; to me come all multitudes;
To my breath they obey; they worship me. I am a goddess & queen."
But listen to Ahania, O ye sons of the Murderd one;
Listen to her whose memory beholds your ancient days;
Listen to her whose eyes behold the dark body of corruptible death

Looking for Urizen in vain; in vain I seek for morning.
The Eternal Man sleeps in the Earth nor feels the vigrous sun
Nor silent moon nor all the hosts of heaven move in his body.

. . .

'O how the horrors of Eternal Death take hold on Man!
His faint groans shake the caves & issue thro the desolate rocks
And the Strong Eagle, now with numming cold blighted of feathers, [P. 109]
Once like the pride of the sun, now flagging in cold night,
Hovers with blasted wings aloft watching with Eager Eye
Till Man shall leave a corruptible body; he famishd hears him groan
And now he fixes his strong talons in the pointed rock
And now he beats the heavy air with his enormous wings.
Beside him lies the Lion dead & in his belly worms
Feast on his death till universal death devours all
And the pale horse seeks for the pool to lie him down & die
But finds the pools filled with serpents devouring one another.
He droops his head & trembling stands & his bright eyes decay.
These are the Visions of My Eyes, the Visions of Ahania.'

Thus cries Ahania. Enion replies from the Caverns of the Grave:

'Fear not, O poor forsaken one! O land of briars & thorns
Where once the Olive flourishd & the Cedar spread his wings!
Once I waild desolate like thee; my fallow fields in fear
Cried to the Churchyards & the Earthworm came in dismal state.
I found him in my bosom & I said "the time of Love
Appears upon the rocks & hills in silent shades" but soon
A voice came in the night, a midnight cry upon the mountains:
"Awake! The bridegroom cometh!" I awoke to sleep no more
But an Eternal Consummation is dark Enion,
The watry grave. O thou Corn field! O thou Vegetater happy!
More happy is the dark consumer; hope drowns all my torment
For I am now surrounded by a shadowy vortex drawing
The Spectre quite away from Enion that I die a death
Of bitter hope altho I consume in these raging waters.

. . .

Listen! I will tell thee what is done in the caverns of the Grave:

"The Lamb of God has rent the Veil of Mystery, soon to return [P. 110]
In Clouds & Fires around the rock & the Mysterious tree.
As the Seed waits Eagerly watching for its flower & fruit,
Anxious its little soul looks out into the clear expanse
To see if hungry winds are abroad with their invisible army,
So Man looks out in tree & herb & fish & bird & beast
Collecting up the scatterd portions of his immortal body
Into the Elemental forms of every thing that grows.

End of the Eighth Night

VALA

Night the Ninth
Being The Last Judgment

. . .

The thrones of Kings are shaken; they have lost their robes & crowns. [P. 117, l. 18]

. . .

The naked warriors rush together down to the sea shore.

. . .

They are become like wintry flocks, like forests stripd of leaves.

. . .

The books of Urizen unroll with dreadful noise; the folding Serpent [P. 118, l. 8]
Of Orc began to Consume in fierce raving fire; his fierce flames
Issud on all sides gathring strength in animating volumes,
Roaming abroad on all the winds, raging intense, reddening
Into resistless pillars of fire rolling round & round, gathering
Strength from the Earth's consumd & heavens & all hidden abysses.

. . .

And all the while the trumpet sounds,
from the clotted gore & from the hollow den
Start forth the trembling millions into flames of mental fire
Bathing their limbs in the bright visions of Eternity.

. . .

Yet pale the just man stands erect & looking up to heaven
Trembling & strucken by the Universal stroke the trees unroot;
The rocks groan horrible & run about; the mountains &
Their rivers cry with a dismal cry; the cattle gather together;
Lowing they kneel before the heavens; the wild beasts of the forests
Tremble; the Lion shuddring asks the Leopard: 'Feelest thou
The dread I feel, unknown before? My voice refuses to roar
And in weak moans I speak to thee. This night
Before the morning's dawn the Eagle called the Vulture,
The Raven calld the hawk. I heard them from my forests black,
Saying "Let us go up far for soon I smell upon the wind
A terror coming from the South." The Eagle & Hawk flew away
At dawn & Eer the sun arose the raven & Vulture followd.
Let us flee also to the north.' They fled. The Sons of Men
Saw them depart in dismal droves. The trumpet sounded loud.

. . .

On this rock lay the faded head of the Eternal Man [P. 119, l. 28]
Enwrapped round with weeds of death, pale cold in sorrow & woe.
He lifts the blue lamps of his Eyes & cries with heavenly voice:

. . .

'O weakness & O weariness! O war within my members!
My Sons exiled from my breast pass to & fro before me.
My birds are silent on my hills, flocks die beneath my branches,
My tents are fallen; my trumpets & the sweet sounds of my harp
Is silent on my clouded hills that belch forth storms & fire.
My milk of cows & honey of bees & fruit of golden harvest
Are gatherd in the scorching heat & in the driving rain.
My robe is turned to confusion & my bright gold to stone.
Where once I sat I weary walk in misery & pain
For from within my witherd breast grown narrow with my woes
The Corn is turnd to thistles & the apples into poison,
The birds of song to murderous crows, My joys to bitter groans,

The voices of children in my tents to cries of helpless infants [P. 120]
And all exiled from the face of light & shine of morning
In this dark world, a narrow House, I wander up & down.
. . .

When shall the Man of future times become as in days of old?
O weary life! why sit I here & give up all my powers
To indolence, to the night of death when indolence & mourning
Sit hovring over my dark threshold? tho I arise, look out
And scorn the war within my members yet my heart is weak
And my head faint. Yet will I look again into the morning.
Whence is this sound of rage of Men drinking each other's blood,
Drunk with the smoking gore & red but not with nourishing-wine?'

The Eternal Man sat on the Rocks & cried with awful voice:
. . .

'Schoolmaster of souls, great opposer of change, arise
That the Eternal worlds may see thy face in peace & joy,
That thou, dread form of Certainty, maist sit in town & village
While little children play around thy feet in gentle awe
Fearing thy frown, loving thy smile, O Urizen prince of light.'

He calld; the deep buried his voice & answer none returnd.

Then wrath burst round; the Eternal Man was wrath; again he cried:

'Arise O stony form of death! O dragon of the Deeps!
Lie down before my feet, O Dragon! let Urizen arise!
. . .

Let Luvah rage in the dark deep even to Consummation
For if thou feedest not his rage it will subside in peace
But if thou darest obstinate refuse my stern behest
Thy crown & scepter I will seize & regulate all my members
In stern severity & cast thee out into the indefinite
Where nothing lives, there to wander, & if thou returnst weary
Weeping at the threshold of Existence I will steel my heart

Against thee to Eternity & never receive thee more.
Thy self destroying beast formd Science shall be thy eternal lot.
My anger against thee is greater than against this Luvah
For war is energy Enslavd but thy religion,
The first author of this war & the distracting of honest minds
Into confused perturbation & strife & honour & pride,
Is a deciet so detestable that I will cast thee out
If thou repentest not & leave thee as a rotten branch to be
burned.'

Urizen wept in the dark deep, anxious his Scaly form [P. 121]
To reassume the human & he wept in the dark deep
Saying 'O that I had never drank the wine nor eat the bread
Of dark mortality nor cast my view into futurity nor turnd
My back, darkning the present, clouding with a cloud
And building arches high & cities turrets & towers & domes
Whose smoke destroyd the pleasant garden & whose running
Kennels
Chokd the bright rivers, burdning with my Ships the angry deep,
Thro chaos seeking for delight & in spaces remote
Seeking the Eternal which is always present to the wise.

. . .

Let Orc consume! let Tharmas rage! let dark Urthona give
All strength to Los & Enitharmon & let Los self cursd
Rend down this fabric as a wall ruind & family extinct.
Rage, Orc! Rage, Tharmas! Urizen no longer curbs your rage.'

So Urizen spoke; he shook his snows from off his Shoulders &
arose
As on a Pyramid of mist, his white robes scattering
The fleecy white; renewd he shook his aged mantles off.

. . .

And the Eternal Man Said, 'Hear my words, O Prince of Light.
Behold Jerusalem in whose bosom the Lamb of God [P. 122]
Is seen; tho slain before her Gates he self renewd remains
Eternal & I thro him awake to life from death's dark vale.
The times revolve; the time is coming when all these delights
Shall be renewd & all these Elements that now consume
Shall reflourish. Then bright Ahania shall awake from death,
A glorious Vision to thine Eyes, a Self renewing Vision.'

. . .

Urizen Said: 'I have Erred & my Error remains with me.
What Chain encompasses? in what Lock is the river of light confind.'

. . .

He ceasd for rivn link from link the bursting Universe explodes.
All things reversd flew from their centers; rattling bones
To bones Join, shaking convulsd the shivering clay breathes;
Each speck of dust to the Earth's center nestles round & round
In pangs of an Eternal Birth: in torment & awe & fear
All spirits deceasd let loose from reptile prisons come in shoals;
Wild furies from the tyger's brain & from the lion's Eyes
And from the ox & ass come moping terrors, from the Eagle
And raven; numerous as the leaves of autumn every species
Flock to the trumpet muttring over the sides of the grave & crying
In the fierce wind round heaving rocks & mountains filld with groans.
And all the marks remain of the slave's scourge & tyrant's [P. 123] Crown
And of the Priest's oergorged Abdomen & of the merchant's thin
Sinewy deception & of the warrior's outbraving & thoughtlessness
In lineaments too extended & in bones too strait & long.
They shew their wounds; they accuse; they seize the oppressor; howlings began
On the golden palace, Songs & joy on the desart; the Cold babe
Stands in the furious air; he cries 'the children of six thousand years
Who died in infancy rage furious; a mighty multitude rage furious,
Naked & pale standing in the expecting air to be deliverd
Rend limb from limb the Warrior & the tyrant, reuniting in pain.'
The furious wind still rends around; they flee in sluggish effort.

. . .

One Planet calls to another & one star enquires of another:
'What flames are these coming from the South? what noise, what dreadful rout

As of a battle in the heavens? hark! heard you not the trumpet
As of fierce battle?' while they spoke the flames come on intense roaring.

They see him whom they have piercd, they wail because of him,
They magnify themselves no more against Jerusalem Nor
Against her little ones; the innocent, accused before the Judges,
Shines with immortal Glory; trembling the Judge springs from his throne
Hiding his face in the dust beneath the prisoner's feet & saying
'Brother of Jesus, what have I done? Intreat thy lord for me!
Perhaps I may be forgiven,' while he speaks the flames roll on
And after the flames appears the Cloud of the Son of Man
Descending from Jerusalem with power & great Glory.
All nations look up to the Cloud & behold him who was Crucified.

. . .

The Cloud is Blood dazling upon the heavens & in the cloud
Above upon its volumes is beheld a throne & a pavement
Of precious stones, surrounded by twenty four venerable patriarchs
And these again surrounded by four wonders of the Almighty
Incomprehensible, pervading all amidst & round about,
Fourfold, each in the other reflected; they are named Life's in Eternity.
Four Starry Universes going forward from Eternity to Eternity
And the Falln Man who was arisen upon the Rock of Ages
Beheld the Vision of God & he arose up from the Rock [P. 124]
And Urizen arose up with him walking thro the flames
To meet the Lord coming to Judgment but the flames repelld them
Still to the Rock; in vain they strove to Enter the Consummation
Together for the Redeemd Man could not enter the Consummation.

. . .

Then Urizen commanded & they brought the Seed of Men.
The trembling souls of All the Dead stood before Urizen
Weak wailing in the troubled air. East, west & north & south

He turnd the horses loose & laid his Plow in the northern corner [P. 125]
Of the wide Universal field, then Stepd forth into the immense.

Then he began to sow the seed; he girded round his loins
With a bright girdle & his skirt filld with immortal souls.
Howling & Wailing fly the souls from Urizen's strong hand

For from the hand of Urizen the myriads fall like stars
Into their own appointed places, driven back by the winds,
The naked warriors rush together down to the sea shores;
They are become like wintry flocks, like forests stripd of leaves.
The Kings & Princes of the Earth cry with a feeble cry,
Driven on the unproducing sands & on the hardend rocks
And all the while the flames of Orc follow the ventrous feet
Of Urizen & all the while the Trump of Tharmas sounds.
Weaping & wailing fly the souls from Urizen's strong hand.
. . .

Then follows the golden harrow in the midst of Mental fires.
To ravishing melody of flutes & harps & softest voice
The seed is harrowd in while flames heat the black mould & cause
The human harvest to begin . . .
. . .

And Lo like the harvest Moon Ahania cast off her death clothes.
She folded them up in care, in silence & her brightning limbs
Bathd in the clear spring of the rock; then from her darksome cave
Issud in majesty divine. Urizen rose up from his couch
On wings of tenfold joy clapping his hands, his feet, his radiant wings
In the immense, as when the Sun dances upon the mountains
A shout of jubilee in lovely notes responding from daughter to daughter,
From son to Son as if the Stars beaming innumerable
Thro night should sing soft warbling filling Earth & heaven
And bright Ahania took her seat by Urizen in songs & joy.

The Eternal Man also sat down upon the Couches of Beulah,
Sorrowful that he could not put off his new risen body

In mental flames; the flames refusd, they drove him back to Beulah.
His body was redeemd to be permanent thro the Mercy Divine.

And now fierce Orc had quite consumd himself in Mental flames, [P. 126]
Expending all his energy against the fuel of fire.
The Regenerate Man stoopd his head over the Universe & in
His holy hands recievd the flaming Demon & Demoness of Smoke
And gave them to Urizen's hands; the Immortal frownd Saying:

'Luvah & Vala, henceforth you are servants; obey & live.
You shall forget your former state; return & Love in peace
Into your Place, the place of seed, not in the brain or heart.
If Gods combine against Man, Setting their Dominion above
The Human form Divine, Thrown down from their high Station
In the Eternal heavens of Human Imagination: buried beneath
In dark oblivion, with incessant pangs ages on ages,
In Enmity & war first weakend, then in stern repentance
They must renew their brightness & their disorganizd functions
Again reorganize till they resume the image of the human,
Cooperating in the bliss of Man, obeying his Will,
Servants to the infinite & Eternal of the Human form.'

. . .

Invisible Luvah in bright clouds hoverd over Vala's head
And thus their ancient golden age renewd, for Luvah spoke:

. . .

'Come forth O Vala from the grass & from the silent Dew,
Rise from the dews of death for the Eternal Man is Risen.'

She rises among flowers & looks toward the Eastern clearness.
She walks, yea runs, her feet are wingd on the tops of the bending grass,
Her garments rejoice in the vocal wind & her hair glistens with dew.

She answerd thus: 'Whose voice is this in the voice of the nourishing air,
In the spirit of the morning awaking the Soul from its grassy bed?

Where dost thou dwell for it is thee I seek & but for thee [P. 127]
I must have slept Eternally nor have felt the dew of thy morning.
Look how the opening dawn advances with vocal harmony!
Look how the beasts foreshew the rising of some glorious power!
The sun is thine, he goeth forth in his majestic brightness,
O thou creating voice that callest & who shall answer thee?'

. . .

'Alas am I but as a flower? then will I sit me down,
Then will I weep, then I'll complain & sigh for immortality
And chide my maker, thee O Sun, that raisedst me to fall.'

So saying she sat down & wept beneath the apple trees.

'O be thou blotted out, thou Sun, that raisedst me to trouble,
That gavest me a heart to crave & raisedst me thy phantom
To feel thy heat & see thy light & wander here alone,
Hopeless if I am like the grass & so shall pass away.'
'Rise sluggish Soul! why sitst thou here? why dost thou sit & weep?
You Sun shall wax old & decay but thou shalt ever flourish,
The fruit shall ripen & fall down & the flowers consume away
But thou shalt still survive; arise, O dry thy dewy tears.'

'Hah! Shall I still survive? whence came that sweet & comforting voice
And whence that voice of sorrow? O sun, thou art nothing now to me.
Go on thy course rejoicing & let us both rejoice together.

. . .

'Rise up, O Sun, most glorious minister & light of day. [P. 128, l. 4]
Flow on, ye gentle airs, & bear the voice of my rejoicing.
Wave freshly clear waters flowing around the tender grass
And thou sweet smelling ground, put forth thy life in fruits & flowers.

. . .

I am not here alone, my flocks, you are my brethren
And you birds that sing & adorn the sky, you are my sisters.
I sing & you reply to my song. I rejoice & you are glad.

. . .

Here I will build myself a house & here I'll call on his name.
Here I'll return when I am weary & take my pleasant rest.'

So spoke the Sinless Soul & laid her head on the downy fleece
Of a curld Ram who stretchd himself in sleep beside his mistress
And soft sleep fell upon her eyelids in the silent noon of day.
Then Luvah passed by & saw the sinless Soul
And said 'Let a pleasant house arise to be the dwelling place
Of this immortal Spirit growing here in lower Paradise.'

He spoke & pillars were builded & walls as white as ivory.
The grass she slept upon was pavd with pavement as of pearl.
Beneath her rose a downy bed & a cieling coverd all.

Vala awoke. 'When in the pleasant gates of sleep I enterd
I saw my Luvah like a spirit stand in the bright air.
Round him stood spirits like me who reard me a bright house
And here I see thee, house, remain in my most pleasant world.'

. . .

She stood in the river & viewd herself within the watry glass [P. 129, l. 14]
And her bright hair was wet with the waters; she rose up from the river
And as she rose her Eyes were opend to the world of waters.
She saw Tharmas sitting upon the rocks beside the wavy sea.
He strokd the water from his beard & mournd faint thro the summer vales
And Vala stood on the rocks of Tharmas & heard his mournful voice:
'O Enion my weary head is in the bed of death
For weeds of death have wrapd around my limbs in the hoary deeps.
I sit in the place of shells & mourn & thou art closd in clouds.
When will the time of Clouds be past & the dismal night of Tharmas?'

. . .

So saying his faint head he laid upon the Oozy rock
And darkness coverd all the deep; the light of Enion faded

Like a faint flame quivering upon the surface of the darkness.
Then Vala lifted up her hands to heaven to call on Enion.
She calld but none could answer her & the Eccho of her voice returnd:

'Where is the voice of God that calld me from the silent dew?
Where is the Lord of Vala? dost thou hide in clefts of the rock?
Why shouldst thou hide thyself from Vala, from the soul that wanders desolate?'

. . .

[She] saw in the door way beneath the trees two little children playing. [P. 130, l. 4]
She drew near to her house & her flocks followd her footsteps.
The Children clung around her knees, she embracd them & wept over them.

'Thou little Boy art Tharmas & thou bright Girl Enion.
How are ye thus renewd & brought into the Gardens of Vala?'
She embracd them in tears, till the sun descended the western hills
And then she enterd her bright house leading her mighty children.

. . .

And in the morning when the Sun arose in the crystal sky
Vala awoke & calld the children from their gentle slumbers:

'Awake O Enion! awake & let thine innocent Eyes
Enlighten all the Crystal house of Vala! awake! awake!
Awake Tharmas! awake awake thou child of dewy tears.
Open the orbs of thy blue eyes & smile upon my gardens.'

The Children woke & smild on Vala; she kneeld by the golden couch.
She presd them to her bosom & her pearly tears dropd down.
'O my sweet Children! Enion, let Tharmas kiss thy Cheek.
Why dost thou turn thyself away from his sweet watry eyes?
Tharmas, henceforth in Vala's bosom thou shalt find sweet peace.
O bless the lovely eyes of Tharmas & the Eyes of Enion!'

He said: 'O Vala I am sick & all this garden of Pleasure [P. 131]
Swims like a dream before my eyes but the sweet smelling fruit
Revives me to new deaths. I fade even like a water lilly
In the sun's heat till in the night on the couch of Enion
I drink new life & feel the breath of sleeping Enion
But in the morning she arises to avoid my Eyes;
Then my loins fade & in the house I sit me down & weep.'
'Chear up thy Countenance, bright boy, & go to Enion.
Tell her that Vala waits her in the shadows of her garden.'

. . .

Thus in Eternal Childhood straying among Vala's flocks
In infant sorrow & joy alternate Enion & Tharmas playd
Round Vala in the Gardens of Vala & by her river's margin.
They are the shadows of Tharmas & of Enion in Vala's world.

. . .

Then Urizen sitting at his repose on beds in the bright South
Cried 'Times are Ended!' he Exulted; he arose in joy, he exulted;
He pourd his light & all his Sons & daughters pourd their light
To exhale the spirits of Luvah & Vala thro the atmosphere
And Luvah & Vala saw the Light; their spirits were Exhald
In all their ancient innocence; the floods depart; the clouds
Dissipate or sink into the Seas of Tharmas. Luvah sat
Above on the bright heavens in peace; the Spirits of Men beneath
Cried out to be deliverd & the Spirit of Luvah wept
Over the human harvest & over Vala the sweet wanderer.

. . .

Then Urizen arose & took his Sickle in his hand. [P. 132, l. 2]
There is A brazen sickle & a scythe of iron hid
Deep in the South guarded by a few solitary stars.
This sickle Urizen took; the scythe his sons embracd
And went forth & began to reap & all his joyful sons
Reapd the wide Universe & bound in Sheaves a wondrous harvest.
They took them into the wide barns with loud rejoicings & triumph
Of flute & harp & drum & trumpet, horn & clarion.

The feast was spread in the bright South & the Regenerate Man
Sat at the feast rejoicing & the wine of Eternity
Was servd round by the flames of Luvah all Day & all the Night

. . .

A whirlwind rose up in the Center & in the Whirlwind a shriek
And in the Shriek a rattling of bones & in the rattling of bones
A dolorous groan & from the dolorous groan in tears
Rose Enion like a gentle light & Enion spoke saying:

'O Dreams of Death! the human form dissolving companied
By beasts & worms & creeping things & darkness & despair.
The clouds fall off from my wet brow, the dust from my cold limbs
Into the Sea of Tharmas. Soon renewd, a Golden Moth
I shall cast off my death clothes & Embrace Tharmas again.'

. . .

Joy thrilld thro all the Furious form of Tharmas humanizing.
Mild he Embracd her whom he sought; he raisd her thro the heavens,
Sounding his trumpet to awake the dead, on high he soard
Over the ruind worlds, the smoking tomb of the Eternal Prophet.

The Eternal Man arose; he welcomd them to the Feast. [P. 133]
The feast was spread in the bright South & the Eternal Man
Sat at the feast rejoicing & the wine of Eternity
Was servd round by the flames of Luvah all day & all the night

. . .

And One of the Eternals spoke. All was silent at the feast.

'Man is a Worm; wearied with joy he seeks the caves of sleep
Among the Flowers of Beulah, in his Selfish cold repose
Forsaking Brotherhood & Universal love, in selfish clay
Folding the pure wings of his mind, seeking the places dark
Abstracted from the roots of Science; then inclosd around
In walls of Gold we cast him like a Seed into the Earth
Till times & spaces have passd over him; duly every morn
We visit him covering with a Veil the immortal seed,
With windows from the inclement sky we cover him & with walls

And hearths protect the Selfish terror till divided all
Ephesians In families we see our shadows born, & thence we know
iii c. 10 v That Man subsists by brotherhood & Universal Love
We fall on one another's necks, more closely we embrace.
Not for ourselves but for the Eternal family we live.
Man liveth not by Self alone but in his brother's face
Each shall behold the Eternal Father & Love & joy abound.'

. . .

'O Mystery,' Fierce Tharmas cries 'Behold thy end is come! [P. 134, l. 5]
Art thou she that made the nations drunk with the cup of Religion?
Go down, ye Kings & Councellors & Giant Warriors,
Go down into the depths, go down & hide yourselves beneath,
Go down with horse & Chariots & Trumpets of hoarse war.

'Lo how the Pomp of Mystery goes down into the Caves!
Her great men howl & throw the dust & rend their hoary hair.
Her delicate women & children shriek upon the bitter wind,
Spoild of their beauty, their hair rent & their skin shrivld up.
Lo, darkness covers the long pomp of banners on the wind
And black horses & armed men & miserable bound captives.
Where shall the graves recieve them all & where shall be their place
And who shall mourn for Mystery who never loosd her Captives?
Let the slave grinding at the mill run out into the field;
Let him look up into the heavens & laugh in the bright air;
Let the inchaind soul shut up in darkness & in sighing
Whose face has never seen a smile in thirty weary years
Rise & look out, his chains are loose, his dungeon doors are open
And let his wife & children return from the oppressor's scourge;
They look behind at every step & believe it is a dream.
Are these the Slaves that groand along the streets of Mystery?
Where are your bonds & task masters? are these the prisoners?
Where are your chains? where are your tears? why do you look around?
If you are thirsty there is the river, go bathe your parched limbs.
The good of all the Land is before you for Mystery is no more.'

Then All the Slaves from every Earth in the wide Universe
Sing a New song drowning confusion in its happy notes
While the flail of Urizen sounded loud & the winnowing wind of Tharmas
So loud, so clear in the wide heavens & the song that they sung was this
Composed by an African Black from the little Earth of Sotha:

'Aha! Aha! how came I here so soon in my sweet native land?
How came I here? Methinks I am as I was in my youth.'

. . .

Then the Eternal Man said: 'Luvah, the Vintage is ripe; arise! [P. 135, l. 5]
The sons of Urizen shall gather the vintage with sharp hooks
And all thy Sons, O Luvah, bear away the families of Earth.
I hear the flail of Urizen; his barns are full; no room
Remains & in the Vineyards stand the abounding sheaves beneath
The falling Grapes that odorous burst upon the winds. Arise,
My flocks & herds trample the Corn, my cattle browze upon
The ripe Clusters. The shepherds shout for Luvah prince of Love.
Let the Bulls of Luvah tread the Corn & draw the loaded waggon
Into the Barn while children glean the Ears around the door.
Then shall they lift their innocent hands & stroke his furious nose
And he shall lick the little girl's white neck & on her head
Scatter the perfume of his breath while from his mountains high
The lion of terror shall come down & bending his bright mane
And couching at their side shall eat from the curld boys white lap
His golden food and in the evening sleep before the Door.'

'Attempting to be more than Man We become less' said Luvah
As he arose from the bright feast drunk with the wine of ages.
His crown of thorns fell from his head, he hung his living Lyre
Behind the seat of the Eternal Man & took his way
Sounding the Song of Los, descending to the Vineyards bright.

. . .

Then fell the Legions of Mystery in maddning Confusion
Down, Down thro the immense with outcry, fury & despair
Into the wine presses of Luvah; howling fell the Clusters

Of human families thro the deep; the wine presses were filld.
O terrible wine presses of Luvah! O caverns of the Grave! [P. 136]
How lovely the delights of those risen again from death!
O trembling joy! excess of joy is like Excess of grief.'

So Sung the Human Odors round the wine presses of Luvah

But in the Wine presses is wailing terror & despair.
Forsaken of their Elements they vanish & are no more,

. . .

How red the Sons & daughters of Luvah! how they tread the Grapes!
Laughing & shouting drunk with odors many fall oerwearied.
Drownd in the wine is many a youth & maiden; those around
Lay them on skins of tygers or the spotted Leopard or wild Ass
Till they revive or bury them in cool Grots making lamentation

But in the Wine Presses the Human Grapes Sing not nor dance.
They howl & writhe in shoals of torment, in fierce flames consuming,
In chains of iron & in dungeons circled with ceaseless fires.

. . .

Timbrils & Violins sport round the Wine Presses; The little Seed
The Sportive root, the Earthworm, the small beetle, the wise Emmet
Dance round the Wine Presses of Luvah; the Centipede is there,
The ground Spider with many Eyes, the Mole clothed in Velvet,
The Earwig armd, the tender maggot emblem of Immortality,
The Slow Slug, the grasshopper that sings & laughs & drinks:
The winter comes, he folds his slender bones without a murmur.
There is the Nettle that stings with soft down & there
The indignant Thistle whose bitterness is bred in his milk
And Who lives in the contempt of his neighbour; there all the idle weeds
That creep about the obscure places shew their various limbs,
Naked in all their beauty dancing round the Wine Presses.

They dance around the Dying & they Drink the howl & groan.
They catch the Shrieks in cups of gold, they hand them to one another. [P. 137]

These are the sports of love & these the sweet delights of
amorous play,
Tears of the grape, the death sweat of the Cluster, the last sigh
Of the mild youth who listens to the luring songs of Luvah.
The Eternal Man darkend with Sorrow & a wintry mantle
Coverd the Hills. He said, 'O Tharmas rise & Urthona!'

. . .

Then Enion & Ahania & Vala & the wife of Dark Urthona
Rose from the feast in joy ascending to their Golden Looms.
There the wingd shuttle Sang, the spindle & the distaff & the
Reel
Rang sweet the praise of industry. Thro all the golden rooms
Heaven rang with winged Exultation. All beneath howld
loud;
With tenfold rout & desolation roard the Chasms beneath
Where the wide woof flowd down & where the Nations are
gathered together.

Then Dark Urthona took the Corn out of the Stores of
Urizen; [P. 138]
He ground it in his rumbling Mills, Terrible the distress
Of all the Nations of Earth ground in the Mills of Urthona.
In his hand Tharmas takes the Storms; he turns the whirlwind
Loose
Upon the wheels; the stormy seas howl at his dread command
And Eddying fierce rejoice in the fierce agitation of the wheels
Of Dark Urthona. Thunders, Earthquakes, Fires, Water, floods
Rejoice to one another; loud their voices shake the Abyss.

. . .

Such are the works of Dark Urthona. Tharmas sifted the corn.
Urthona made the Bread of Ages & he placed it
In golden & in silver baskets in heavens of precious stone
And then took his repose in Winter in the night of Time.

The Sun has left his blackness & has found a fresher
morning
And the mild moon rejoices in the clear & cloudless night
And Man walks forth from midst of the fires; the evil is all
consumd.
His eyes behold the Angelic spheres arising night & day,

The stars consumd like a lamp blown out & in their stead behold
The Expanding Eyes of Man beholds the depths of wondrous worlds.

. . .

'How is it we have walkd thro fires & yet are not consumd?
How is it that all things are changd even as in ancient times?'

The Sun arises from his dewy bed & the fresh airs [P. 139]
Play in his smiling beams giving the seeds of life to grow
And the fresh Earth beams forth ten thousand thousand springs of life.
Urthona is arisen in his strength, no longer now
Divided from Enitharmon, no longer the Spectre Los.
Where is the Spectre of Prophecy? where the delusive phantom?
Departed & Urthona rises from the ruinous walls
In all his ancient strength to form the golden armour of science
For intellectual War. The war of swords departed now,
The dark religions are departed & sweet Science reigns.

End of The Dream

Letters
1800–1803

To John Flaxman, 12 September 1800

To My Dearest Friend John Flaxman these lines:

I bless thee O Father of Heaven & Earth that ever I saw Flaxman's face.
Angels stand round my Spirit in Heaven, the blessed of Heaven are my friends upon Earth.
When Flaxman was taken to Italy, Fuseli was giv'n to me for a season
And now Flaxman hath given me Hayley his friend to be mine. Such my lot upon Earth.
Now my lot in the Heavens is this; Milton lovd me in childhood & shewd me his face;
Ezra came with Isaiah the Prophet, but Shakespeare in riper years gave me his hand;
Paracelsus & Behmen appeard to me, terrors appear'd in the Heavens above
And in Hell beneath & a mighty & awful change threatend the Earth.
The American War began. All its dark horrors passd before my face
Across the Atlantic to France. Then the French Revolution commencd in thick clouds
And My Angels have told me that Seeing such visions I could not Subsist on the Earth
But by my conjunction with Flaxman who knows to forgive Nervous Fear.

Catherine Blake to Nancy Flaxman, 14 September 1800

To my dear Friend Mrs Anna Flaxman

This Song to the flower of Flaxman's joy,
To the blossom of hope for a sweet decoy;
Do all that you can or all that you may
To entice him to Felpham & far away.

Away to Sweet Felpham for Heaven is there;
The Ladder of Angels descends thro the air;
On the Turret its spiral does softly descend,
Thro the village then winds, at My Cot it does end.

You stand in the Village & look up to heaven;
The precious stones glitter on flights Seventy Seven
And My Brother is there & My Friend & Thine
Descend & ascend with the Bread & the Wine.

The Bread of sweet Thought & the Wine of Delight
Feeds the Village of Felpham by day & by night
And at his own door the blessd Hermit does stand
Dispensing Unceasing to all the whole Land.

W Blake

To Thomas Butts, 2 October 1800

To my Friend Butts I write
My first Vision of Light
On the yellow sands sitting.
The Sun was Emitting
His Glorious beams
From Heaven's high Streams.
Over Sea, over Land
My Eyes did Expand
Into regions of air
Away from all Care,
Into regions of fire
Remote from Desire;

The Light of the Morning
Heaven's Mountains adorning.
In particles bright
The jewels of Light
Distinct shone & clear –
Amazd & in fear
I each particle gazed
Astonishd, Amazed
For each was a Man
Human formd. Swift I ran,
For they beckond to me
Remote by the Sea
Saying: 'Each grain of Sand,
Every Stone on the Land,
Each rock & each hill,
Each fountain & rill,
Each herb & each tree,
Mountain, hill, Earth & Sea,
Cloud, Meteor & Star
Are Men Seen Afar.'
I stood in the Streams
Of Heaven's bright beams
And Saw Felpham sweet
Beneath my bright feet
In soft Female charms
And in her fair arms
My Shadow I knew
And my wife's shadow too
And My Sister & Friend.
We like Infants descend
In our Shadows on Earth
Like a weak mortal birth.
My Eyes more & more
Like a Sea without shore
Continue Expanding,
The Heavens commanding,
Till the Jewels of Light,
Heavenly Men beaming bright,
Appeard as One Man
Who Complacent began

My limbs to infold
In his beams of bright gold,
Like drops purgd away
All my mire & my clay.
Soft consumd in delight
In his bosom Sun bright
I remaind. Soft he smild,
And I heard his voice Mild
Saying 'This is My Fold
O thou Ram hornd with gold
Who awakest from Sleep
On the Sides of the Deep.
On the Mountains around
The roarings resound
Of the lion & wolf,
The loud Sea & deep gulf.
These are guards of My Fold,
O thou Ram hornd with gold.'
And the voice faded mild.
I remain'd as a Child.
All I ever had known
Before me bright Shone.
I saw you & your wife
By the fountains of life.
Such the Vision to me
Appeard on the Sea.

To Thomas Butts, 22 November 1802

With happiness stretchd across the hills
In a cloud that dewy sweetness distills,
With a blue sky spread over with wings
And a mild Sun that mounts & sings,
With trees & fields full of Fairy elves
And little devils who fight for themselves;
Remembring the Verses that Hayley sung
When my heart knockd against the root of my tongue;
With Angels planted in Hawthorn bowers
And God himself in the passing hours,
With Silver Angels across my way
And Golden Demons that none can stay,

With my Father hovering upon the wind
And my Brother Robert just behind
And my Brother John the evil one
In a black cloud making his mone;
Tho dead they appear upon my path
Notwithstanding my terrible wrath.
They beg, they intreat, they drop their tears
Filld full of hopes, filld full of fears;
With a thousand Angels upon the Wind
Pouring disconsolate from behind
To drive them off & before my way
A frowning Thistle implores my stay.
What to others a trifle appears
Fills me full of smiles or tears
For double the vision my Eyes do see
And a double vision is always with me.
With my inward Eye 'tis an old Man grey,
With my outward a Thistle across my way.
'If thou goest back,' the thistle said
'Thou art to endless woe betrayd
For here does Theotormon lower
And here is Enitharmon's bower
And Los the terrible thus hath sworn
"Because thou backward dost return
Poverty, Envy, old age & fear
Shall bring thy Wife upon a bier;
And Butts shall give what Fuseli gave,
A dark black Rock & a gloomy Cave." '
I struck the Thistle with my foot
And broke him up from his delving root.
'Must the duties of life each other cross?
Must every joy be dung & dross?
Must my dear Butts feel cold neglect
Because I give Hayley his due respect?
Must Flaxman look upon me as wild
And all my friends be with doubts beguild?
Must my Wife live in my Sister's Bane
Or my Sister survive on my Love's pain?
The curses of Los the terrible shade
And his dismal terrors make me afraid.'

So I spoke & struck in my wrath
The old man weltering upon my path.
Then Los appeard in all his power;
In the Sun he appeard descending before
My face in fierce flames; in my double sight
Twas outward a Sun: inward Los in his might.

'My hands are labourd day & night
And Ease comes never in my sight.
My Wife has no indulgence given
Except what comes to her from heaven.
We eat little, we drink less;
This Earth breeds not our happiness.
Another Sun feeds our life's streams,
We are not warmed with thy beams;
Thou measurest not the Time to me
Nor yet the Space that I do see;
My Mind is not with thy light arrayd.
Thy terrors shall not make me afraid.'

When I had my Defiance given
The Sun stood trembling in heaven,
The Moon that glowd remote below
Became leprous & white as snow,
And every Soul of men on the Earth
Felt affliction & sorrow & sickness & dearth.
Los flamd in my path & the Sun was hot
With the bows of my Mind & the Arrows of Thought.
My bow string fierce with Ardour breathes,
My arrows glow in their golden sheaves;
My brothers & father march before;
The heavens drop with human gore.

Now I a fourfold vision see
And a fourfold vision is given to me;
Tis fourfold in my supreme delight
And three fold in soft Beulah's night
And twofold Always. May God us keep
From Single vision & Newton's Sleep!

To Thomas Butts, 16 August 1803

O why was I born with a different face?
Why was I not born like the rest of my race?
When I look each one starts! when I speak I offend;
Then I'm silent & passive & lose every Friend.

Then my verse I dishonour, My pictures despise,
My person degrade & my temper chastise;
And the pen is my terror, the pencil my shame;
All my Talents I bury, and dead is my Fame.

I am either too low or too highly prizd;
When Elate I am Envyd, When Meek I'm Despisd.

MILTON

a Poem in 2 Books

To Justify the Ways of God to Men

([London:] The Author & Printer W Blake 1804)

PREFACE

And did those feet in ancient time [Pl. 2]
Walk upon England's mountains green;
And was the holy Lamb of God
On England's pleasant pastures seen!

And did the Countenance Divine
Shine forth upon our clouded hills?
And was Jerusalem builded here,
Among these dark Satanic Mills?

Bring me my Bow of burning gold:
Bring me my Arrows of desire:
Bring me my Spear: O clouds, unfold:
Bring me my Chariot of Fire!

I will not cease from Mental Fight,
Nor shall my Sword sleep in my hand:
Till we have built Jerusalem,
In England's green & pleasant Land.

'Would to God that all the Lord's people were Prophets.'
Numbers XI Ch 29 v.

BOOK THE FIRST

'If you account it Wisdom when you are angry to be silent and [Pl. a, l. 5]
Not to shew it: I do not account that Wisdom but Folly.
Every Man's Wisdom is peculiar to his own Individuality.
Lo Satan, my youngest born, art thou not Prince of the Starry Hosts

And of the Wheels of Heaven, to turn the Mills day & night?
Art thou not Newton's Pantocrator weaving the Woof of Locke?
To Mortals thy Mills seem every thing & the Harrow of Shaddai
A Scheme of Human conduct invisible & incomprehensible.
Get to thy Labours at the Mills & leave me to my wrath.'

. . .

Ah weak & wide astray: Ah shut in narrow doleful form [Pl. f, l. 19]
Creeping in reptile flesh upon the bosom of the ground:
The Eye of Man a little narrow orb closd up & dark
Scarcely beholding the great light, conversing with the Void:
The Ear a little shell in small volutions shutting out
All melodies & comprehending only Discord & Harmony;
The Tongue a little moisture Fills, a little food it cloys,
A little sound it utters & its cries are faintly heard,
Then brings forth Moral Virtue the cruel Virgin Babylon.

'Can such an Eye judge of the stars? & looking thro its tubes
Measure the sunny rays that point their spears in Udanadan?
Can such an Ear filld with the vapours of the yawning pit
Judge of the pure melodious harp struck by a hand divine:
Can such closed Nostrils feel a joy? or tell of autumn fruits
When grapes & figs burst their covering to the joyful air?
Can such a Tongue boast of the living waters? or take in
Ought but the Vegetable Ratio & loathe the faint delight?
Can such gross Lips percieve? alas, folded within themselves
They touch not ought but pallid turn & tremble at every wind.'

. . .

For Satan flaming with Rintrah's fury hidden beneath his own mildness [Pl. 7, l. 19]
Accus'd Palamabron before the Assembly of ingratitude: of malice:
He created Seven deadly Sins drawing out his infernal scroll
Of Moral laws and cruel punishments upon the clouds of Jehovah
To pervert the Divine voice in its entrance to the earth
With thunder of war & trumpets' sound, with armies of disease,
Punishments & deaths musterd & number'd; 'Saying I am God alone;
There is no other: let all obey my principles of moral individuality.

I have brought them from the uppermost innermost recesses
Of my Eternal Mind, transgressors I will rend off for ever,
As now I rend this accursed Family from my covering.'

Thus Satan rag'd amidst the Assembly: and his bosom grew
Opake against the Divine Vision, the paved terraces of
His bosom inwards shone with fires, but the stones becoming opake
Hid him from sight, in an extreme blackness and darkness,
And there a World of deeper Ulro was opend, in the midst
Of the Assembly. In Satan's bosom a vast unfathomable Abyss.

Astonishment held the Assembly in an awful silence: and tears
Fell down as dews of night, & a loud solemn universal groan
Was utter'd from the east & from the west & from the south
And from the north; and Satan stood opake immeasurable
Covering the east with solid blackness, round his hidden heart
With thunders utterd from his hidden wheels: accusing loud
The Divine Mercy for protecting Palamabron in his tent.

Rintrah rear'd up walls of rocks and pourd rivers & moats
Of fire round the walls: columns of fire guard around
Between Satan and Palamabron in the terrible darkness.

And Satan not having the Science of Wrath, but only of Pity
Rent them asunder, and wrath was left to wrath, & pity to pity.
He sunk down a dreadful Death, unlike the slumbers of Beulah.

The Separation was terrible: the Dead was repos'd on his Couch
Beneath the Couch of Albion, on the seven mountains of Rome
In the whole place of the Covering Cherub, Rome, Babylon & Tyre.
His Spectre raging furious descended into its Space.

. . .

'Let the Bard himself witness. Where hadst thou this terrible Song?' [Pl. 11, l. 50]

The Bard replied: 'I am Inspired! I know it is Truth! for I Sing
According to the inspiration of the Poetic Genius [Pl. 12]
Who is the eternal all-protecting Divine Humanity
To whom be Glory & Power & Dominion Evermore Amen.'

. . .

Then Milton rose up from the heavens of Albion ardorous!
The whole Assembly wept prophetic, seeing in Milton's face
And in his lineaments divine the Shades of Death & Ulro.
He took off the robe of the promise, & ungirded himself from
the oath of God.

And Milton said, 'I go to Eternal Death! The Nations still
Follow after the detestable Gods of Priam; in pomp
Of warlike selfhood, contradicting and blaspheming.
When will the Resurrection come; to deliver the sleeping body
From corruptibility; O when, Lord Jesus, wilt thou come?
Tarry no longer; for my soul lies at the gates of death.
I will arise and look forth for the morning of the grave.
I will go down to the sepulcher to see if morning breaks!
I will go down to self annihilation and eternal death,
Lest the Last Judgment come & find me unannihilate
And I be siez'd & givn'n into the hands of my own Selfhood.
The Lamb of God is seen thro' mists & shadows, hov'ring
Over the sepulchers in clouds of Jehovah & winds of Elohim,
A disk of blood, distant; & heav'ns & earths roll dark between.
What do I here before the Judgment? without my Emanation?
With the daughters of memory, & not with the daughters of
inspiration?
I in my Selfhood am that Satan: I am that Evil One!
He is my Spectre! in my obedience to loose him from my Hells,
To claim the Hells, my Furnaces, I go to Eternal Death.'

. . .

Four Universes round the Mundane Egg remain [Pl. 17, l. 15]
Chaotic,
One to the North, named Urthona: One to the South, named
Urizen:
One to the East, named Luvah: One to the West, named
Tharmas.
They are the Four Zoa's that stood around the Throne
Divine:
But when Luvah assum'd the World of Urizen to the South:
And Albion was slain upon his mountains, & in his tent:
All fell towards the Center in dire ruin, sinking down.
And in the South remains a burning fire; in the East a void;

In the West, a world of raging waters; in the North a solid,
Unfathomable: without end. But in the midst of these
Is built eternally the Universe of Los and Enitharmon:

. . .

Now Albion's sleeping Humanity began to turn upon his Couch, [Pl. 18, l. 25]
Feeling the electric flame of Milton's awful precipitate descent.
Seest thou the little winged fly, smaller than a grain of sand?
It has a heart like thee: a brain open to heaven & hell,
Withinside wondrous & expansive; its gates are not clos'd,
I hope thine are not: hence it clothes itself in rich array:
Hence thou art cloth'd with human beauty, O thou mortal man.
Seek not thy heavenly father then beyond the skies;
There Chaos dwells & ancient Night & Og & Anak old:
For every human heart has gates of brass & bars of adamant,
Which few dare unbar because dread Og & Anak guard the gates
Terrific! and each mortal brain is walld and moated round
Within: and Og & Anak watch here: here is the Seat
Of Satan in its Webs; for in brain and heart and loins
Gates open behind Satan's Seat to the City of Golgonooza
Which is the spiritual fourfold London, in the loins of Albion.

. . .

And Ololon said, 'Let us descend also, and let us give [Pl. 19, l. 45]
Ourselves to death in Ulro among the Transgressors,
Is Virtue a Punisher? O no! how is this wondrous thing?
This World beneath, unseen before: this refuge from the wars
Of Great Eternity! unnatural refuge! unknown by us till now,
Or are these the pangs of repentance? let us enter into them.'

Then the Divine Family said: 'Six Thousand Years are now
Accomplish'd in this World of Sorrow; Milton's Angel knew
The Universal Dictate: and you also feel this Dictate.
And now you know this World of Sorrow, and feel Pity. Obey
The Dictate! Watch over this World, and with your brooding wings
Renew it to Eternal Life: Lo! I am with you alway
But you cannot renew Milton; he goes to Eternal Death.'

So spake the Family Divine as One Man even Jesus
Uniting in One with Ololon & the appearance of One Man
Jesus the Saviour appeard coming in the clouds of Ololon:
Tho driven away with the Seven Starry Ones into the Ulro [Pl. 20]
Yet the Divine Vision remains Every-where For-ever. Amen.
And Ololon lamented for Milton with a great lamentation.

While Los heard indistinct in fear, what time I bound my sandals
On: to walk forward thro' Eternity, Los descended to me:
And Los behind me stood; a terrible flaming Sun: just close
Behind my back: I turned round in terror, and behold,
Los stood in that fierce glowing fire; & he also stoop'd down
And bound my sandals on in Udan-Adan; trembling I stood
Exceedingly with fear & terror, standing in the Vale
Of Lambeth; but he kissed me and wishd me health,
And I became One Man with him arising in my strength:
Twas too late now to recede. Los had enterd into my soul:
His terrors now posses'd me whole! I arose in fury & strength.

'I am that Shadowy Prophet who Six Thousand Years ago
Fell from my station in the Eternal bosom. Six Thousand Years
Are finish'd. I return! both Time & Space obey my will.
I in Six Thousand Years walk up and down; for not one Moment
Of Time is lost, nor one Event of Space unpermanent
But all remain: every fabric of Six Thousand Years
Remains permanent: tho' on the Earth where Satan
Fell, and was cut off all things vanish & are seen no more;
They vanish not from me & mine, we guard them first & last.
The generations of men run on in the tide of Time
But leave their destind lineaments permanent for ever & ever.'

. . .

O Swedenborg! strongest of men, the Samson shorn by the Churches:
Shewing the Transgressors in Hell, the proud Warriors in Heaven:
Heaven as a Punisher & Hell as One under Punishment:
With Laws from Plato & his Greeks to renew the Trojan Gods
In Albion: & to deny the value of the Saviour's blood.

But then I rais'd up Whitefield, Palamabron raisd up Westley,
And these are the cries of the Churches before the two Witnesses'
Faith in God the dear Saviour who took on the likeness of men:
Becoming obedient to death, even the death of the Cross.
The Witnesses lie dead in the Street of the Great City:
No Faith is in all the Earth: the Book of God is trodden under Foot:
He sent his two Servants Whitefield & Westley: were they Prophets
Or were they Idiots or Madmen? shew us Miracles!
Can you have greater Miracles than these? Men who devote [Pl. 22]
Their life's whole comfort to intire scorn & injury & death?
Awake thou sleeper on the Rock of Eternity! Albion awake!
The trumpet of Judgment hath twice sounded: all Nations are Awake
But thou art still heavy and dull: Awake, Albion, Awake!

. . .

Los is by mortals nam'd Time, Enitharmon is nam'd space [Pl. 23, l. 68]
But they depict him bald & aged who is in eternal youth
All powerful and his locks flourish like the brows of morning.
He is the Spirit of Prophecy, the ever apparent Elias.
Time is the mercy of Eternity; without Time's swiftness
Which is the swiftest of all things: all were eternal torment,
All the Gods of the Kingdoms of Earth labour in Los's Halls.
Every one is a fallen Son of the Spirit of Prophecy.
He is the Fourth Zoa that stood around the Throne Divine.

. . .

Timbrels & violins sport round the Wine-presses: the little Seed: [Pl. 24, l. 11]
The sportive Root, the Earth-worm, the gold Beetle: the wise Emmet;
Dance round the Wine-presses of Luvah: the Centipede is there:
The ground Spider with many eyes: the Mole clothed in velvet:
The ambitious Spider in his sullen web: the lucky golden Spinner:
The Earwig armd: the tender Maggot emblem of immortality:
The Flea: Louse: Bug: the Tape-Worm: all the Armies of Disease:
Visible or invisible to the slothful vegetating Man.

The slow Slug: the Grasshopper that sings & laughs & drinks:
Winter comes, he folds his slender bones without a murmur.
The cruel Scorpion is there: the Gnat: Wasp: Hornet & the Honey Bee:
The Toad & venemous Newt: the Serpent clothd in gems & gold:
They throw off their gorgeous raiment: they rejoice with loud jubilee
Around the Wine-presses of Luvah, naked & drunk with wine.

There is the Nettle that stings with soft down: and there
The indignant Thistle: whose bitterness is bred in his milk:
Who feeds on contempt of his neighbour: there all the idle Weeds
That creep around the obscure places, shew their various limbs,
Naked in all their beauty dancing round the Wine-presses.

But in the Wine-presses the Human grapes sing not, nor dance.
They howl & writhe in shoals of torment; in fierce flames consuming,
In chains of iron & in dungeons circled with ceaseless fires,
In pits & dens & shades of death: in shapes of torment & woe;
The plates & screws & wracks & saws & cords & fires & cisterns,
The cruel joys of Luvah's Daughters lacerating with knives
And whips their Victims & the deadly sport of Luvah's Sons.

They dance around the dying, & they drink the howl & groan.
They catch the shrieks in cups of gold, they hand them to one another.
These are the sports of love, & these the sweet delights of amorous play,
Tears of the grape, the death sweat of the cluster, the last sigh
Of the mild youth who listens to the lureing songs of Luvah.

. . .

But in Eternity the Four Arts: Poetry, Painting, Music
And Architecture which is Science: are the Four Faces of Man.
Not so in Time & Space: there Three are shut out, and only
Science remains thro Mercy: & by means of Science the Three
Become apparent in Time & Space in the Three Professions
Poetry is Religion: Music, Law: Painting, in Physic & Surgery:

That Man may live upon Earth till the time of his awaking,
And from these Three, Science derives every Occupation of Men,
And Science is divided into Bowlahoola & Allamanda.

. . .

'Fellow Labourers! The Great Vintage & Harvest is now upon Earth. [Pl. 25, l. 17]
The whole extent of the Globe is explored: Every scatterd Atom
Of Human Intellect now is flocking to the sound of the Trumpet.
All the Wisdom which was hidden in caves & dens from ancient
Time: is now sought out from Animal & Vegetable & Mineral.
The Awakener is come, outstretchd over Europe: the Vision of God is fulfilled.
The Ancient Man upon the Rock of Albion Awakes.
He listens to the sounds of War astonishd & ashamed:
He sees his Children mock at Faith & deny Providence.
Therefore you must bind the Sheaves not by Nations or Families;
You shall bind them in Three Classes; according to their Classes
So shall you bind them, Separating What has been Mixed
Since Men began to be Wove into Nations by Rahab & Tirzah,
Since Albion's Death & Satan's Cutting off from our awful Fields,
When under pretence to benevolence the Elect Subdud All
From the Foundation of the World. The Elect is one Class: You
Shall bind them separate: they cannot Believe in Eternal Life
Except by Miracle & a New Birth. The other two Classes:
The Reprobate who never cease to Believe, and the Redeemd,
Who live in doubts & fears perpetually tormented by the Elect:
These you shall bind in a twin-bundle for the Consummation
But the Elect must be saved from fires of Eternal Death,
To be formed into the Churches of Beulah that they destroy not the Earth
For in every Nation & every Family the Three Classes are born
And in every Species of Earth, Metal, Tree, Fish, Bird & Beast.
We form the Mundane Egg, that Spectres coming by fury or amity,
All is the same, & every one remains in his own energy.
Go forth, reapers, with rejoicing, you sowed in tears
But the time of your refreshing cometh, only a little moment
Still abstain from pleasure & rest in the labours of eternity
And you shall Reap the whole Earth, from Pole to Pole! from Sea to Sea

Beginning at Jerusalem's Inner Court, Lambeth ruin'd and given
To the detestable Gods of Priam, to Apollo: and at the Asylum
Given to Hercules, who labour in Tirzah's Looms for bread,
Who set Pleasure against Duty: who Create Olympic crowns
    To make Learning a burden & the Work of the Holy Spirit: Strife:
The Thor & cruel Odin who first reard the Polar Caves.
Lambeth mourns calling Jerusalem, she weeps & looks abroad
For the Lord's coming, that Jerusalem may overspread all Nations.
Crave not for the mortal & perishing delights, but leave them
To the weak, and pity the weak as your infant care; Break not
Forth in your wrath lest you also are vegetated by Tirzah.
Wait till the Judgment is past, till the Creation is consumed
And then rush forward with me into the glorious spiritual
Vegetation; the Supper of the Lamb & his Bride; and the
Awaking of Albion our friend and ancient companion.'

So Los spoke, But lightnings of discontent broke on all sides round
And murmurs of thunder rolling heavy long & loud over the mountains
While Los calld his Sons around him to the Harvest & the Vintage.

Thou seest the Constellations in the deep & wondrous Night.
They rise in order and continue their immortal courses
Upon the mountains & in vales with harp & heavenly song,
With flute & clarion; with cups & measures filld with foaming wine.
Glittring the streams reflect the Vision of beatitude
And the Calm Ocean joys beneath & smooths his awful waves:
These are the Sons of Los, & these the Labourers of the Vintage. [Pl. 26]
Thou seest the gorgeous clothed Flies that dance & sport in summer.
Upon the sunny brooks & meadows: every one the dance
Knows in its intricate mazes of delight artful to weave:
Each one to sound his instruments of music in the dance.
To touch each other & recede; to cross & change & return.
These are the Children of Los; thou seest the Trees on mountains,
The wind blows heavy, loud they thunder thro' the darksom day

Uttering prophecies & speaking instructive words to the sons
Of men: These are the Sons of Los! These the Visions of Eternity
But we see only as it were the hem of their garments
When with our vegetable eyes we view these wond'rous Visions.

. . .

The Sky is an immortal Tent built by the Sons of Los [Pl. 28, l. 4]
And every space that a Man views around his dwelling-place,
Standing on his own roof, or in his garden on a mount
Of twentyfive cubits in height, such space is his Universe:
And on its verge the Sun rises & sets, the Clouds bow
To meet the flat Earth & the Sea in such an orderd Space:
The Starry heavens reach no further but here bend and set
On all sides & the two Poles turn on their valves of gold:
And if he move his dwelling-place, his heavens also move
Wher'eer he goes & all his neighbourhoods bewail his loss:
Such are the Spaces called Earth & such its dimension:
As to that false appearance which appears to the reasoner
As of a Globe rolling thro Voidness, it is a delusion of Ulro.
The Microscope knows not of this nor the Telescope, they alter
The ratio of the Spectator's Organs but leave the Objects untouchd
For every Space larger than a red Globule of Man's blood
Is visionary: and is created by the Hammer of Los
And every space smaller than a Globule of Man's blood opens
Into Eternity of which this vegetable Earth is but a shadow;
The red Globule is the unwearied Sun by Los created
To measure Time and Space to mortal Men every morning.

. . .

BOOK THE SECOND

Thou hearest the Nightingale begin the Song of Spring: [Pl. 31, l. 27]
The Lark sitting upon his earthy bed: just as the morn
Appears: listens silent: then springing from the waving Cornfield! loud
He leads the Choir of Day! trill, trill, trill, trill,
Mounting upon the wings of light into the Great Expanse,
Reechoing against the lovely blue & shining heavenly Shell:
His little throat labours with inspiration; every feather

On throat & breast & wings vibrates with the effluence Divine.
All Nature listens silent to him & the awful Sun
Stands still upon the Mountain looking on this little Bird
With eyes of soft humility, & wonder, love & awe.
Then loud from their green covert all the Birds begin their Song:
The Thrush, the Linnet & the Goldfinch, Robin & the Wren
Awake the Sun from his sweet reverie upon the Mountain:
The Nightingale again assays his song & thro the day
And thro the night warbles luxuriant: every Bird of Song
Attending his loud harmony with admiration & love.
This is a Vision of the lamentation of Beulah over Ololon:

Thou percievest the Flowers put forth their precious Odors:
And none can tell how from so small a center comes such sweets
Forgetting that within that Center Eternity expands
Its ever during doors that Og & Anak fiercely guard.
First eer the morning breaks joy opens in the flowery bosoms,
Joy even to tears, which the Sun rising dries; first the Wild Thyme
And Meadow-sweet downy & soft waving among the reeds,
Light springing on the air lead the sweet Dance: they wake
The Honeysuckle sleeping on the Oak: she flaunting beauty
Revels along upon the wind; the White-thorn lovely May
Opens her many lovely eyes: listening the Rose still sleeps,
None dare to wake her; soon she bursts her crimson curtaind bed
And comes forth in the majesty of beauty; every Flower:
The Pink, the Jessamine, the Wall-flower, the Carnation,
The Jonquil, the mild Lilly opes her heavens: every Tree
And Flower & Herb soon fill the air with an innumerable Dance,
Yet all in order sweet & lovely, Men are sick with Love;
Such is a Vision of the lamentation of Beulah over Ololon.

. . .

In the eastern porch of Satan's Universe Milton stood & said: [Pl. 39, l. 28]

'Satan! my Spectre! I know my power thee to annihilate
And be a greater in thy place, & be thy Tabernacle,
A covering for thee to do thy will, till one greater comes
And smites me as I smote thee & becomes my covering.
Such are the Laws of thy false Heavns; but Laws of Eternity

Are not such: know thou: I come to Self Annihilation.
Such are the Laws of Eternity that each shall mutually
Annihilate himself for others' good, as I for thee.
Thy purpose & the purpose of thy Priests & of thy Churches
Is to impress on men the fear of death: to teach
Trembling & fear, terror, constriction: abject selfishness.
Mine is to teach Men to despise death & to go on
In fearless majesty annihilating Self, laughing to scorn
Thy Laws & terrors, shaking down thy Synagogues as webs.
I come to discover before Heavn & Hell the Self righteousness
In all its Hypocritic turpitude, opening to every eye
These wonders of Satan's holiness shewing to the Earth
The Idol Virtues of the Natural Heart, & Satan's Seat
Explore in all its Selfish Natural Virtue & put off
In Self annihilation all that is not of God alone:
To put off Self & all I have ever & ever Amen.'

Satan heard! Coming in a cloud with trumpets & flaming fire
Saying: 'I am God the judge of all, the living & the dead.
Fall therefore down & worship me, submit thy supreme
Dictate to my eternal Will & to my dictate bow.
I hold the Balances of Right & Just & mine the Sword.
Seven Angels bear my Name & in those Seven I appear
But I alone am God & I alone in Heaven & Earth
Of all that live dare utter this, others tremble & bow
Till All Things become One Great Satan in Holiness [Pl. 40]
Oppos'd to Mercy, and the Divine Delusion Jesus be no more.'

. . .

But turning toward Ololon in terrible majesty Milton [Pl. 42, l. 28]
Replied: 'Obey thou the Words of the Inspired Man.
All that can be annihilated must be annihilated
That the Children of Jerusalem may be saved from slavery.
There is a Negation, there is a Contrary;
The Negation must be destroyd to redeem the Contraries.
The Negation is the Spectre; the Reasoning Power in Man.
This is a false Body: an Incrustation over my Immortal
Spirit: a Selfhood which must be put off & annihilated alway
To cleanse the Face of my Spirit by Self-examination,
To bathe in the Waters of Life: to wash off the Not [Pl. 43]
Human,
I come in Self-annihilation & the grandeur of Inspiration

To cast off Rational Demonstration by Faith in the Saviour,
To cast off the rotten rags of Memory by Inspiration,
To cast off Bacon, Locke & Newton from Albion's covering,
To take off his filthy garments, & clothe him with Imagination,
To cast aside from Poetry, all that is not Inspiration
That it no longer shall dare to mock with aspersion of Madness
Cast on the Inspired, by the tame high finisher of paltry Blots
Indefinite or paltry Rhymes; or paltry Harmonies,
Who creeps into State Government like a catterpiller to destroy;
To cast off the idiot Questioner who is always questioning,
But never capable of answering: who sits with a sly grin
Silent plotting when to question, like a thief in a cave:
Who publishes doubt & calls it knowledge: whose Science is Despair;
Whose pretence to knowledge is Envy: whose whole Science is
To destroy the wisdom of ages to gratify ravenous Envy
That rages round him like a Wolf day & night without rest.
He smiles with condescension; he talks of Benevolence & Virtue
And those who act with Benevolence & Virtue, they murder time on time.
These are the destroyers of Jerusalem; these are the murderers
Of Jesus, who deny the Faith & mock at Eternal Life:
Who pretend to Poetry that they may destroy Imagination:
By imitation of Nature's Images drawn from Remembrance.
These are the Sexual Garments, the Abomination of Desolation,
Hiding the Human Lineaments as with an Ark & curtains
Which Jesus rent: & now shall wholly purge away with Fire
Till Generation is swallowd up in Regeneration.'

. . .

Terror struck in the Vale I stood at that immortal sound. [Pl. 44, l. 24]
My bones trembled. I fell outstretchd upon the path
A moment, & my Soul returnd into its mortal state
To Resurrection & Judgment in the Vegetable Body
And my sweet Shadow of Delight stood trembling by my side.

Immediately the Lark mounted with a loud trill from Felpham's Vale
And the Wild Thyme from Wimbleton's green & impurpled Hills
And Los & Enitharmon rose over the Hills of Surrey.
Their clouds roll over London with a south wind, soft Oothoon
Pants in the Vales of Lambeth weeping oer her Human Harvest.

Los listens to the Cry of the Poor Man: his Cloud
Over London in volume terrific, low bended in anger.

Rintrah & Palamabron view the Human Harvest beneath.
Their Wine-presses & Barns stand open; the Ovens are prepard,
The Waggons ready: terrific Lions & Tygers sport & play.
All Animals upon the Earth, are prepared in all their strength
To go forth to the Great Harvest & Vintage of the Nations. [Pl. 45, l. 1]

Finis

Jerusalem

The Emanation of The Giant Albion
([London:] Printed by W Blake Sth Molton S^{t} 1804)

Reader! lover of books! lover of heaven, [Pl. 3]
And of the God from whom all books are given,
Who in mysterious Sinai's awful cave
To Man the wondrous art of writing gave,
Again he speaks in thunder and in fire!
Thunder of Thought, & flames of fierce desire;
Even from the depths of Hell his voice I hear
Within the unfathomd caverns of my Ear.
Therefore I print; nor vain my types shall be:
Heaven, Earth & Hell, henceforth shall live in harmony.

Jerusalem

Chap: 1

Of the Sleep of Ulro! and of the passage through Eternal Death! And of the awaking to Eternal Life. [Pl. 4]

This theme calls me in sleep night after night, & ev'ry morn
Awakes me at sun-rise, then I see the Saviour over me
Spreading his beams of love, & dictating the words of this mild song.

Awake! awake, O sleeper of the land of shadows, wake! expand!
I am in you and you in me, mutual in love divine:
Fibres of love from man to man thro Albion's pleasant land.
In all the dark Atlantic vale down from the hills of Surrey
A black water accumulates, return, Albion! return!
Thy brethren call thee, and thy fathers, and thy sons,
Thy nurses and thy mothers, thy sisters and thy daughters
Weep at thy soul's disease, and the Divine Vision is darkend;
Thy Emanation that was wont to play before thy face,
Beaming forth with her daughters into the Divine bosom.
Where hast thou hidden thy Emanation, lovely Jerusalem,
From the vision and fruition of the Holy-one?

I am not a God afar off, I am a brother and friend;
Within your bosoms I reside, and you reside in me:
Lo! we are One, forgiving all Evil; Not seeking recompense!
Ye are my members, O ye sleepers of Beulah, land of shades!

But the perturbed Man away turns down the valleys dark;

'Phantom of the over heated brain! shadow of immortality!
Seeking to keep my soul a victim to thy Love! which binds
Man the enemy of man into deceitful friendships:
Jerusalem is not! her daughters are indefinite:
By demonstration man alone can live, and not by faith.
My mountains are my own, and I will keep them to myself;
The Malvern and the Cheviot, the Wolds, Plinlimmon & Snowdon
Are mine, here will I build my Laws of Moral Virtue:
Humanity shall be no more: but war & princedom & victory!'

. . .

Trembling I sit day and night, my friends are astonish'd at me, [Pl. 5, l. 16]
Yet they forgive my wanderings, I rest not from my great task!
To open the Eternal Worlds, to open the immortal Eyes
Of Man inwards into the Worlds of Thought; into Eternity
Ever expanding in the Bosom of God, the Human Imagination.
O Saviour, pour upon me thy Spirit of meekness & love:
Annihilate the Selfhood in me, be thou all my life!
Guide thou my hand which trembles exceedingly upon the rock of ages

. . .

'I must Create a System, or be enslav'd by another Man's. [Pl. 10, l. 20]
I will not Reason & Compare: my business is to Create.'

. . .

So Los in fury & strength; in indignation & burning wrath.

. . .

And Los said: 'I behold the finger of God in terrors! [Pl. 12, l. 5]
Albion is dead! his Emanation is divided from him!
But I am living! yet I feel my Emanation also dividing.

Such thing was never known! O pity me, thou all-piteous-one!
What shall I do! or how exist, divided from Enitharmon?
Yet why despair! I saw the finger of God go forth
Upon my Furnaces, from within the Wheels of Albion's Sons:
Fixing their Systems permanent: by mathematic power
Giving a body to Falsehood that it may be cast off for ever,
With Demonstrative Science piercing Apollyon with his own bow!
God is within & without! he is even in the depths of Hell!'

. . .

I see the Four-fold Man, The Humanity in deadly sleep [Pl. 15, l. 6]
And its fallen Emanation, The Spectre & its cruel Shadow.
I see the Past, Present & Future, existing all at once
Before me; O Divine Spirit, sustain me on thy wings!
That I may awake Albion from his long & cold repose
For Bacon & Newton sheathd in dismal steel their terrors hang
Like iron scourges over Albion, Reasonings like vast Serpents
Infold around my limbs, bruising my minute articulations.

I turn my eyes to the Schools & Universities of Europe
And there behold the Loom of Locke whose Woof rages dire
Washd by the Water-wheels of Newton; black the cloth
In heavy wreathes folds over every Nation; cruel Works
Of many Wheels I view, wheel without wheel, with cogs tyrannic
Moving by compulsion each other: not as those in Eden: which
Wheel within Wheel in freedom revolve in harmony & peace.

His Children exil'd from his breast pass to and fro before him, [Pl. 19]
His birds are silent on his hills, flocks die beneath his branches,
His tents are fall'n; his trumpets, and the sweet sound of his harp
Are silent on his clouded hills, that belch forth storm & fire
His milk of Cows, & honey of Bees, & fruit of golden harvest
Is gather'd in the scorching heat & in the driving rain:
Where once he sat he weary walks in misery and pain:
His Giant beauty and perfection fallen into dust:
Till from within his witherd breast grown narrow with his woes:
The corn is turn'd to thistles & the apples into poison:
The birds of song to murderous crows, his joys to bitter groans:
The voices of children in his tents to cries of helpless infants:
And self-exiled from the face of light & shine of morning,

In the dark world a narrow house! he wanders up and down,
Seeking for rest and finding none! and hidden far within,
His Eon weeping in the cold and desolated Earth.

. . .

'When winter rends the hungry family and the snow falls: [Pl. 20, l. 12]
Upon the ways of men hiding the paths of man and beast,
Then mourns the wanderer: then he repents his wandering & eyes
The distant forest; then the slave groans in the dungeon of stone,
The captive in the mill of the stranger, sold for scanty hire.
They view their former life: they number moments over and over:
Stringing them on their remembrance as on a thread of sorrow.
Thou art my sister and my daughter: thy shame is mine also:
Ask me not of my griefs! thou knowest all my griefs.'

Jerusalem answer'd with soft tears over the valleys:

'O Vala, what is sin? that thou shudderest and weepest
At sight of thy once lov'd Jerusalem! What is Sin but a little
Error & fault that is soon forgiven; but mercy is not a Sin
Nor pity nor love nor kind forgiveness: O! if I have Sinned
Forgive & pity me! O! unfold thy Veil in mercy and love!

'Slay not my little ones, beloved Virgin daughter of Babylon,
Slay not my infant loves & graces, beautiful daughter of Moab!
I cannot put off the human form. I strive but strive in vain.'

'Albion, thy fear has made me tremble; thy terrors have surrounded me. [Pl. 22]
Thy Sons have naild me on the Gates, piercing my hands & feet:
Till Skofield's Nimrod, the mighty Huntsman Jehovah came,
With Cush his Son & took me down. He in a golden Ark,
Bears me before his Armies tho my Shadow hovers here.
The flesh of multitudes fed & nourishd me in my childhood.
My morn & evening food were prepard in Battles of Men.
Great is the cry of the Hounds of Nimrod along the Valley
Of Vision, they scent the odor of War in the Valley of Vision.
All Love is lost! terror succeeds & Hatred instead of Love
And stern demands of Right & Duty instead of Liberty.

Once thou wast to me the loveliest Son of heaven; but now
Where shall I hide from thy dread countenance & searching eyes?
I have looked into the secret Soul of him I loved
And in the dark recesses found Sin & can never return.'

Albion again utterd his voice beneath the silent Moon:

'I brought Love into light of day to pride in chaste beauty;
I brought Love into light & fancied Innocence is no more.'

Then spoke Jerusalem: 'O Albion! my Father Albion!
Why wilt thou number every little fibre of my Soul,
Spreading them out before the Sun like stalks of flax to dry?
The Infant Joy is beautiful, but its anatomy
Horrible ghast & deadly! nought shalt thou find in it
But dark despair & everlasting brooding melancholy!'

. . .

Thy Sons came to Jerusalem with gifts; she sent them away [Pl. 24, l. 38]
With blessings on their hands & on their feet, blessings of gold
And pearl & diamond; thy Daughters sang in her Courts:
They came up to Jerusalem; they walked before Albion:
In the Exchanges of London every Nation walkd
And London walkd in every Nation mutual in love & harmony.
Albion coverd the whole Earth, England encompassd the Nations,
Mutual each within other's bosom in Visions of Regeneration:
Jerusalem coverd the Atlantic Mountains & the Erythrean,
From bright Japan & China to Hesperia, France & England.
Mount Zion lifted his head in every Nation under heaven:
And the Mount of Olives was beheld over the whole Earth:
The footsteps of the Lamb of God were there: but now no more,
No more shall I behold him, he is closed in Luvah's Sepulcher.
Yet why these smitings of Luvah, the gentlest mildest Zoa?
If God was Merciful this could not be: O Lamb of God,
Thou art a delusion and Jerusalem is my Sin! O my Children
I have educated you in the crucifying cruelties of Demonstration
Till you have assum'd the Providence of God & slain your Father.

The fields from Islington to Marybone, [Pl. 27]
To Primrose Hill and Saint John's Wood:
Were builded over with pillars of gold,
And there Jerusalem's pillars stood.

Her Little-ones ran on the fields,
The Lamb of God among them seen
And fair Jerusalem his Bride:
Among the little meadows green.

Pancras & Kentish-town repose
Among her golden pillars high;
Among her golden arches which
Shine upon the starry sky.

The Jew's-harp-house & the Green Man;
The Ponds where Boys to bathe delight:
The fields of Cows by Willans farm:
Shine in Jerusalem's pleasant sight.

She walks upon our meadows green:
The Lamb of God walks by her side:
And every English Child is seen,
Children of Jesus & his Bride.

Forgiving trespasses and sins
Lest Babylon with cruel Og
With Moral & Self-righteous Law
Should Crucify in Satan's Synagogue!

What are those golden Builders doing
Near mournful ever-weeping Paddington
Standing above that mighty Ruin
Where Satan the first victory won,

Where Albion slept beneath the Fatal Tree
And the Druid's golden Knife,
Rioted in human gore,
In Offerings of Human Life?

They groand aloud on London Stone,
They groan'd aloud on Tyburn's Brook,
Albion gave his deadly groan,
And all the Atlantic Mountains shook.

Albion's Spectre from his Loins
Tore forth in all the pomp of War:
Satan his name: in flames of fire
He stretch'd his Druid Pillars far.

Jerusalem fell from Lambeth's Vale
Down thro Poplar & Old Bow;
Thro Malden & across the Sea,
In War & howling, death & woe,

The Rhine was red with human blood:
The Danube rolld a purple tide:
On the Euphrates Satan stood:
And over Asia stretch'd his pride.

He witherd up sweet Zion's Hill
From every Nation of the Earth:
He witherd up Jerusalem's Gates,
And in a dark Land gave her birth.

He witherd up the Human Form,
By laws of sacrifice for sin:
Till it became a Mortal Worm:
But O! translucent all within.

The Divine Vision still was seen,
Still was the Human Form Divine
Weeping in weak & mortal clay,
O Jesus, still the Form was thine.

And thine the Human Face & thine
The Human Hands & Feet & Breath
Entering thro' the Gates of Birth
And passing thro' the Gates of Death

And O thou Lamb of God, whom I
Slew in my dark self-righteous pride:
Art thou returned to Albion's Land!
And is Jerusalem thy Bride?

Come to my arms & never more
Depart; but dwell for ever here:
Create my Spirit to thy Love:
Subdue my Spectre to thy Fear.

Spectre of Albion! Warlike Fiend!
In clouds of blood & ruin roll'd:
I here reclaim thee as my own,
My Selfhood! Satan! armd in gold.

Is this thy soft Family-Love,
Thy cruel Patriarchal pride
Planting thy Family alone,
Destroying all the World beside?

A man's worst enemies are those
Of his own house & family;
And he who makes his law a curse,
By his own law shall surely die.

In my Exchanges every Land
Shall walk & mine in every Land,
Mutual shall build Jerusalem;
Both heart in heart & hand in hand.

Jerusalem

Chap: 2.

'What shall I do? What could I do, if I could find these Criminals? [Pl. 31, l. 29]
I could not dare to take vengeance; for all things are so constructed
And builded by the Divine hand that the sinner shall always escape,
And he who takes vengeance alone is the criminal of Providence;

If I should dare to lay my finger on a grain of sand
In way of vengeance: I punish the already punishd; O whom
Should I pity if I pity not the sinner who is gone astray;
O Albion, if thou takest vengeance; if thou revengest thy wrongs
Thou art forever lost! What can I do to hinder the Sons
Of Albion from taking vengeance? or how shall I them
perswade?'

. . .

'I am your Rational Power, O Albion, & that Human Form [Pl. 33, l.5]
You call Divine is but a Worm seventy inches long
That creeps forth in a night & is dried in the morning sun
In fortuitous concourse of memorys accumulated & lost.
It plows the Earth in its own conceit, it overwhelms the Hills
Beneath its winding labyrinths, till a stone of the brook
Stops it in midst of its pride among its hills & rivers.
Battersea & Chelsea mourn, London & Canterbury tremble:
Their place shall not be found as the wind passes over.
The ancient Cities of the Earth remove as a traveller
And shall Albion's Cities remain when I pass over them
With my deluge of forgotten remembrances over the tablet?'

So spoke the Spectre to Albion: he is the Great Selfhood
Satan: Worshipd as God by the Mighty Ones of the Earth.

. . .

Vala replied in clouds of tears Albion's garment embracing: [Pl. 33, l. 35]

'I was a City & a Temple built by Albion's Children.
I was a Garden planted with beauty. I allured on hill & valley
The River of Life to flow against my walls & among my trees.
Vala was Albion's Bride & Wife in great Eternity,
The loveliest of the daughters of Eternity when in day-break
I emanated from Luvah over the Towers of Jerusalem
And in her Courts among her little Children offering up
The Sacrifice of fanatic love? why loved I Jerusalem:
Why was I one with her embracing in the Vision of Jesus?
Wherefore did I loving create love, which never yet
Immingled God & Man, when thou & I hid the Divine Vision
In cloud of secret gloom which behold involves me round about?

Know me now, Albion; look upon me. I alone am Beauty.
The Imaginative Human Form is but a breathing of Vala;
I breathe him forth into the Heaven from my secret Cave
Born of the Woman to obey the Woman, O Albion the mighty,
For the Divine appearance is Brotherhood, but I am Love.

. . .

'I hear the screech of Childbirth loud pealing, & the groans [Pl. 34, l. 23]
Of Death in Albion's clouds dreadful utterd over all the Earth.
What may Man be? who can tell! but what may Woman be?
To have power over Man from Cradle to corruptible Grave?
There is a Throne in every Man, it is the Throne of God;
This Woman had claimd as her own & Man is no more!
Albion is the Tabernacle of Vala & her Temple
And not the Tabernacle & Temple of the Most High.
O Albion, why wilt thou Create a Female Will?
To hide the most evident God in a hidden covert, even
In the shadows of a Woman & a secluded Holy Place
That we may pry after him as after a stolen treasure
Hidden among the Dead & mured up from the paths of life.

. . .

'Albion goes to Eternal Death: In Me all Eternity [Pl. 35, l. 9]
Must pass thro' condemnation and awake beyond the Grave!
No individual can keep these Laws, for they are death
To every energy of man, and forbid the springs of life;
Albion hath enterd the State Satan! Be permanent, O State!
And be thou for ever accursed! that Albion may arise again:
And be thou created into a State! I go forth to Create
States: to deliver Individuals evermore! Amen.'

. . .

And many of the Eternal Ones laughed after their manner: [Pl. 36, l. 42]

'Have you known the Judgment that is arisen among the
Zoas of Albion? where a Man dare hardly to embrace
His own Wife, for the terrors of Chastity that they call
By the name of Morality? their Daughters govern all
In hidden deceit! they are Vegetable, only fit for burning.
Art & Science cannot exist but by Naked Beauty displayd.'

Then those in Great Eternity who contemplate on Death
Said thus: 'What seems to Be: Is! To those to whom
It seems to Be, & is productive of the most dreadful
Consequences to those to whom it seems to Be: even of
Torments, Despair, Eternal Death; but the Divine Mercy
Steps beyond and Redeems Man in the Body of Jesus. Amen.
And Length, Bredth, Highth again Obey the Divine Vision.
Hallelujah.'

. . .

. . . 'Albion! Our wars are wars of life, & wounds of love, [Pl. 38, l. 14]
With intellectual spears; & long winged arrows of thought:
Mutual in one another's love and wrath all renewing
We live as One Man; for contracting our infinite senses
We behold multitude; or expanding: we behold as one,
As One Man all the Universal Family; and that One Man
We call Jesus the Christ; and he in us, and we in him
Live in perfect harmony in Eden the land of life,
Giving, recieving, and forgiving each others' trespasses.
He is the Good shepherd, he is the Lord and master:
He is the Shepherd of Albion, he is all in all,
In Eden: in the garden of God; and in heavenly Jerusalem.
If we have offended, forgive us, take not vengeance against us.'

Thus speaking: the Divine Family follow Albion:
I see them in the Vision of God upon my pleasant valleys,
I behold London; a Human awful wonder of God!
He says: 'Return, Albion, return! I give myself for thee:
My Streets are my Ideas of Imagination.
Awake, Albion, awake! and let us awake up together.
My Houses are Thoughts: my Inhabitants; Affections,
The children of my thoughts walking within my blood-vessels,
Shut from my nervous form which sleeps upon the verge of Beulah
In dreams of darkness, while my vegetating blood in veiny pipes
Rolls dreadful thro' the Furnaces of Los, and the Mills of Satan.
For Albion's sake and for Jerusalem thy Emanation
I give myself, and these my brethren give themselves for Albion.'

So spoke London, immortal Guardian! I heard in Lambeth's shades;
In Felpham I heard and saw the Visions of Albion.
I write in South Molton Street what I both see and hear
In regions of Humanity, in London's opening streets.

. . .

There is a grain of sand in Lambeth that Satan cannot find [Pl. 41, l. 15]
Nor can his Watch Fiends find it: tis translucent & has many Angles
But he who finds it will find Oothoon's palace, for within
Opening into Beulah every angle is a lovely heaven
But should the Watch Fiends find it, they would call it Sin
And lay its Heavens & their inhabitants in blood of punishment.

. . .

Los answerd: 'Righteousness & justice I give thee in return [Pl. 42, l. 19]
For thy righteousness! but I add mercy also, and bind
Thee from destroying these little ones; am I to be only
Merciful to thee and cruel to all that thou hatest?
Thou wast the Image of God surrounded by the Four Zoas.
Three thou hast slain! I am the Fourth: thou canst not destroy me.
Thou art in Error; trouble me not with thy righteousness.
I have innocence to defend and ignorance to instruct.'

. . .

Ah! weak & wide astray! Ah! shut in narrow doleful form! [Pl. 49, l. 32]
Creeping in reptile flesh upon the bosom of the ground!
The Eye of Man, a little narrow orb, closd up & dark,
Scarcely beholding the Great Light: conversing with the ground:
The Ear, a little shelf, in small volutions shutting out
True Harmonies, & comprehending great as very small:
The Nostrils, bent down to the earth & clos'd with senseless flesh,
That odours cannot them expand, nor joy on them exult:
The Tongue, a little moisture fills, a little food it cloys
A little sound it utters, & its cries are faintly heard.

Therefore they are removed; therefore they have taken root
In Egypt & Philistea: in Moab & Edom & Aram:
In the Erythrean Sea their Uncircumcision in Heart & Loins
Be lost for ever & ever; then they shall arise from Self
By Self Annihilation into Jerusalem's Courts & into Shiloh.

. . .

Expanding on wing, the Daughters of Beulah replied in sweet response: [Pl. 50, l. 21]

'Come, O thou Lamb of God, and take away the remembrance of Sin.
To Sin & to hide the Sin in sweet deceit is lovely!
To Sin in the open face of day is cruel & pitiless! But
To record the Sin for a reproach: to let the Sun go down
In a remembrance of the Sin, is a Woe & a Horror!
A brooder of an Evil Day and a Sun rising in blood!
Come then, O Lamb of God, and take away the remembrance of Sin.'

End of Chap: 2^{d}

I saw a Monk of Charlemaine [Pl. 52]
Arise before my sight;
I talkd with the Grey Monk as we stood
In beams of infernal light.

Gibbon arose with a lash of steel
And Voltaire with a wracking wheel;
The Schools in clouds of learning rolld
Arose with war in iron & gold.

'Thou lazy Monk,' they sound afar,
'In vain condemning glorious War
And in your Cell you shall ever dwell;
Rise War & bind him in his Cell.'

The blood red ran from the Grey Monk's side;
His hands & feet were wounded wide,
His body bent, his arms & knees
Like to the roots of ancient trees.

When Satan first the black bow bent
And the Moral Law from the Gospel rent
He forgd the Law into a Sword
And spilld the blood of mercy's Lord.

Titus! Constantine! Charlemaine!
O Voltaire! Rousseau! Gibbon! Vain
Your Grecian Mocks & Roman Sword
Against this image of his Lord!

For a Tear is an Intellectual thing!
And a Sigh is the Sword of an Angel King
And the bitter groan of a Martyr's woe
Is an Arrow from the Almighties Bow!

Jerusalem

Chap 3

In Great Eternity, every particular Form gives forth or Emanates [Pl. 54]
Its own peculiar Light; & the Form is the Divine Vision
And the Light is his Garment. This is Jerusalem in every Man,
A Tent & Tabernacle of Mutual Forgiveness, Male & Female Clothings.
And Jerusalem is called Liberty among the Children of Albion

But Albion fell down, a Rocky fragment from Eternity hurld
By his own Spectre, who is the Reasoning Power in every Man,
Into his own Chaos which is the Memory between Man & Man.

The silent broodings of deadly revenge springing from the
All powerful parental affection, fills Albion from head to foot;
Seeing his Sons assimilate with Luvah, bound in the bonds
Of spiritual Hate, from which springs Sexual Love as iron chains,
He tosses like a cloud outstretchd among Jerusalem's Ruins
Which overspread all the Earth, he groans among his ruind porches

But the Spectre like a hoar frost & a Mildew rose over Albion
Saying, 'I am God, O Sons of Men! I am your Rational Power!
Am I not Bacon & Newton & Locke who teach Humility to Man!
Who teach doubt & Experiment & my two Wings: Voltaire: Rousseau?
Where is that Friend of Sinners! that Rebel against my Laws!
Who teaches Belief to the Nations & an unknown Eternal Life?
Come hither into the Desart & turn these stones to bread.
Vain Foolish Man! wilt thou believe without Experiment?
And build a World of Phantasy upon my Great Abyss?
A World of Shapes in craving lust & devouring appetite.'

. . .

Loud! loud! the Mountains lifted up their voices, loud the Forests; [Pl. 55, l. 23]
Rivers thunderd against their banks, loud Winds furious fought;
Cities & Nations contended in fires & clouds & tempests.
The Seas raisd up their voices & lifted their hands on high;
The Stars in their courses fought, the Sun! Moon! Heaven! Earth!
Contending for Albion & for Jerusalem his Emanation
And for Shiloh, the Emanation of France & for lovely Vala.

Then far the greatest number were about to make a Separation
And they Elected Seven, calld the Seven Eyes of God;
Lucifer, Molech, Elohim, Shaddai, Pahad, Jehovah, Jesus.
They namd the Eighth; he came not, he hid in Albion's Forests
But first they said: (& their Words stood in Chariots' array
Curbing their Tygers with golden bits & bridles of silver & ivory)

'Let the Human Organs be kept in their perfect Integrity
At will Contracting into Worms, or Expanding into Gods
And then behold! what are these Ulro Visions of Chastity?
Then as the moss upon the tree: or dust upon the plow:
Or as the sweat upon the labouring shoulder: or as the chaff
Of the wheat-floor or as the dregs of the sweet wine-press,
Such are these Ulro Visions, for tho we sit down within
The plowed furrow listning to the weeping of the clods till we
Contract or Expand Space at will: or if we raise ourselves

Upon the chariots of the morning, Contracting or Expanding Time:
Every one knows, we are One Family! One Man blessed for ever.'

Silence remaind & every one resumd his Human Majesty
And many conversed on these things as they labourd at the furrow
Saying; 'It is better to prevent misery than to release from misery:
It is better to prevent error than to forgive the criminal!
Labour well the Minute Particulars, attend to the Little-ones:
And those who are in misery cannot remain so long
If we do but our duty: labour well the teeming Earth.'

They Plow'd in tears, the trumpets sounded before the golden Plow
And the voices of the Living Creatures were heard in the clouds of heaven
Crying; 'Compell the Reasoner to Demonstrate with unhewn Demonstrations,
Let the Indefinite be explored, and let every Man be Judged
By his own Works, Let all Indefinites be thrown into Demonstrations
To be pounded to dust & melted in the Furnaces of Affliction:
He who would do good to another must do it in Minute Particulars.
General Good is the plea of the Scoundrel hypocrite & flatterer:
For Art & Science cannot exist but in minutely organized Particulars
And not in generalizing Demonstrations of the Rational Power,
The Infinite alone resides in Definite & Determinate Identity;
Establishment of Truth depends on destruction of Falsehood continually,
On Circumcision: not on Virginity, O Reasoners of Albion!'

So cried they at the Plow. Albion's Rock frowned above
And the Great Voice of Eternity rolled above terrible in clouds
Saying, 'Who will go forth for us! & Who shall we send before our face?'

Then Los heaved his thundring Bellows on the Valley of Middlesex [Pl. 56]
And thus he chaunted his Song: the Daughters of Albion reply:

'What may Man be? who can tell! But what may Woman Be?
To have power over Man from Cradle to corruptible Grave.
He who is an Infant, and whose Cradle is a Manger
Knoweth the Infant sorrow; whence it came, and where it goeth:
And who weave it a Cradle of the grass that withereth away.
This World is all a Cradle for the erred wandering Phantom:
Rock'd by Year, Month, Day & Hour; and every two Moments
Between dwells a Daughter of Beulah, to feed the Human Vegetable.
Entune: Daughters of Albion, your hymning Chorus mildly!
Cord of affection thrilling extatic on the iron Reel:
To the golden Loom of Love! to the moth-labourd Woof,
A Garment and Cradle weaving for the infantine Terror:
For fear; at entering the gate into our World of cruel
Lamentation: it flee back & hide in Non-Entity's dark wild
Where dwells the Spectre of Albion: destroyer of Definite Form.
The Sun shall be a Scythed Chariot of Britain: the Moon, a Ship
In the British Ocean! Created by Los's Hammer, measured out
Into Days & Nights & Years & Months, to travel with my feet
Over these desolate rocks of Albion: O daughters of despair!
Rock the Cradle, and in mild melodies tell me where found
What you have enwoven with so much tears & care? so much
Tender artifice: to laugh: to weep: to learn: to know:
Remember! recollect! what dark befel in wintry days.'

. . .

'I gave thee liberty and life, O lovely Jerusalem, [Pl. 60, l. 10]
And thou hast bound me down upon the Stems of Vegetation.
I gave thee Sheep-walks upon the Spanish Mountains, Jerusalem:
I gave thee Priam's City and the Isles of Grecia lovely:
I gave thee Hand & Scofield & the Counties of Albion:
They spread forth like a lovely root into the Garden of God:
They were as Adam before me: united into One Man,
They stood in innocence & their skiey tent reachd over Asia
To Nimrod's Tower, to Ham & Canaan walking with Mizraim
Upon the Egyptian Nile, with solemn songs to Grecia
And sweet Hesperia, even to Great Chaldea & Tesshina
Following thee as a Shepherd by the Four Rivers of Eden.

Why wilt thou rend thyself apart, Jerusalem?
And build this Babylon & sacrifice in secret Groves,
Among the Gods of Asia: among the fountains of pitch & nitre?
Therefore thy Mountains are become barren, Jerusalem!
Thy Valleys, Plains of burning sand; thy Rivers: waters of death.
Thy Villages die of the Famine and thy Cities
Beg bread from house to house, lovely Jerusalem.
Why wilt thou deface thy beauty & the beauty of thy little-ones
To please thy Idols, in the pretended chastities of Uncircumcision?
Thy Sons are lovelier than Egypt or Assyria; wherefore
Dost thou blacken their beauty by a Secluded place of rest
And a peculiar Tabernacle to cut the integuments of beauty
Into veils of tears and sorrows, O lovely Jerusalem!
They have perswaded thee to this, therefore their end shall come
And I will lead thee thro the Wilderness in shadow of my cloud
And in my love I will lead thee, lovely Shadow of Sleeping Albion.'

This is the Song of the Lamb, sung by Slaves in evening time.

. . .

the Divine Voice replied:

'Mild Shade of Man, pitiest thou these Visions of terror & woe!
Give forth thy pity & love; fear not! lo I am with thee always.
Only believe in me that I have power to raise from death
Thy Brother who Sleepeth in Albion! fear not, trembling shade.
Behold: in the Visions of Elohim Jehovah, behold Joseph & Mary [Pl. 61]
And be comforted, O Jerusalem, in the Visions of Jehovah Elohim.'

She looked & saw Joseph the Carpenter in Nazareth & Mary
His espoused Wife. And Mary said, 'If thou put me away from thee
Dost thou not murder me?' Joseph spoke in anger & fury: 'Should I
Marry a Harlot & an Adulteress?' Mary answered: 'Art thou more pure

Than thy Maker who forgiveth Sins & calls again Her that is Lost?
Tho She hates, he calls her again in love. I love my dear Joseph
But he driveth me away from his presence; yet I hear the voice of God
In the voice of my Husband; tho he is angry for a moment, he will not
Utterly cast me away; if I were pure, never could I taste the sweets
Of the Forgiveness of Sins: if I were holy: I never could behold the tears
Of love! of him who loves me in the midst of his anger in furnace of fire.'

'Ah my Mary:' said Joseph: weeping over & embracing her closely in
His arms: 'Doth he forgive Jerusalem & not exact Purity from her who is
Polluted? I heard his voice in my sleep & his Angel in my dream:
Saying: "Doth Jehovah Forgive a Debt only on condition that it shall
Be Payed? Doth he Forgive Pollution only on conditions of Purity?
That Debt is not Forgiven! That Pollution is not Forgiven!
Such is the Forgiveness of the Gods, the Moral Virtues of the
Heathen, whose tender Mercies are Cruelty. But Jehovah's Salvation
Is without Money & without Price, in the Continual Forgiveness of Sins,
In the Perpetual Mutual Sacrifice in Great Eternity! for behold!
There is none that liveth & Sinneth not! And this is the Covenant
Of Jehovah: If you Forgive one-another, so shall Jehovah Forgive You:
That He Himself may Dwell among You. Fear not then to take
To thee Mary thy Wife for she is with Child by the Holy Ghost."'

. . .

For in the depths of Albion's bosom in the eastern heaven, [Pl. 65, l. 5]
They sound the clarions strong! they chain the howling Captives:
They cast the lots into the helmet: they give the oath of blood in Lambeth,

They vote the death of Luvah & they naild him to Albion's Tree in Bath:
They staind him with poisonous blue, they inwove him in cruel roots
To die a death of Six thousand years bound round with vegetation.
The sun was black & the moon rolld a useless globe thro Britain.

Then left the Sons of Urizen the plow & harrow, the loom,
The hammer & the chisel & the rule & compasses; from London fleeing,
They forg'd the sword on Cheviot, the chariot of war & the battle-ax,
The trumpet fitted to mortal battle, & the Flute of summer in Annandale
And all the Arts of Life they changd into the Arts of Death in Albion.
The hour-glass contemnd because its simple workmanship
Was like the workmanship of the plowman, & the water wheel
That raises water into cisterns broken & burnd with fire:
Because its workmanship was like the workmanship of the shepherd,
And in their stead, intricate wheels invented, wheel without wheel:
To perplex youth in their outgoings, & to bind to labours in Albion
Of day & night the myriads of eternity that they may grind
And polish brass & iron hour after hour, laborious task:
Kept ignorant of its use, that they might spend the days of wisdom
In sorrowful drudgery, to obtain a scanty pittance of bread:
In ignorance to view a small portion & think that All,
And call it Demonstration: blind to all the simple rules of life.

'Now: now the battle rages round thy tender limbs, O Vala!
Now smile among thy bitter tears: now put on all thy beauty.
Is not the wound of the sword sweet: & the broken bone delightful?
Wilt thou now smile among the scythes when the wounded groan in the field?
We were carried away in thousands from London; & in tens
Of thousands from Westminster & Marybone in ships closd up

Chaind hand & foot, compelld to fight under the iron whips
Of our captains; fearing our officers more than the enemy.
Lift up thy blue eyes, Vala, & put on thy sapphire shoes:
O melancholy Magdalen, behold the morning over Malden break:
Gird on thy flaming zone, descend into the sepulcher of
Canterbury.
Scatter the blood from thy golden brow, the tears from thy silver
locks:
Shake off the waters from thy wings! & the dust from thy white
garments.
Remember all thy feigned terrors on the secret couch of
Lambeth's Vale
When the sun rose in glowing morn, with arms of mighty hosts
Marching to battle who was wont to rise with Urizen's harps
Girt as a sower with his seed to scatter life abroad over Albion.
Arise, O Vala! bring the bow of Urizen: bring the swift arrows of
light.
How rag'd the golden horses of Urizen, compelld to the chariot
of love,
Compelld to leave the plow to the ox, to snuff up the winds of
desolation,
To trample the corn fields in boastful neighings; this is no gentle
harp,
This is no warbling brook, nor shadow of a mirtle tree:
But blood and wounds and dismal cries, and shadows of the oak:
And hearts laid open to the light by the broad grizly sword:
And bowels hid in hammerd steel ripd quivering on the ground.
Call forth thy smiles of soft deceit: call forth thy cloudy tears:
We hear thy sighs in trumpets shrill when morn shall blood
renew.'

So saying the Spectre Sons of Albion round Luvah's Stone of
Trial.

. . .

They become like what they behold! Yet immense in [Pl. 65, l. 79]
strength & power,

In awful pomp & gold, in all the precious unhewn stones [Pl. 66]
of Eden
They build a stupendous Building on the Plain of Salisbury; with
chains

Of rocks round London Stone: of Reasonings: of unhewn Demonstrations
In labyrinthine arches (Mighty Urizen the Architect) thro which
The Heavens might revolve & Eternity be bound in their chain.
Labour unparalleld! a wondrous rocky World of cruel destiny,
Rocks piled on rocks reaching the stars; stretching from pole to pole.
The Building is Natural Religion & its Altars Natural Morality,
A building of eternal death: whose proportions are eternal despair.
Here Vala stood turning the iron Spindle of destruction
From heaven to earth: howling! invisible! but not invisible
Her Two Covering Cherubs afterwards named Voltaire & Rousseau:
Two frowning Rocks: on each side of the Cove & Stone of Torture:
Frozen Sons of the feminine Tabernacle of Bacon, Newton & Locke,
For Luvah is France; the Victim of the Spectres of Albion.

. . .

'O thou poor Human Form!' said she. 'O thou poor child of woe! [Pl. 67, l. 44]
Why wilt thou wander away from Tirzah: why me compel to bind thee?
If thou dost go away from me I shall consume upon these Rocks.
These fibres of thine eyes that used to beam in distant heavens
Away from me: I have bound down with a hot iron.
These nostrils that expanded with delight in morning skies
I have bent downward with lead melted in my roaring furnaces
Of affliction; of love: of sweet despair: of torment unendurable.
My soul is seven furnaces, incessant roars the bellows
Upon my terribly flaming heart, the molten metal runs
In channels thro my fiery limbs: O love: O pity: O fear:
O pain! O the pangs, the bitter pangs of love forsaken!
Ephraim was a wilderness of joy where all my wild beasts ran.
The River Kanah wanderd by my sweet Manasseh's side
To see the boy spring into heavens sounding from my sight!
Go, Noah, fetch the girdle of strong brass; heat it red-hot:
Press it around the loins of this ever expanding cruelty.
Shriek not so, my only love; I refuse thy joys; I drink
Thy shrieks because Hand & Hyle are cruel & obdurate to me.

O Skofield, why are thou cruel? Lo Joseph is thine! to make [Pl. 68]
You One: to weave you both in the same mantle of skin.
Bind him down, Sisters, bind him down on Ebal, Mount of cursing:
Malah, come forth from Lebanon: & Hoglah from Mount Sinai:
Come circumscribe this tongue of sweets & with a screw of iron
Fasten this ear into the rock: Milcah, the task is thine!
Weep not so, Sisters: weep not so: our life depends on this
Or mercy & truth are fled away from Shechem & Mount Gilead
Unless my beloved is bound upon the Stems of Vegetation.'

. . .

What is Above is Within, for every-thing in Eternity is translucent: [Pl. 71, l. 6]
The Circumference is Within: Without is formed the Selfish Center
And the Circumference still expands going forward to Eternity,
And the Center has Eternal States: these States we now explore.

. . .

For all are Men in Eternity; Rivers, Mountains, Cities, Villages,
All are Human & when you enter into their Bosoms you walk
In Heavens & Earths; as in your own Bosom you bear your Heaven
And Earth, & all you behold; tho it appears Without it is Within
In your Imagination of which this World of Mortality is but a Shadow.

The Four Zoas clouded rage; Urizen stood by Albion [Pl. 74]
With Rintrah and Palamabron and Theotormon and Bromion:
These Four are Verulam & London & York & Edinburgh
And the Four Zoas are Urizen & Luvah & Tharmas & Urthona
In opposition deadly, and their Wheels in poisonous
And deadly stupor turnd against each other loud & fierce
Entering into the Reasoning Power, forsaking Imagination
They became Spectres: & their Human Bodies were reposed
In Beulah, by the Daughters of Beulah with tears & lamentations.

The Spectre is the Reasoning Power in Man; & when separated
From Imagination and closing itself as in steel, in a Ratio
Of the Things of Memory, It thence frames Laws & Moralities
To destroy Imagination! The Divine Body, by Martyrdoms &
Wars.

Teach me, O Holy Spirit, the Testimony of Jesus! let me
Comprehend wonderous things out of the Divine Law!
I behold Babylon in the opening Streets of London, I behold
Jerusalem in ruins wandering about from house to house.
This I behold; the shudderings of death attend my steps.
I walk up and down in Six Thousand Years: their Events are
present before me
To tell how Los in grief & anger, whirling round his Hammer
on high
Drave the Sons & Daughters of Albion from their ancient
mountains.
They became the Twelve Gods of Asia Opposing the Divine
Vision.

I give you the end of a golden string; [Pl. 77]
Only wind it into a ball:
It will lead you in at Heaven's gate,
Built in Jerusalem's wall.

I stood among my valleys of the south
And saw a flame of fire, even as a Wheel
Of fire surrounding all the heavens; it went
From west to east against the current of
Creation and devourd all things in its loud
Fury & thundering course round heaven & earth.
By it the Sun was rolld into an orb:
By it the Moon faded into a globe
Travelling thro the night: for from its dire
And restless fury, Man himself shrunk up
Into a little root a fathom long,
And I asked a Watcher & a Holy-One
Its Name? he answered: 'It is the Wheel of Religion.'
I wept & said: 'Is this the law of Jesus,
This terrible devouring sword turning every way?'

He answerd: 'Jesus died because he strove
Against the current of this Wheel: its Name
Is Caiaphas, the dark Preacher of Death,
Of Sin, of sorrow, & of punishment;
Opposing Nature! It is Natural Religion
But Jesus is the bright Preacher of Life
Creating Nature from this fiery Law,
By self-denial & forgiveness of Sin.
Go therefore, cast out devils in Christ's name,
Heal thou the sick of spiritual disease,
Pity the evil, for thou art not sent
To smite with terror & with punishments
Those that are sick, like to the Pharisees
Crucifying & encompassing sea & land
For proselytes to tyranny & wrath.
But to the Publicans & Harlots go!
Teach them True Happiness, but let no curse
Go forth out of thy mouth to blight their peace
For Hell is opend to Heaven; thine eyes beheld
The dungeons burst & the Prisoners set free.'

England! awake! awake! awake!
    Jerusalem thy Sister calls!
Why wilt thou sleep the sleep of death?
    And close her from thy ancient walls?

. . .

Thy hills & valleys felt her feet
    Gently upon their bosoms move:
Thy gates beheld sweet Zion's ways;
    Then was a time of joy and love.

And now the time returns again:
    Our souls exult & London's towers
Receive the Lamb of God to dwell
    In England's green & pleasant bowers.

Jerusalem.

C[hap:] 4

. . .

'I know I am Urthona keeper of the Gates of Heaven, [Pl. 82, l. 81]
And that I can at will expatiate in the Gardens of bliss;
But pangs of love draw me down to my loins which are
Become a fountain of veiny pipes: O Albion! my brother!
Corruptibility appears upon thy limbs, and never more [Pl. 83]
Can I arise and leave thy side, but labour here incessant
Till thy awaking! yet alas I shall forget Eternity!
Against the Patriarchal pomp and cruelty, labouring incessant
I shall become an Infant horror, Enion! Tharmas! friends
Absorb me not in such dire grief: O Albion, my brother!
Jerusalem hungers in the desart; affection to her children!
The scorn'd and contemnd youthful girl, where shall she fly?
Sussex shuts up her Villages: Hants, Devon & Wilts
Surrounded with masses of stones in orderd form: determine then
A form for Vala and a form for Luvah, here on the Thames
Where the Victim nightly howls beneath the Druid's knife
A Form of Vegetation, nail them down on the stems of Mystery:
O when shall the Saxon return with the English his redeemed brother:
O when shall the Lamb of God descend among the Reprobate!'

. . .

. . . 'from Lambeth [Pl. 84, l. 3]
We began our Foundations: lovely Lambeth! O lovely Hills
Of Camberwell, we shall behold you no more in glory & pride
For Jerusalem lies in ruins & the Furnaces of Los are builded there.
You are now shrunk up to a narrow Rock in the midst of the Sea
But here we build Babylon on Euphrates, compelld to build
And to inhabit, our Little-ones to clothe in armour of the gold
Of Jerusalem's Cherubims & to forge them swords of her Altars.
I see London blind & age-bent begging thro the Streets
Of Babylon, led by a child; his tears run down his beard.
The voice of Wandering Reuben ecchoes from street to street

In all the Cities of the Nations, Paris, Madrid, Amsterdam.
The Corner of Broad Street weeps; Poland Street languishes;
To Great Queen Street & Lincoln's Inn all is distress & woe.'

. . .

And thus Los replies upon his Watch: the Valleys listen silent: [Pl. 85, l. 14]
The stars stand still to hear: Jerusalem & Vala cease to mourn:
His voice is heard from Albion: the Alps & Appenines
Listen: Hermon & Lebanon bow their crowned heads:
Babel & Shinar look toward the Western Gate, they sit down
Silent at his voice: they view the red Globe of fire in Los's hand
As he walks from Furnace to Furnace directing the Labourers
And this is the Song of Los, the Song that he sings on his Watch:

'O lovely mild Jerusalem! O Shiloh of Mount Ephraim!
I see thy Gates of precious stones; thy Walls of gold & silver.
Thou art the soft reflected Image of the Sleeping Man
Who stretchd on Albion's rocks reposes amidst his Twenty-eight
Cities: where Beulah lovely terminates, in the hills & valleys of Albion,
Cities not yet embodied in Time and Space: plant ye
The Seeds, O Sisters, in the bosom of Time & Space's womb
To spring up for Jerusalem: lovely Shadow of Sleeping Albion.
Why wilt thou rend thyself apart & build an Earthly Kingdom
To reign in pride & to opress & to mix the Cup of Delusion?
O thou that dwellest with Babylon! Come forth O lovely-one!'

. . .

And Enitharmon like a faint rainbow waved before him [Pl. 86, l. 50]
Filling with Fibres from his loins which reddend with desire
Into a Globe of blood beneath his bosom trembling in darkness
Of Albion's clouds, he fed it with his tears & bitter groans,
Hiding his Spectre in invisibility from the timorous Shade
Till it became a separated cloud of beauty, grace & love
Among the darkness of his Furnaces dividing asunder till
She separated stood before him a lovely Female weeping,
Even Enitharmon separated outside, & his Loins closed

And heal'd after the separation: his pains he soon forgot:
Lured by her beauty outside of himself in shadowy grief.
Two Wills they had: Two Intellects: & not as in times of old.

Los answered sighing like the Bellows of his Furnaces: [Pl. 88]

'I care not! the swing of my Hammer shall measure the starry round.
When in Eternity Man converses with Man they enter
Into each other's Bosom (which are Universes of delight)
In mutual interchange, and first their Emanations meet
Surrounded by their Children; if they embrace & comingle
The Human Four-fold Forms mingle also in thunders of Intellect
But if the Emanations mingle not; with storms & agitations
Of earthquakes & consuming fires they roll apart in fear
For Man cannot unite with Man but by their Emanations
Which stand both Male & Female at the Gates of each Humanity.
How then can I ever again be united as Man with Man
While thou my Emanation refusest my Fibres of dominion?
When Souls mingle & join thro all the Fibres of Brotherhood
Can there be any secret joy on Earth greater than this?'

Enitharmon answerd: 'This is Woman's World nor need she any
Spectre to defend her from Man. I will Create secret places
And the masculine names of the places Merlin & Arthur.
A triple Female Tabernacle for Moral Law I weave
That he who loves Jesus may loathe terrified Female love
Till God himself becomes a Male subservient to the Female.'

. . .

The Man who respects Woman shall be despised by Woman [Pl. 88, l. 37]
And deadly cunning & mean abjectness only shall enjoy them
For I will make their places of joy & love excrementious,
Continually building, continually destroying in Family feuds.
While you are under the dominion of a jealous Female
Unpermanent for ever because of love & jealousy,
You shall want all the Minute Particulars of Life.'

Thus joyd the Spectre in the dusky fires of Los's Forge, eyeing
Enitharmon who at her shining Looms sings lulling cadences

While Los stood at his Anvil in wrath, the victim of their love
And hate: dividing the Space of Love with brazen Compasses.

'It is easier to forgive an Enemy than to forgive a Friend: [Pl. 91]
The man who permits you to injure him deserves your vengeance:
He also will recieve it: go Spectre: obey my most secret desire:
Which thou knowest without my speaking: Go to these Fiends of Righteousness:
Tell them to obey their Humanities, & not pretend Holiness:
When they are murderers; as far as my Hammer & Anvil permit.
Go, tell them that the Worship of God, is honouring his gifts
In other men; & loving the greatest men best, each according
To his Genius; which is the Holy Ghost in Man; there is no other
God than that God who is the intellectual fountain of Humanity:
He who envies or calumniates which is murder & cruelty,
Murders the Holy-one: Go tell them this & overthrow their cup,
Their bread, their altar-table, their incense & their oath:
Their marriage & their baptism; their burial & consecration:
I have tried to make friends by corporeal gifts but have only
Made enemies: I never made friends but by spiritual gifts:
By severe contentions of friendship & the burning fire of thought.
He who would see the Divinity must see him in his Children,
One first, in friendship & love; then a Divine Family, & in the midst
Jesus will appear; so he who wishes to see a Vision; a perfect Whole
Must see it in its Minute Particulars: Organized & not as thou
O Fiend of Righteousness pretendest: thine is a Disorganized
And snowy cloud: brooder of tempests & destructive War.
You smile with pomp & rigor: you talk of benevolence & virtue:
I act with benevolence & Virtue & get murderd time after time:
You accumulate Particulars, & murder by analyzing, that you
May take the aggregate: & you call the aggregate Moral Law:
And you call that swelld & bloated Form: a Minute Particular.
But General Forms have their vitality in Particulars: & every
Particular is a Man: a Divine Member of the Divine Jesus.'

So Los cried at his Anvil in the horrible darkness weeping.

. . .

Terrified Los sat to behold trembling & weeping & howling:
'I care not whether a Man is Good or Evil; all that I care
Is whether he is a Wise Man or a Fool. Go! put off Holiness
And put on Intellect: or my thundrous Hammer shall drive thee
To wrath which thou condemnest: till thou obey my voice.'

Her voice pierc'd Albion's clay cold ear; he moved upon the Rock. [Pl. 95]
The Breath Divine went forth upon the morning hills. Albion mov'd
Upon the Rock, he opend his eyelids in pain; in pain he mov'd
His stony members, he saw England. Ah! shall the Dead live again?

The Breath Divine went forth over the morning hills. Albion rose
In anger: the wrath of God breaking bright flaming on all sides around
His awful limbs; into the Heavens he walked clothed in flames
Loud thundring, with broad flashes of flaming lightning & pillars
Of fire, speaking the Words of Eternity in Human Forms in direful
Revolutions of Action & Passion, thro the Four Elements on all sides
Surrounding his awful Members. Thou seest the Sun in heavy clouds
Struggling to rise above the Mountains; in his burning hand
He takes his Bow, then chooses out his arrows of flaming gold;
Murmuring the Bowstring breathes with ardor! clouds roll round the
Horns of the wide Bow, loud sounding winds sport on the mountain brows
Compelling Urizen to his Furrow: & Tharmas to his Sheepfold:
And Luvah to his Loom: Urthona he beheld mighty labouring at
His Anvil, in the Great Spectre Los unwearied labouring & weeping.
Therefore the Sons of Eden praise Urthona's Spectre in songs
Because he kept the Divine Vision in time of trouble.

. . .

Jesus replied: 'Fear not Albion; unless I die thou canst not live [Pl. 96, l. 14]
But if I die I shall arise again & thou with me.
This is Friendship & Brotherhood; without it Man Is Not.'

So Jesus spoke: the Covering Cherub coming on in darkness
Overshadowd them & Jesus said: 'Thus do Men in Eternity
One for another to put off by forgiveness every sin.'

Albion replyd: 'Cannot Man exist without Mysterious
Offering of Self for Another? is this Friendship & Brotherhood?
I see thee in the likeness & similitude of Los my Friend.'

Jesus said: 'Wouldest thou love one who never died
For thee or ever die for one who had not died for thee?
And if God dieth not for Man & giveth not himself
Eternally for Man, Man could not exist, for Man is Love:
As God is Love: every kindness to another is a little Death
In the Divine Image nor can Man exist but by Brotherhood!'

'Awake! Awake Jerusalem! O lovely Emanation of Albion, [Pl. 97]
Awake and overspread all Nations as in Ancient Time
For lo! the Night of Death is past and the Eternal Day
Appears upon our Hills: Awake, Jerusalem, and come away!'

So spake the Vision of Albion & in him so spake in my hearing
The Universal Father. Then Albion stretchd his hand into Infinitude
And took his Bow. Fourfold the Vision for bright beaming Urizen
Layd his hand on the South & took a breathing Bow of carved Gold:
Luvah his hand stretchd to the East & bore a Silver Bow bright shining:
Tharmas Westward a Bow of Brass pure flaming richly wrought:
Urthona Northward in thick storms a Bow of Iron terrible thundering

And the Bow is a Male & Female & the Quiver of the arrows of Love
Are the Children of this Bow: a Bow of Mercy & Loving-kindness: laying

Open the hidden Heart in Wars of mutual Benevolence, Wars of Love
And the Hand of Man grasps firm between the Male & Female Loves
And he Clothed himself in Bow & Arrows in awful state Fourfold
In the midst of his Twenty-eight Cities each with his Bow breathing.

Then each an Arrow flaming from his Quiver fitted carefully; [Pl. 98]
They drew fourfold the unreprovable String, bending thro the wide Heavens
The horned Bow Fourfold, loud sounding flew the flaming Arrow fourfold.

Murmuring the Bowstring breathes with ardor. Clouds roll round the horns
Of the wide Bow, loud sounding Winds sport on the Mountain's brows:
The Druid Spectre was Annihilate, loud thundring, rejoicing terrific, vanishing,
Fourfold Annihilation & at the clangor of the Arrows of Intellect
The innumerable Chariots of the Almighty appeard in Heaven
And Bacon & Newton & Locke, & Milton & Shakspear & Chaucer,
A Sun of blood red wrath surrounding heaven on all sides around
Glorious incomprehensible by Mortal Man & each Chariot was Sexual Threefold

And every Man stood Fourfold; each Four Faces had: One to the West,
One toward the East, One to the South, One to the North, the Horses Fourfold
And the dim Chaos brightend beneath, above, around! Eyed as the Peacock
According to the Human Nerves of Sensation, the Four Rivers of the Water of Life.

. . .

The Four Living Creatures, Chariots of Humanity Divine Incomprehensible,
In beautiful Paradises expand. These are the Four Rivers of Paradise
And the Four faces of Humanity fronting the Four Cardinal Points
Of Heaven, going forward forward irresistible from Eternity to Eternity

And they conversed together in Visionary forms dramatic which bright
Redounded from their Tongues in thunderous majesty, in Visions
In new Expanses, creating exemplars of Memory and of Intellect,
Creating Space, Creating Time according to the wonders Divine
Of Human Imagination, throughout all the Three Regions immense
Of Childhood, Manhood & Old Age & all the tremendous unfathomable NonEns
Of Death was seen in regenerations terrific or complacent, varying
According to the subject of discourse & every Word & Every Character
Was Human according to the Expansion or Contraction, the Translucence or
Opakeness of Nervous fibres: such was the variation of Time & Space
Which vary according as the Organs of Perception vary & they walked
To & fro in Eternity as One Man reflecting each in each & clearly seen
And seeing: according to fitness & order. And I heard Jehovah speak
Terrific from his Holy Place & saw the Words of the Mutual Covenant Divine
On Chariots of gold & jewels with Living Creatures starry & flaming
With every Colour, Lion, Tyger, Horse, Elephant, Eagle, Dove, Fly, Worm,

And all the wondrous Serpent clothd in gems & rich array
Humanize
In the Forgiveness of Sins according to the Covenant of Jehovah.
They Cry:

'Where is the Covenant of Priam, the Moral Virtues of the
Heathen?
Where is the Tree of Good & Evil that rooted beneath the cruel
heel
Of Albion's Spectre, the Patriarch Druid! where are all his
Human Sacrifice
For Sin in War & in the Druid Temples of the accuser of Sin;
beneath
The Oak Groves of Albion that coverd the whole Earth beneath
his Spectre?
Where are the Kingdoms of the World & all their glory that grew
on Desolation,
The Fruit of Albion's Poverty Tree when the Triple Headed
Gog-Magog Giant
Of Albion Taxed the Nations into Desolation & then gave the
Spectrous Oath?'

Such is the Cry from all the Earth, from the Living Creatures of
the Earth
And from the great city of Golgonooza in the Shadowy
Generation
And from the Thirty-two Nations of the Earth among the Living
Creatures.

All Human Forms identified, even Tree, Metal, Earth & [Pl. 99]
Stone: all
Human Forms identified, living, going forth & returning wearied
Into the Planetary lives of Years, Months, Days & Hours;
reposing
And then Awaking into his Bosom in the Life of Immortality
And I heard the Name of their Emanations: they are named
Jerusalem.

The End of The Song of Jerusalem

To the Queen

Dedication of the illustrations to Robert Blair, *The Grave* (1808)

The Door of Death is made of Gold,
That Mortal Eyes cannot behold;
But, when the Mortal Eyes are clos'd,
And cold and pale the Limbs repos'd,
The Soul awakes and, wondring, sees
In her mild Hand the golden Keys:
The Grave is Heaven's golden Gate,
And rich and poor around it wait;
O Shepherdess of England's Fold,
Behold this Gate of Pearl and Gold!

To dedicate to England's Queen
The Visions that my Soul has seen,
And, by Her kind permission, bring
What I have borne on solemn Wing,
From the vast regions of the Grave,
Before Her Throne my Wings I wave;
Bowing before my Sov'reign's Feet,
'The Grave produc'd these Blossoms sweet
In mild repose from Earthly strife;
The Blossoms of Eternal Life!'

WILLIAM BLAKE

The Ballads (or Pickering) Manuscript
([?after 1807])

The Mental Traveller

I traveld thro' a Land of Men,
A Land of Men & Women too
And heard & saw such dreadful things
As cold Earth wanderers never knew

For there the Babe is born in joy
That was begotten in dire woe
Just as we Reap in joy the fruit
Which we in bitter tears did Sow

And if the Babe is born a Boy
He's given to a Woman Old
Who nails him down upon a rock,
Catches his Shrieks in Cups of gold.

She binds iron thorns around his head,
She pierces both his hands & feet,
She cuts his heart out at his side
To make it feel both cold & heat.

Her fingers number every Nerve
Just as a Miser counts his gold;
She lives upon his shrieks & cries
And She grows young as he grows old

Till he becomes a bleeding youth
And she becomes a Virgin bright;
Then he rends up his Manacles
And binds her down for his delight.

He plants himself in all her Nerves
Just as a Husbandman his mould
And She becomes his dwelling place
And Garden fruitful Seventy fold.

An aged Shadow soon he fades
Wandring round an Earthly Cot
Full filled all with gems & gold
Which he by industry had got

And these are the gems of the Human Soul,
The rubies & pearls of a lovesick eye,
The countless gold of the akeing heart,
The martyr's groan & the lover's sigh.

They are his meat, they are his drink;
He feeds the Beggar & the Poor
And the way faring Traveller;
For ever open is his door.

His grief is their eternal joy;
They make the roofs & walls to ring
Till from the fire on the hearth
A little Female Babe does spring

And she is all of solid fire
And gems & gold that none his hand
Dares stretch to touch her Baby form
Or wrap her in his swaddling-band

But She comes to the Man she loves
If young or old or rich or poor;
They soon drive out the aged Host
A Beggar at another's door.

He wanders weeping far away
Untill some other take him in
Oft blind & age-bent, sore distrest
Until he can a Maiden win

And to allay his freezing Age
The Poor Man takes her in his arms;
The Cottage fades before his Sight,
The garden & its lovely Charms.

The Guests are scatterd thro' the land
For the Eye altering alters all;
The Senses roll themselves in fear
And the flat Earth becomes a Ball;

The Stars, Sun, Moon all shrink away
A desart vast without a bound
And nothing left to eat or drink
And a dark desart all around.

The honey of her Infant lips,
The bread & wine of her sweet smile,
The wild game of her roving Eye
Does him to Infancy beguile

For as he eats & drinks he grows
Younger & younger every day
And on the desart wild they both
Wander in terror & dismay.

Like the wild Stag she flees away,
Her fear plants many a thicket wild
While he pursues her night & day
By various arts of Love beguild,

By various arts of Love & Hate
Till the wide desart planted oer
With Labyrinths of wayward Love
Where roams the Lion, Wolf & Boar

Till he becomes a wayward Babe
And she a weeping Woman Old.
Then many a Lover wanders here;
The Sun & Stars are nearer rolld.

The tree brings forth sweet Extacy
To all who in the desart roam
Till many a City there is Built
And many a pleasant Shepherd's home

But when they find the frowning Babe
Terror strikes thro the region wide;
They cry 'the Babe, the Babe is Born'
And flee away on Every side

For who dare touch the frowning form
His arm is witherd to its root;
Lions, Boars, Wolves all howling flee
And every Tree does shed its fruit

And none can touch the frowning form
Except it be a Woman Old;
She nails him down upon the Rock
And all is done as I have told.

The Land of Dreams

'Awake, awake my little Boy!
Thou wast thy Mother's only joy;
Why dost thou weep in thy gentle Sleep?
Awake! thy Father does thee keep.'

'O what Land is the Land of Dreams?
What are its Mountains & what are its Streams?
O Father, I saw my Mother there
Among the Lillies by waters fair.

'Among the Lambs clothed in white
She walkd with her Thomas in sweet delight.
I wept for joy, like a dove I mourn!
O when Shall I again return?'

'Dear Child, I also by pleasant Streams
Have wanderd all Night in the Land of Dreams
But tho calm & warm the waters wide
I could not get to the other side.'

'Father, O Father, what do we here
In this Land of unbelief & fear?
The Land of Dreams is better far
Above the light of the Morning Star.'

The Crystal Cabinet

The Maiden caught me in the Wild
Where I was dancing merrily;
She put me into her Cabinet
And Lockd me up with a golden Key.

This Cabinet is formd of Gold
And Pearl & Crystal Shining bright
And within it opens into a World
And a little lovely Moony Night.

Another England there I saw,
Another London with its Tower,
Another Thames & other Hills
And another pleasant Surrey Bower,

Another Maiden like herself
Translucent lovely shining clear
Threefold each in the other closd;
O what a pleasant trembling fear!

O what a smile, a threefold Smile
Filld me that like a flame I burnd;
I bent to Kiss the lovely Maid
And found a Threefold Kiss returnd.

I strove to seize the inmost Form
With ardor fierce & hands of flame
But burst the Crystal Cabinet
And like a Weeping Babe became;

A weeping Babe upon the wild
And Weeping Woman pale reclind
And in the outward air again
I filld with woes the passing Wind.

Auguries of Innocence

To see a World in a Grain of Sand
And a Heaven in a Wild Flower,
Hold Infinity in the palm of your hand
And Eternity in an hour.
A Robin Red breast in a Cage
Puts all Heaven in a Rage.
A dove house filld with doves & Pigeons
Shudders Hell thro all its regions.
A dog starvd at his Master's gate
Predicts the ruin of the State.
A Horse misusd upon the Road
Calls to Heaven for Human blood.
Each outcry of the hunted Hare
A fibre from the Brain does tear.
A sky lark wounded in the wing,
A Cherubim does cease to sing.
The Game Cock clipd & armd for fight
Does the Rising Sun affright.
Every Wolf 's & Lion's howl
Raises from Hell a Human Soul.
The wild deer wandring here & there
Keeps the Human Soul from Care.
The Lamb misusd breeds Public strife
And yet forgives the Butcher's Knife.
The Bat that flits at close of Eve
Has left the Brain that won't Believe.
The Owl that calls upon the Night
Speaks the Unbeliever's fright.
He who shall hurt the little Wren
Shall never be belovd by Men.
He who the Ox to wrath has movd
Shall never be by Woman lovd.
The wanton Boy that kills the Fly
Shall feel the Spider's enmity.
He who torments the Chafer's sprite
Weaves a Bower in endless Night.
The Caterpiller on the Leaf
Repeats to thee thy Mother's grief

Kill not the Moth nor Butterfly
For the Last Judgment draweth nigh.
He who shall train the Horse to War
Shall never pass the Polar Bar.
The Begger's Dog & Widow's Cat,
Feed them & thou wilt grow fat.
The Gnat that sings his Summer's song
Poison gets from Slander's tongue.
The poison of the Snake & Newt
Is the sweat of Envy's Foot.
The Poison of the Honey Bee
Is the Artist's Jealousy.
The Prince's Robes & Beggar's Rags
Are Toadstools on the Miser's Bags.
A truth that's told with bad intent
Beats all the Lies you can invent.
It is right it should be so;
Man was made for Joy & Woe
And when this we rightly Know
Thro the World we safely go.
Joy & Woe are woven fine
A Clothing for the soul divine;
Under every grief & pine
Runs a joy with silken twine.
The Babe is more than Swadling Bands;
Throughout all these Human Lands
Tools were made & Born were hands,
Every Farmer Understands.
Every Tear from Every Eye
Becomes a Babe in Eternity;
This is caught by Females bright
And returnd to its own delight.
The Bleat, the Bark, Bellow & Roar
Are Waves that Beat on Heaven's Shore.
The Babe that weeps the Rod beneath
Writes Revenge in realms of death.
The Beggar's Rags fluttering in Air
Does to Rags the Heavens tear.
The Soldier armd with Sword & Gun
Palsied strikes the Summer's Sun.
The poor Man's Farthing is worth more
Than all the Gold on Afric's Shore.

One Mite wrung from the Labrer's hands
Shall buy & sell the Miser's Lands
Or if protected from on high
Does that whole Nation sell & buy.
He who mocks the Infant's Faith
Shall be mock'd in Age & Death.
He who shall teach the Child to Doubt
The rotting Grave shall neer get out.
He who respects the Infant's Faith
Triumphs over Hell & Death.
The Child's Toys & the Old Man's Reasons
Are the Fruits of the Two seasons.
The Questioner who sits so sly
Shall never Know how to Reply.
He who replies to words of Doubt
Doth put the Light of Knowledge out.
The Strongest Poison ever known
Came from Caesar's Laurel Crown.
Nought can deform the Human Race
Like to the Armour's iron brace.
When Gold & Gems adorn the Plow
To peaceful Arts shall Envy bow.
A Riddle or the Cricket's Cry
Is to Doubt a fit Reply.
The Emmet's Inch & Eagle's Mile
Make Lame Philosophy to smile.
He who Doubts from what he sees
Will neer Believe, do what you Please.
If the Sun & Moon should doubt
They'd immediately Go out.
To be in a Passion you Good may do
But no Good if a Passion is in you.
The Whore & Gambler by the State
Licencd build that Nation's Fate.
The Harlot's cry from Street to Street
Shall weave Old England's winding Sheet.
The Winner's Shout, the Loser's Curse
Dance before dead England's Hearse.
Every Night & every Morn
Some to Misery are Born.
Every Morn & every Night
Some are Born to sweet delight,

Some are Born to sweet delight,
Some are Born to Endless Night.
We are led to Believe a Lie
When we see not Thro the Eye
Which was Born in a Night to perish in a Night
When the Soul Slept in Beams of light.
God Appears & God is Light
To those poor Souls who dwell in Night
But does a Human Form Display
To those who Dwell in Realms of day.

THE GHOST OF ABEL

A Revelation In the Vision of Jehovah
Seen by William Blake
([London:] 1822 W Blake's Original Stereotype was 1788)

To LORD BYRON in the Wilderness:
What dost thou here, Elijah?

Can a Poet doubt the Visions of Jehovah? Nature has no Outline: but Imagination has. Nature has no Time: but Imagination has. Nature has no Supernatural & dissolves: Imagination is Eternity. Scene A rocky Country. Eve fainted over the dead body of Abel which lays near a Grave. Adam kneels by her. Jehovah stands above.

Jehovah– Adam!
Adam– I will not hear thee more thou Spiritual Voice.
Is this Death?
Jehovah– Adam!
Adam– It is in vain: I will not hear thee
Henceforth! Is this thy Promise that the Woman's Seed
Should bruise the Serpent's head: Is this the Serpent?
Ah!

Eve revives.

Eve Is this the Promise of Jehovah! O it is all a vain delusion,
This Death & this Life & this Jehovah!
Jehovah– Woman! lift
thine eyes!

A Voice is heard coming on.

Voice O Earth, cover not thou my Blood! cover not thou my
Blood!

Enter the Ghost of Abel.

Eve– Thou Visionary Phantasm, thou art not the real Abel
Abel Among the Elohim a Human Victim I wander: I am their
House
Prince of the Air, & our dimensions compass Zenith &
Nadir.
Vain is thy Covenant, O Jehovah! I am the Accuser &
Avenger
Of Blood. O Earth, Cover not thou the Blood of Abel.
Jehovah What Vengeance dost thou require?
Abel– Life for Life! Life for Life!
Jehovah He who shall take Cain's life must also Die, O Abel.
And who is he? Adam wilt thou, or Eve thou do this?

Adam — It is all a Vain delusion of the all creative Imagination.
Eve come away & let us not believe these vain delusions.
Abel is dead & Cain slew him! We shall also Die a Death
And then! what then! be as poor Abel a Thought: or as
This? O what shall I call thee, Form Divine: Father of Mercies
That appearest to my Spiritual Vision; Eve, seest thou also?

Eve– — I see him plainly with my Mind's Eye. I see also Abel living:
Tho terribly afflicted as We also are, yet Jehovah sees him
Alive & not Dead: were it not better to believe Vision
With all our might & strength tho we are fallen & lost?

Adam– — Eve thou hast spoken truly; let us kneel before his feet.

They Kneel before Jehovah.

Abel — Are these the Sacrifices of Eternity, O Jehovah, a Broken Spirit
And a Contrite Heart? O I cannot Forgive! the Accuser hath
Enterd into Me as into his House & I loathe thy Tabernacles.
As thou has said, so is it come to pass: My desire is unto Cain
And He doth rule over Me: therefore My Soul in fumes of Blood
Cries for Vengeance: Sacrifice on Sacrifice, Blood on Blood!

Jehovah — Lo, I have given you a Lamb for an Atonement instead
Of the Transgressor, or no Flesh or Spirit could ever Live.

Abel– — Compelled I cry, O Earth, cover not the Blood of Abel!

Abel sinks down into the Grave, from which arises Satan
Armed in glittering scales and with a Crown & a Spear.

Satan — I will have Human Blood & not the blood of Bulls or Goats
And no Atonement, O Jehovah! the Elohim live on Sacrifice
Of Men: hence I am God of Men: Thou Human, O Jehovah.
By the Rock & Oak of the Druid creeping Mistletoe & Thorn

Cain's City built with Human Blood, not Blood of Bulls & Goats,
Thou shalt Thyself be Sacrificed to Me thy God on Calvary.

Jehovah Such is My Will Thunders.
That Thou Thyself go to Eternal Death
In Self Annihilation even till Satan Self-subdud Put off Satan
Into the Bottomless Abyss whose torment arises for ever & ever.

On each side a Chorus of Angels entering Sing the following:

The Elohim of the Heathen Swore Vengeance for Sin! Then Thou stoodst
Forth O Elohim Jehovah! in the midst of the darkness of the Oath! All Clothed
In Thy Covenant of the Forgiveness of Sins: Death O Holy! Is this Brotherhood?
The Elohim saw their Oath Eternal Fire: they rolled apart trembling over The
Mercy Seat: each in his station fixt in the Firmament by Peace, Brotherhood and Love.

The Curtain falls.
The voice of Abel's Blood

For the Sexes: *The Gates of Paradise* ([London, ?1826])

What is Man!

The Sun's Light when he unfolds it. [Pl. 1]
Depends on the Organ that beholds it.

Mutual Forgiveness of each Vice, [Pl. 2]
Such are the Gates of Paradise.
Against the Accuser's chief desire
Who walkd among the Stones of Fire
Jehovah's Finger Wrote the Law
Then Wept! Then rose in Zeal & Awe
And the Dead Corpse from Sinai's heat
Buried beneath his Mercy Seat.
O Christians, Christians! Tell me Why
You rear it on your Altars high.

The Keys

The Caterpiller on the Leaf [Pl. 19]
Reminds thee of thy Mother's Grief.

Of the Gates

1 My Eternal Man set in Repose,
The Female from his darkness rose
And She found me beneath a Tree,
A Mandrake, & in her Veil hid me.
Serpent Reasonings us entice
Of Good & Evil, Virtue & Vice.
2 Doubt Self Jealous, Watry folly
3 Struggling thro Earth's Melancholy,
4 Naked in Air in Shame & Fear
5 Blind in Fire with shield & spear,
Two Horn'd Reasoning Cloven Fiction
In Doubt which is Self contradiction,
A dark Hermaphrodite We stood,
Rational Truth Root of Evil & Good,
Round me flew the Flaming Sword;
Round her snowy Whirlwinds roard

Freezing her Veil the Mundane Shell.
6 I rent the Veil where the Dead dwell.
When weary Man enters his Cave
He meets his Saviour in the Grave. [Pl. 20]
Some find a Female Garment there
And some a Male woven with care
Lest the Sexual Garments sweet
Should grow a devouring Winding sheet.
7 One Dies! Alas! the Living & Dead,
One is slain & One is fled.
8 In Vain-glory hatcht & nurst,
By double Spectres Self Accurst,
My Son! my Son! Thou treatest me
But as I have instructed thee.
9 On the shadows of the Moon
Climbing thro Night's highest noon
10 In Time's Ocean falling drownd
In Aged Ignorance profound
11 Holy & cold I clipd the Wings
Of all Sublunary Things
12 And in depths of my Dungeon's
Closd the father & the Sons
13 But when once I did descry
The Immortal Man that cannot Die
14 Thro evening shades I haste away
To close the Labours of my Day.
15 The Door of Death I open found
And the Worm Weaving in the Ground.
16 Thou'rt my Mother from the Womb,
Wife, Sister, Daughter to the Tomb
Weaving to Dreams the Sexual strife
And Weeping over the Web of Life.

To The Accuser who is [Pl. 21]
The God of This World

Truly My Satan thou art but a Dunce
And dost not know the Garment from the Man.
Every Harlot was a Virgin once
Nor canst thou ever change Kate into Nan.

Tho thou art Worshipd by the Names Divine
Of Jesus & Jehovah: thou art still
The Son of Morn in weary Night's decline,
The lost Traveller's Dream under the Hill.

Bibliography

FACSIMILES OF BLAKE'S WRITING

The Complete Graphic Works of William Blake, edited by David Bindman, assisted by Deirdre Toomey with 765 illustrations (London: Thames and Hudson, 1978, 1986). Includes Blake's commercial engravings.

The Complete Illuminated Books, Introduction by David Bindman (London: Thames & Hudson in association with The William Blake Trust, 2000). Colour reproductions, most true size.

An Island in the Moon: A Facsimile of the Manuscript, edited by Michael Phillips with a Preface by Haven O'More (Cambridge: Cambridge University Press, 1987). True size.

The Notebook of William Blake: A Photographic and Typographic Facsimile, edited by David V. Erdman with the assistance of Donald K. Moore (Oxford: Clarendon Press, 1973). True size.

The Pickering Manuscript, Introduction by Charles Ryskamp (New York: Pierpont Morgan Library, 1972). True size.

Tiriel: Facsimile and Transcript of the Manuscript, Reproduction of the Drawings and a Commentary on the Poem by G. E. Bentley, Jr (Oxford: Clarendon Press, 1967). True size of the manuscript.

Vala or The Four Zoas: A Facsimile of the Manuscript, a Transcript of the Poem and a Study of its Growth and Significance by G. E. Bentley, Jr (Oxford: Clarendon Press, 1963). True size.

William Blake's Works in Conventional Typography, edited by G. E. Bentley, Jr (Delmar, New York: Scholars' Facsimiles and Reprints, 1984).

TYPOGRAPHIC EDITIONS

The Complete Poems, edited by Alicia Ostriker (Harmondsworth: Penguin Books, 1977, 1981).

The Complete Writings of William Blake, with Variant Readings, edited by Geoffrey Keynes (Oxford, New York, Toronto: Oxford University Press, 1966 ff.). Revised from his *The Writings of William Blake* in three volumes (1925) and *Poetry and Prose of William Blake* complete in one volume

(London: Nonesuch Press, 1927). Most frequently quoted in Britain and her former colonies.

The Poetry and Prose of William Blake, edited by David V. Erdman. Commentary by Harold Bloom (Garden City, New York: Doubleday and Co., 1965; revised, 1982, 1988). The standard edition in North America.

The William Blake Archive, edited by Morris Eaves, Robert N. Essick and Joseph Viscomi. Online at the University of Virginia (<http//iath.virginia.edu/blake>) with colour reproductions of (usually) multiple copies of Blake's works, mostly in Illuminated Printing but including some MSS and graphic series.

William Blake's Writings: Volume I: Engraved and Etched Writings; Volume II: Writings in Conventional Typography and in Manuscript, edited by G. E. Bentley, Jr (Oxford: Clarendon Press, 1978). With reproductions of all the significant designs in Illuminated Printing.

CONCORDANCE

A Concordance to the Writings of William Blake, two volumes, edited by David V. Erdman, with the assistance of John E. Thiesmeyer and Richard J. Wolfe; also G. E. Bentley, Jr, Palmer Brown, Robert F. Gleckner, George Mills Harper, Karl Kiralis, Martin K. Nurmi and Paul M. Zall (Ithaca: Cornell University Press, 1967). Based on the Keynes edition.

BLAKE'S ART

Butlin, Martin, *The Paintings and Drawings of William Blake* (New Haven and London: Yale University Press, 1981). A magisterial catalogue raisonnée (Vol. I) with admirable reproductions of hundreds of designs (Vol. II).

Essick, Robert N., *William Blake's Commercial Book Illustrations: A Catalogue and Study of the Plates Engraved by Blake after Designs by Other Artists* (Oxford: Clarendon Press, 1991). Includes reproductions of all the designs.

Essick, Robert N., *The Separate Plates of William Blake: A Catalogue* (Princeton: Princeton University Press, 1983). Includes reproductions of all the designs, many in colour.

Grant, John E., Edward J. Rose, Michael J. Tolley, David V. Erdman, *William Blake's Designs for Young's* Night Thoughts*: A Complete edition*, two volumes (Oxford: Clarendon Press, 1980). Mostly in black-and-white, not true size.

BIBLIOGRAPHY

Bentley, G. E., Jr, *Blake Books: Annotated Catalogues of William Blake's Writings in Illuminated Printing, in Conventional Typography and in Manuscript and Reprints thereof, Reproductions of his Designs, Books with his Engravings, Catalogues, Books he owned, and Scholarly and Critical Works about him* (Oxford: Clarendon Press, 1977).

Bentley, G. E., Jr, *Blake Books Supplement: A Bibliography of Publications and Discoveries about William Blake 1971–1992 being a Continuation of* Blake Books (1977) (Oxford: Clarendon Press, 1995).

Bentley, G. E., Jr, with the assistance of Keiko Aoyama (1994–2002) and Hikari Sato (2003) for Japanese publications, 'William Blake and His Circle', *Blake: An Illustrated Quarterly* (1994 ff.).

BIOGRAPHY

Ackroyd, Peter, *Blake* (London: Sinclair-Stevenson, 1995).

Bentley, G. E., Jr, *Blake Records*, second edition: *Documents (1714–1841) Concerning the Life of William Blake (1757–1827) and his Family Incorporating* Blake Records *(1969),* Blake Records Supplement *(1988) and Extensive Discoveries since 1988* (New Haven and London: Yale University Press for the Paul Mellon Centre for Studies in British Art, 2004).

Bentley, G. E., Jr, *The Stranger from Paradise: A Biography of William Blake* (New Haven and London: Yale University Press, 2001, 2003).

Gilchrist, Alexander, *Life of William Blake, 'Pictor Ignotus'. With Selections from his Poems and Other Writings. Illustrated from Blake's Own Works, in Facsimile by W. J. Linton, and in Photolithography; with a Few of Blake's Original Plates.* Two volumes (London and Cambridge: Macmillan, 1863). A New and Enlarged Edition, with Additional Letters (1880), edited by Ruthven Todd (London and New York: Everyman, 1942, 1945).

CRITICISM

Bindman, David, *Blake as an artist* (Oxford: Phaidon, 1977).

Blake: An Illustrated Quarterly, edited by M. D. Paley and Morris Eaves (1967 ff.; until 1977 it was called *Blake Newsletter*).

Damon, S. Foster, *A Blake Dictionary: The Ideas and Symbols of William Blake* (Providence, Rhode Island: Brown University Press, 1965).

De Luca, Vincent Arthur, *Words of Eternity: Blake and the Poetics of the Sublime* (Princeton: Princeton University Press, 1991).

Eaves, Morris, *The Counter Arts Conspiracy: Art and Industry in the Age of Blake* (Ithaca and London: Cornell University Press, 1992).

Erdman, David V., *Blake: Prophet Against Empire: A Poet's Interpretation of the History of his Own Times* (Princeton: Princeton University Press, 1954); revised edition (Garden City, New York: Anchor, 1969). A wonderfully influential work on Blake's political context.

Essick, Robert N., *William Blake Printmaker* (Princeton: Princeton University Press, 1980).

Frye, Northrop, *Fearful Symmetry: A Study of William Blake* (Princeton: Princeton University Press, 1947). The most lastingly influential study of Blake.

Gleckner, Robert F., *The Piper and the Bard: A Study of William Blake* (Detroit: Wayne State University Press, 1959).

Heppner, Christopher, *Reading Blake's Designs* (Cambridge: Cambridge University Press, 1995).

Hilton, Howard Nelson, *Literal Imagination: Blake's Vision of Words* (Berkeley, Los Angeles, London: University of California Press, 1983).

Hobson, Christopher Z., *The Chained Boy: Orc and Blake's Idea of Revolution* (Lewisburg: Bucknell University Press; London: Associated University Presses, 1999).

Holloway, John, *Blake: The Lyric Poetry* (London, 1968).

Lincoln, Andrew, *Spiritual History: A Reading of William Blake's* Vala *or* The Four Zoas (Oxford: Clarendon Press, 1995).

Lindberg, Bo, *William Blake's Illustrations to the Book of Job* (Åbo, Finland: Åbo Akademi, 1973).

Mitchell, W. J. T., *Blake's Composite Art: A Study of the Illuminated Poetry* (Princeton: Princeton University Press, 1978).

Paley, Morton, *Energy and Imagination: A Study of the Development of Blake's Thought* (Oxford: Clarendon Press, 1970).

Tannenbaum, Leslie W., *Biblical Tradition and Blake's Early Prophecies: The Great Code of Art* (Princeton: Princeton University Press, 1982).

Thompson, E. P., *Witness Against the Beast: William Blake and the Moral Law* (Cambridge: Cambridge University Press, 1993).

Viscomi, Joseph, *William Blake and the Idea of the Book* (Princeton: Princeton University Press, 1993).

Wittreich, Joseph Anthony, Jr, *Angel of the Apocalypse: Blake's Idea of Milton* (Madison: University of Wisconsin Press, 1975).

INSTITUTIONS WITH MAJOR COLLECTIONS OF BLAKE'S ORIGINAL BOOKS AND MANUSCRIPTS

England

British Library (London)
British Museum Department of Prints and Drawings (London)
Cambridge University Library (Cambridge)
Fitzwilliam Museum (Cambridge)

Germany

Bayerisch Staatsbibliothek (Munich)

United States of America

Harvard University Libraries (Cambridge, Massachusetts)
Huntington Library (San Marino, California)
Library of Congress (Washington, DC)
New York Public Library (chiefly the Berg Collection)
Pierpont Morgan Library (New York)
Yale University Libraries and Yale Centre for British Art (New Haven, Connecticut)

INSTITUTIONS WITH MAJOR COLLECTIONS OF BLAKE'S PAINTINGS AND DRAWINGS

England

British Museum Department of Prints and Drawings (London)
Fitzwilliam Museum (Cambridge)
Tate Britain (London)

United States of America

Huntington Library and Art Gallery (San Marino, California)

Notes

The Bible is cited throughout from the Authorized King James version.

Poetical Sketches

Printed in 1783 in conventional typography (in a volume of 76 pages) for Blake's friends the Reverend Anthony Stephen Mathew (husband of Blake's patroness Harriet Mathew) and the sculptor John Flaxman in about fifty copies (twenty-three survive) and 'given to Blake to sell to friends, or publish, as he might think proper', according to his friend J. T. Smith in 1828 (*Blake Records*, second edition, 2004, p. 606). Blake made inconsistent manuscript corrections in eleven copies which he and the Flaxmans gave away to friends, but he still had a few uncorrected copies when he died forty-four years later.

Facsimiles were printed in 1890 and 1927 and in *William Blake's Works in Conventional Typography*, edited by G. E. Bentley, Jr (1984).

The 'Advertisement' is by the Revd Anthony Stephen Mathew, who, with Blake's friend the young sculptor John Flaxman, defrayed the expenses of printing *Poetical Sketches*.

Song ['How sweet I roam'd']

'Song' was 'written before the age of fourteen', according to B. H. Malkin (1806) (*Blake Records*, p. 605).

To the Muses

Ida is a mountain in central Crete. The nine Greek muses of inspiration wander through the four elements, fire ('The chambers of the sun'), earth, air and water. A. C. Swinburne wrote that in 'To the Muses' 'The Eighteenth Century died to music' (*William Blake* [1869], p. 8).

An Island in the Moon

Composed *c.* 1784. The verses are sung in response to a call for 'an Anthem'.

Blake's manuscript (in the Fitzwilliam Museum, Cambridge, England) known as 'An Island in the Moon' (from its opening words, not quoted here) is a satire on contemporary intellectual and social pretensions, perhaps focusing on the Mathew salon which patronized Blake around 1783. It is a discontinuous narrative with interspersed songs, mostly satiric, including three early versions of poems etched in *Songs of Innocence* such as 'Holy Thursday'. It is reproduced in facsimile in the edition by Michael Philips (1987).

1. *Doctor Johnson*: Dr Samuel Johnson (1709–84) was an imperious critic, scholar and dictionary-maker.
2. *Scipio africanus*: General Publius Cornelius Scipio Africanus Major (?237–183 BC), conqueror of Hannibal, or his adopted grandson General Publius Cornelius Scipio Aemilianus Africanus Minor (?185–129 BC), conqueror of Carthage. Probably chosen because of the ribald rhyme possibilities of his name.

Songs by Shepherds

Composed *c.* 1787. The original has not been traced; a contemporary manuscript transcription was copied into Nancy Flaxman's copy of *Poetical Sketches* (F), now in the Turnbull Library, Wellington, New Zealand, and reproduced in *William Blake's Works in Conventional Typography* (1984). One of the poems in it is adapted in *Songs of Innocence.*

'Song 2^{d} by a Young Shepherd' is an early version of 'Laughing Song' in *Innocence.*

Tiriel

Composed *c.* 1789. The manuscript in the British Library Department of Manuscripts consists of eight leaves, with sections numbered 1–8. There are many minor alterations including thirty-nine lines deleted. Twelve separate designs for it are now widely scattered, and three have not been traced since 1863. Some of the designs illustrate the text closely, and some depict incidents not in the poem, such as Har and Heva bathing. The manuscript and the surviving illustrations are reproduced in facsimile in *Tiriel*, edited by G. E. Bentley, Jr (1967).

Some of the strange names in *Tiriel* have been plausibly traced to earlier sources:

1. *Tiriel*: Is 'the Intelligence of *Mercury*' and *Zazel* is 'The spirit of *Saturn*', according to Cornelius Agrippa, *Three Books of Occult Philosophy*, tr. J. F. (1651), p. 243.
24. *Heuxos*: Probably related to the historical nomadic enemies of Egypt

called 'Hicksoes' or 'Hyxoes'; 'Hicksoes' appear in *The Captive of the Castle of Sennaar* (1798) by Blake's friend George Cumberland.

55. *Har*: 'Mountain' in Hebrew, according to Jacob Bryant, *A New System, or, an Analysis of Ancient Mythology* (1774), I, p. 94, a book which Blake probably illustrated.

56. *Heva*: In Scandinavian mythology Heva/Hela is 'the Goddess of Death', according to the *Poems of* [Thomas] *Gray* (1776), p. 105.

62. *Mnetha*: May be related to Mnemosyne, the Greek goddess of memory (cf. 'mnemonic' and 'Mne Seraphim' in *Thel*, l. 1); Blake remarks that 'The Greek Muses are daughters of Mnemosyne, or Memory' (*Descriptive Catalogue* [1809], ¶11).

150. *Ijim*: Translated as 'satyr' in the King James translation of Isaiah 13: 21; represented as 'diabolical Love' or 'Love of Self' in Swedenborg, *True Christian Religion*, tr. J. Clowes (1781), pp. 65–6.

Songs of Innocence

First printed in 1789. From 1789 to 1818, Blake printed twenty-six copies of the separate *Songs of Innocence*, which have survived, and twenty-four more were bound with *Songs of Innocence and of Experience*. Before about 1818, the plates in each copy of *Innocence* are arranged in a different, unique order, but thereafter they were given in the order found here. Four poems in early copies of *Songs of Innocence* were later moved to *Songs of Experience* – 'The Little Girl Lost' and 'The Little Girl Found', 'The School Boy', and 'The Voice of the Ancient Bard' – indicating that Blake found qualities of both innocence and experience in them. In early copies, the marginal designs were very simply coloured and the cost in 1793 was 5 shillings (around 25p today), but after about 1800 the Blakes coloured them more heavily, sometimes obscuring the text, and the cost was raised enormously to £3 3s in 1818 and £5 5s in 1827. The colouring sometimes vitally affects one's understanding of the poems. In early copies of 'The Little Black Boy', the left child is pink, while in late copies he is black or grey. In early copies of 'The Little Girl Lost', the boy is naked, while in late copies he is clothed.

The poems of *Innocence* were admired by some of the most distinguished of Blake's contemporaries – Coleridge, Wordsworth, Lamb and Hazlitt – but most readers were probably more interested in the designs than in the poems.

Notice who speaks in the poems – a shepherd, a little black boy, a nurse, a mother with her baby, a school boy, a baby two days old, an ancient bard, even an emmet and a glow-worm. The poems do not show Blake's version of the truth; they represent rather what the sub-title to *Songs of Innocence and of Experience* calls 'the Two Contrary States of the Human Soul'. Each sees the world differently.

The Frontispiece shows a flock of grazing sheep with their shepherd in tights holding a flute and looking upward at a naked child lying on a cloud beneath the trees.

The title page design represents a seated woman in a mob cap with two children standing at her knees, looking at a book on her lap.

The Lamb

The form of the catechism in 'The Lamb' is echoed in 'The Tyger' of *Experience.*

The Blossom

The design shows not sparrows and robins but winged cherubs flying in a huge flame-like plant.

The Chimney Sweeper

In most trades, the father paid the master to apprentice his child, but for the dangerous trade of chimney sweepers, who began work as young as four years old in order to be able to climb the narrow, twisting flues, the master paid the father. The youngest sweeps could not yet pronounce the 's' of their call through the streets: 'sweep, sweep'. The children slept among their bags of soot, which were the perquisite of the trade (soot was used in making ink). The complement of this poem appears in 'The Chimney Sweeper' of *Songs of Experience.*

The Little Boy lost

Drafted in 'An Island in the Moon' (?1784).

Laughing Song

Drafted in 'Song 2^{d} by a Young Shepherd'.

The Divine Image

Echoed in 'The Human Abstract' and 'A Divine Image' in *Songs of Experience.* Never printed by Blake and known only from posthumously printed copies.

Holy Thursday

Holy Thursday was first celebrated in St Paul's Cathedral on Ascension Day, 2 May 1782, when 6,000 charity school children sang movingly in celebration of the charity they had received. In the design, girls walk in a file separate from that of the boys. The poem was drafted in 'An Island in the Moon' (?1784) and echoed in 'Holy Thursday' of *Songs of Experience.*

Nurse's Song

Sung as 'my mother's song' in 'An Island in the Moon' (?1784) and echoed in 'Nurse's Song' in *Songs of Experience*.

Infant Joy

In the design, an enormous blossom encloses a child with moth wings standing before a seated woman with a baby in her lap. The poem is echoed in 'Infant Sorrow' in *Songs of Experience*.

The Little Girl Lost

The design represents an adolescent girl and boy embracing; in early copies the boy is naked, but when the poem was transferred to *Songs of Experience* he is usually clothed.

The Little Girl Found

Later transferred to *Songs of Experience*.

The School Boy

Later transferred to *Songs of Experience*.

The Voice of the Ancient Bard

Later transferred to *Songs of Experience*.

The Book of Thel

First printed in 1789. *The Book of Thel* survives in sixteen copies, all coloured, mostly very lightly. They were offered for sale at 3s in 1793, £2 2s in 1818, and £3 3s in 1827. Blake's own income was probably between 20s and 30s a week.

'Thel's Motto' is missing in one copy and was numbered and bound after the text in two copies.

The title page design shows Thel, with a shepherd's long crook, watching a naked man flying from a blossom to embrace a tiny clothed woman from another blossom. Erasmus Darwin's *Botanic Garden* (entered at Stationers' Hall in March 1789) described in very human terms 'The [Sexual] Loves of the Plants' and Blake made engravings for it dated 1791. Thel seeks advice from the water lily (Part I), the cloud of air (Part II), the earthworm (Part III) and the grave (Part IV).

1. *Mne Seraphim*: May be related to Mnetha in *Tiriel*, to Mnemosyne the Greek goddess of memory, and to 'Bne Seraphim', the Intelligence

of Mercury in Cornelius Agrippa, *Three Books of Occult Philosophy*, tr. J. F. (1651), p. 243.

4. *Adona*: According to Jacob Bryant, *A New System . . . of Ancient Mythology* (1775), Vol. I, p. 376: 'Adon, or Adonis . . . is the name of one of the principal rivers in Canaan . . . where the death of Thamuz was particularly lamented'.

29. *o'erfired*: Was perhaps intended as 'o'ertired'.

83. *Har*: See the notes for *Tiriel*.

121–3. *Why . . . shriek*: Erased from two copies but are still present in copies printed later.

124. After the last line of text is a design of a large, cheerful serpent harnessed by three naked children riding on its back.

The Marriage of Heaven and Hell

First printed *c.* 1790. *The Marriage* was perhaps created in sections, not in the final printed order as given here, in part as a satire on the Swedish visionary Emanuel Swedenborg and his followers. The nine surviving copies were printed 1790(?) to 1827. It was offered at 7s 6d in 1793 but did not appear on Blake's lists of works for sale in 1818 and 1827, though he created a copy for the dilettante and poisoner Thomas Griffiths Wainewright in 1827 – before his poisonous propensities were publicly known.

On the title page at the top, above 'Heaven', are leafless trees, while at the bottom, by 'and Hell', are embracing naked couples surrounded by flames.

¶1. *thirty-three years since its advent*: Above this is added '1790' in one copy. Swedenborg had announced that the Last Judgment took place in 1757, coincidentally the year Blake was born. Thirty-three was the age of Blake in 1790 and of Christ at his death.

Swedenborg: Emanuel Swedenborg (1688–1772) was a Swedish scientist and religious visionary, whose New Jerusalem Church Blake and his wife joined at its founding in 1787. Blake annotated Swedenborg's writings at first with studious approval – 'Excellent', 'Good & Evil are here both Good & the two contraries married' (*The Wisdom of Angels Concerning Divine Love and Divine Wisdom* [1788], pp. 56, 58) – and later with vigorous indignation – 'Is not this Predestination?', 'Lies & Priestcraft!', 'Cursed Folly!' (*The Wisdom of Angels Concerning The Divine Providence*, tr. N. Tucker, 1790, pp. v, xix, 434).

the tomb and *the linen clothes folded up*: Are those of Christ.

Isaiah XXXIV & XXXV: Concerns 'the day of the Lord's vengeance' when 'he will come and save you' and 'the desert shall rejoice, and blossom as the rose'.

¶4. Below this line is a design of a nude woman giving birth.

¶11. Below the text, the design shows a naked man flying across the sea with a naked child in his arms, while a naked man in flames and chained by the ankle tries to reach them. Blake called one copy of this design 'Good and Evil Angels'.

¶19. Early illustrations of *Paradise Lost* showed the Devil with horns, a tail and cloven hooves, but by the 1770s artists were depicting him as a naked heroic man.

¶20. *shewn in the Gospel*: In John 14:16, Jesus says 'I will pray the Father, and he shall give you another Comforter'.

he who dwells in flaming fire: 'God out of Christ is a Consuming Fire' according to Blake's notes on his design (after 1808) of the 'Epitome of Hervey's *Meditations among the Tombs*'.

¶21. *Milton*: The idea that Milton was 'of the Devil's party without knowing it' was becoming commonplace among artists but was a novelty among literary critics in 1790.

A Memorable Fancy

A Memorable Fancy: Blake's 'Memorable Fancies' are parodies of Swedenborg's 'Memorable Relations'.

¶24. In Blake's copy of Thomas Chatterton's *Poems, supposed to have been written . . . by Thomas Rowley, and Others* (1778), p. 51, Blake would have read:

> How dydd I know that evry darte,
> That cut the airie waie,
> Mighte nott fynde passage toe my harte,
> And close myne eyes for aie?

Proverbs of Hell

6. *The cut worm*: In a deleted stanza of 'The Fly' in his Notebook, p. 101, Blake wrote:

> The cut worm
> Forgives the plow
> And dies in peace
> And so do thou.

66. *Improvent*: The misspelling 'improvent' was deliberate, for it was never corrected.

70. Below the text is a design of a naked kneeling man with bat wings pointing to a long unrolled scroll, which is apparently being copied by clothed, seated scribes on either side of him.

A Memorable Fancy

¶37. *Isaiah*: 'Isaiah hath walked naked and barefoot three years for a sign and wonder upon Egypt and upon Ethiopia' (Isaiah 20:3).

¶38. *Diogenes the Grecian*: Diogenes the Cynic (?412–323 BC).

¶39. *Ezekiel*: The spirit said, 'lie thou ... upon thy left side ... three hundred and ninety days ... And when thou has accomplished them, lie again on thy right side ... forty days ... Lo, I have given thee cow's dung ... and thou shalt prepare thy bread therewith' (Ezekiel 4:4, 6, 15).

¶40. Archbishop James Usher (1581–1656) had determined that the world was created in 4004 BC, so 6,000 years would be accomplished in 1996.

¶41. *cherub*: When Adam was driven out, God 'placed at the east of the garden of Eden, Cherubims, and a flaming sword which turned every way, to keep the way of the tree of life' (Genesis 3:24).

¶43. *printing in the infernal method*: Blake's works in Illuminated Printing, like *The Marriage*, were created by writing and drawing on copper in a liquid impervious to acid and then bathing the surface in acid so that the words and designs were left in relief for printing.

¶49. *Eagle*: The design at the bottom of the plate represents an eagle with outspread wings holding a serpent in his talons, a symbol of the accomplishment of the alchemical work.

Above ¶53. The design represents a stone prison with a bearded old man and two young men on either side of him sitting on the ground with their heads bowed over their knees. A similar design in *For Children: The Gates of Paradise* (1793), entitled 'Does thy God O Priest take such vengeance as this?' clearly refers to Dante's Ugolino and his sons and grandsons imprisoned and left to starve to death.

the weak in courage is strong in cunning: See proverb 49 above.

¶59. *I came not to send Peace but a Sword*: 'When the Son of man shall come in his glory ... before him shall be gathered all nations: and he shall separate them one from another, as a shepherd divideth his sheep from the goats'; 'I came not to send peace, but a sword' (Matthew 25:31–5; 10:34).

¶63. See Swedenborg, *The Apocalypse Revealed* (tr. N. Tucker) (1791), p. 565:

> The FIRST MEMORABLE RELATION: I once heard there [in the spiritual world] a Sound ... of a Mill ... I recollected that by Mill ... in the Word is meant to collect from the Word what is serviceable or subservient to Doctrine ... Therefore I went to the Place, where the Sound was heard, and ... I saw ... a House ... into which there was a Passage through a Cavern; on seeing which I descended and went in, and ... saw an old Man ... with the

Word before him, and collecting out of it Passages in support of his Doctrine . . .

¶66. *looking east*: Paris is 'east, distant about three degrees' from London.

¶70. *picking the flesh off of his own tail*: In a letter of 21 October 1827, Coleridge refers to 'what the Apes . . . are said to do, when hungry, – i.e. eat a joint or two of the extremity of their tail' (*Collected Letters*, edited by E. L. Griggs, 1971, vol. VI, p. 704).

Between ¶72 and ¶73 is a design of a huge, open-mouthed serpent coiling through the sea.

Above ¶74 is a design of a naked man with splayed legs sitting on a little hill with his knee on a human skull. A very similar figure appears in *America* above l. 37.

¶80. *Paracelsus or Jacob Behmen*: Paracelsus is Theophrastus Bombastus von Hohenheim (1490–1541), a German alchemist, and Behmen is Jakob Boehme (1575–1624), a German peasant mystic whose *Works* (1764–81) Blake praised in 1825: 'Boehmen was . . . a divinely inspired man' (*Blake Records*, p. 423).

¶86. *bray a fool . . . wheat*: This is an echo of Proverbs 27:22: 'Though thou shouldest bray a fool among wheat with a pestle, yet will not his foolishness depart from him'.

'The Everlasting Gospel' extends this portrait of an antinomian Jesus.

¶89. *The Bible of Hell*: May be the 'Proverbs of Hell' or 'A Song of Liberty' in *The Marriage*, but Blake also made a title page for 'The Bible of Hell, in Nocturnal Visions collected Vol. I Lambeth' (where he lived 1790–1800).

Between ¶89 and ¶90 is a design of an old man, naked except for a crown, crawling beside huge tree trunks. The same figure appears in a colour-print called *Nebuchadnezzar* (1795), representing the sixth century BC King of Babylon who was reported in the Old Testament to have been reduced to eating grass like the beasts of the field (like primitive man in the Gilgamesh epic).

¶90. *One Law for the Lion & Ox*: Cf. 'Why is one law given to the lion & the patient Ox' (*Tiriel*, 334) and 'is there not one law for both the lion and the ox?' (*Visions of the Daughters of Albion*, 108).

A Song of Liberty

8. *On these infinite . . . barr'd out*: Cf. 'Those vast shady hills between America & Albion's shore: Now barr'd out by the Atlantic sea' (*America*, 107–108).

20. *Empire is no more*: 'Empire is no more, and now the Lion & Wolf shall cease' appears in *America*, 51.

Chorus

¶91. Repeated in Blake's annotations to Lavater's *Aphorisms* (1788), ¶309, *Visions of the Daughters of Albion*, 215, *America*, 71, and *Vala*, p. 34, l. 79.

'A Fairy leapt'

Composed *c.* 1793. The poem is written in pencil on the back of Blake's drawing of 'The Infant Hercules Throttling Serpents' (Library of Congress), which may not be relevant to the poem.

For another fairy poem, see the introduction to *Europe*.

VISIONS of the Daughters of Albion

First printed in 1793. Blake made sketches for *Visions of the Daughters of Albion* in his Notebook, but no manuscript text of the poem survives there – or anywhere else. Seventeen surviving copies were printed from 1793 to about 1821. The colouring of early copies is fairly slight and uniform. They were offered at 7s 6d in 1793, £3 3s in 1818 and £5 5s in 1827.

The explicit eroticism of *Visions of the Daughters of Albion* is an attack upon Locke's philosophy of the five senses, suggesting that we perceive far more than we can account for from our senses of touch, taste, smell, hearing and sight.

The frontispiece shows a cave-mouth overlooking the sea, with Oothoon, nude and kneeling, chained back to back with Bromion, while Theotormon, also naked, crouches by them with his arms wrapped around his head.

The title page represents a rainbow over the sea across which flees a nude woman pursued by a flying bearded god whose heavy wings are in flames.

8. Below 'The Argument' is a design of Oothoon, nude, kneeling and holding her breasts as she kisses a small nude figure flying from a flower (?a marigold), with a sunrise in the background.

21. *Stampt with my signet*: Slaves were sometimes branded with the name of their owner; Blake engraved a plate (1792) of a *Family of Negro Slaves from Loango*, showing on them the owner's branded initials 'J.G.S.' for his friend J. G. Stedman's *Narrative of a five years' expedition, against the Revolted Negroes of Surinam* (1796).

23. Below the line is a design of a naked man and woman sprawling on their backs in exhaustion.

86. Above the line is a design of an enormous eagle attacking the midriff of a nude woman on a cloud.

87. Above the line is a design of a clothed man seated on the sea-shore, while above him in a wave hovers a nude woman chained by the ankle.

108. *And is there not one law*: Cf. *Tiriel*, 360 and *The Marriage*, ¶90.

114. *Urizen*: Urizen (perhaps from 'Your Reason' or 'Horizon') represents Reason in Blake's later myth.
175. Beneath the line is a design of a naked man lying on a cloud and holding a studded whip, while a nude woman hurries away from him with her face in her hands. The man may be Theotormon flagellating himself and the weeping woman Oothoon. He could not reach her with his whip.
176. Above the line is a confused design of three or more seated women huddled together, perhaps representing the Daughters of Albion.
215. *Arise . . . that lives is holy*: See *The Marriage*, ¶92.
218. Below the line at the end of the poem is a design of three seated women clutching one another on the sea-shore as they look up at a mournful man floating on a cloud amid flames; probably the design represents the Daughters of Albion watching Theotormon.

AMERICA *a Prophecy*

First printed in 1793. *America* and its companion *Europe*, which are often bound together, are Blake's most ambitiously illustrated works. Their folio size gave him great scope, and on most of the plates half or more of the space is devoted to designs, often surrounding the text. There are sketches for *America* in Blake's Notebook, but no manuscript draft text is known.

Pl. e with the word 'Preludium' was omitted in four copies (A–B, M, O) and in posthumous copies, but added in manuscript in copy M. In pl. 4, ll. 38–41 were masked so that they did not print in most copies (B–F, H–M, R) or erased from the paper after printing (G). In copy B, pl. 4 and 9 with ll. 21–41, 52–8 are missing and replaced by facsimiles so accurate that they were not detected until 1983.

Blake produced fourteen copies of *America*, and three more (N, P, Q) were printed after his death by his disciple Frederick Tatham. Only copies A, K, M, O and R were coloured, sometimes years after they were printed. *America* was offered at 10s 6d in 1793, £5 5s in 1818, and £6 6s in 1827.

America is a visionary history of US independence, not a public record. As Blake wrote of his pictures, 'The Artist has endeavoured to emulate the grandeur of those seen in his vision, and to apply it to modern Heroes, on a smaller scale' (*Descriptive Catalogue* [1809], ¶10).

The frontispiece shows a naked man with heavy wings sitting in a breach in a stone wall with his head on his knees and his manacled hands on the ground, and beside him sits a naked woman with her arms around two naked children.

The title page represents a woman passionately kissing a prostrate corpse with a sword in its hand.

Above Preludium l. 1 a design shows a naked couple (Los and Enitharmon) lamenting over a naked boy (Orc) manacled to the ground. Urthona is apparent to fallen men as Los, who in Blake's later myth is explicitly the imagination.

A Prophecy

Beside 'A Prophecy' a naked man with broken chains rises through the sky.

4. *Washington . . . Green*: The colonial patriots George Washington (1732–99), Benjamin Franklin (1706–90), John Warren (1741–75), Horatio Gates (1728–1806), John Hancock (1737–93), Nathaniel Greene (1742–86) and the English pamphleteer Tom Paine (1737–1809) were never in the same place together. In his indignant marginalia to Bishop Watson's *Apology for the Bible* (1797), Blake wrote of Paine's *Common Sense*: 'Is it a greater miracle to feed five thousand men with five loaves than to overturn all the armies of Europe with a small pamphlet?'

8. Below the line a naked flying man blows a trumpet which emits flames.

15–17. Beside the lines a naked man, woman and child flee from flames.

18. Below the line, a winged serpentine dragon (a wyvern) chases a falling man in a trailing gown down the left margin.

29. Below the line a naked kneeling man holds his head in his hands, and beside him a naked man holds a naked child.

30. Above the line, at the right a flying long-haired nude woman carries by the blade a huge flaming sword; to her left a naked man bends under the weight of another naked man on his shoulders; and to their left a flying long-haired naked man holds a balance or scales, the left side of which unbalances down the left margin.

31–4. *The terror . . . sphere*: These astronomical hypotheses are apparently unique to Blake.

36. Below the line flames rise from the bottom margin, and into them fall a naked man with his hands behind his head at left and, in the centre, another naked man surrounded by the coils of a giant serpent in the form of a question-mark.

37. Above the line is a naked man with his legs splayed beside a skull on a hillock, very like the figure in *The Marriage*, pl. 21.

37. Below the line is a design of a naked man or youth extricating himself from the earth.

38–41. *The grave . . . are burst*: The lines are masked or erased in all but two copies of *America* printed by Blake.

42–8. *Let the slave . . . dream*: Lines were copied in *Vala*, p. 134, ll. 18–24.

49–50. *The Sun . . . night*: Lines are adapted in *Vala*, p. 138, ll. 20–21.

51. *For empire . . . cease*: Is repeated from l. 20 of 'A Song of Liberty' in *The Marriage*.

52–8. Lines are surrounded on three sides by an idyllic scene of a birch tree overarching the text with long-tailed, exotic birds among the leaves, while at the bottom two naked boys sleep beside and on the back of a huge sleeping ram. The clangour of the text contrasts powerfully with the harmony of the design, as if representing a different point of view.

55. *Stands at the gate ... devour her children*: In Revelation 12:4, the great red 'dragon stood before the woman which was ready to be delivered, for to devour her child as soon as it was born'. Blake made two separate watercolours of *The Great Red Dragon and The Woman Clothed with the Sun.*

59. Above the line, a heavily bearded man in a long robe sits with outstretched arms on a massive cloud which surrounds the text.

71. *For every thing ... life*: The line also appears in *The Marriage*, ¶92.

72. *Because the soul ... defil'd*: The line appears as Proverb 54 in *The Marriage.*

74–5. *Amidst the lustful fires ... gold*: Nebuchadnezzar dreamed of a man 'whose head was of fine gold, his breast and his arms of silver, his belly and thighs of brass. His legs of iron, his feet part of iron and part of clay' (Daniel 2:32–3).

102. Beside and below the line a field of grain swirls round the body of a rigid, naked, prostrate child.

108. *Now barr'd out by the Atlantic sea*: In 'A Song of Liberty', 8 in *The Marriage* appear 'these infinite mountains of light now barr'd out by the atlantic sea'.

112. *Ariston*: Ariston, King of Sparta, tricked his friend Agetus into allowing Ariston to marry the wife of Agetus (*Herodotus*, translated by J. E. Powell, 1949, Book VI, ll. 61–2). Many other Greeks were named Ariston.

114. Below the line a naked, kneeling youth embraces surging flames. His position mirrors that of the old man above 59.

117. Below the line a naked, backward-looking man with a bridle rides a huge flying swan.

129. Below the line a huge, harnessed serpent is ridden in the same direction as the swan above by three naked children, a scene repeated almost exactly, though reversed, from the design at the end of *The Book of Thel.*

141. Below the line a bearded old man in a long robe, leaning on a crutch, seems to be blown into a stone doorway beneath a massive tree. An almost identical scene reappears in *For Children: The Gates of Paradise* (1793) and among Blake's designs for Blair's *The Grave* (1808), each of them called 'Death's Door'.

142. Above the line a huge eagle with outspread wings seems to devour the midriff of a nude woman prone on the shore (a similar scene appears in *Visions* above, l. 86).

143. *Bernard's house*: Sir Francis Bernard (?1711–79) was British Governor of Massachusetts in 1760–71.

157. Below the line the body of a naked man at the bottom of the sea is attacked by eels and fish.
158. *Gates & Lee*: Richard Henry Lee (1732–94) was a leading colonial patriot.
166. Below the line, beneath a huge tree, a naked woman (?) with a snake between her legs gestures towards a youth reclining on what seems to be a pile of books, with his hands joined as if in prayer.
177. Below the line, below 'the red fires rag'd', a stubby fish-like serpent belches flame.
203. Below the line, ending 'the tender grape appears', are a bunch of ripe grapes and naked women and children who crouch in flames. The Song of Solomon 7:12 has 'the tender grape appear[s]'.
204. Above the line crouches a huge, kneeling, robed figure with clasped hands and long hair which seems to turn to water flowing down the right margin. On the figure's head and feet are tiny embracing couples, and on its thigh a tiny man plays a flute. Behind the figure are bare trees in oddly human shapes.
223. *Filled with blasting fancies . . . mildews of despair*: In Deuteronomy 28:22 and Amos 4:5, Moses and God threaten the disobedient Jews with 'blasting and mildews'.

Notebook

Composed between 1793 and 1826. Blake's Notebook (in the British Library Department of Manuscripts) belonged first to his beloved younger brother Robert (d. 1787), who made some sketches in it. When Blake began adding to it, he made memoranda and jottings ('Tuesday Jan^{ry}. 20, 1807 between Two & Seven in the Evening – Despair'), poems including some which were later etched in *Songs of Experience* and 'The Everlasting Gospel', prose such as 'Vision of the Last Judgment' (1810) and 'Public Address' (1810–11), and drawings including some for *For Children: The Gates of Paradise* (1793), *The Marriage of Heaven and Hell* ([1790]), *Visions of the Daughters of Albion* (1793), *America* (1793), *Songs of Experience* (1794), *The First Book of Urizen* (1794), and *The Song of Los* (1795). Four leaves of the manuscript are missing.

'The Everlasting Gospel' is on pages scattered through the Notebook and on a leaf in the Rosenbach Foundation (Philadelphia). The poem was repeatedly redrafted and never finished.

There were facsimiles of the Notebook, edited by Geoffrey Keynes (1937) and D. V. Erdman (1973).

I have omitted drafts of poems printed in *Songs of Experience*, except for 'London', 'The Tyger', and 'Infant Sorrow', where the manuscript versions differ in particularly interesting ways from the printed versions.

'My Spectre around me'

67–8. *The Woman that . . . your smiles*: Compare: 'She who adores not your frowns will only loathe your smiles' (*Jerusalem*, pl. 95, l. 24).

'When Klopstock England defied'

In 1800, Blake painted for Hayley's library a portrait of the German poet Gottlieb Friedrich Klopstock (1724–1802). Hayley wrote on 11 August 1800 of Klopstock as the 'Milton of Germany', and on 26 March 1802 he 'read Klopstock into English to Blake'.

8. *At Lambeth*: Blake lived in Lambeth in 1790–1800.

On the Virginity of the Virgin Mary & Johanna Southcott

In October 1802 Joanna Southcott (1750–1814) announced that she would bring forth Shiloh, and in 1813 she said that she was pregnant by the Holy Ghost. She died of dropsy next year.

'Beneath the white thorn'

The marginal numbers indicate how Blake thought of reordering the lines. Similar numbers appear in 'Several Questions Answerd', 'Let the Brothels of Paris be opend' and 'O I cannot cannot find'.

To F—

'F—' is probably Blake's friend, the sculptor John Flaxman (1756–1826).

'Cr— loves artists'

'Cr—' is almost certainly the publisher Robert Hartley Cromek (1770–1812), who cheated Blake of the promised commission to engrave Blake's designs (1805) for Blair's *The Grave* (1808) and tried to cheat him over his design for Chaucer's Canterbury Pilgrims.

'The Angel that presided oer my birth'

For another pronouncement of 'an Angel at my birth', see 'Now Art has lost its mental Charms', below, ll. 1–3.

On F— & S—

'F—' is probably Flaxman (as in 'To F—' above) and 'S—' is probably the artist Thomas Stothard (1755–1834), whom Blake suspected of having stolen his design for Chaucer's Canterbury Pilgrims.

'P— lovd me not'

'P—' is probably the publisher Richard Phillips (1767–1840), Blake's partner-employer in the publication of Hayley's *Ballads* (1805) with designs by Blake.

'The only Man that eer I knew'

'When Flaxman was taken to Italy [in 1787], Fuseli was giv'n to me for a Season' (letter of 12 September 1800). Henry Fuseli (1741–1825) was a splenetic Swiss artist living in London, whose style of painting the heroic supernatural made contemporaries think that Blake was his follower.

William Cowper Esq[re]

William Cowper (1731–1800) was a domestic and religious poet who believed that God was his personal enemy. Hayley befriended him, and Blake illustrated Hayley's biography of Cowper (1802–3).

'The Caverns of the Grave I've seen'

2. *England's Queen*: Blake's designs for Blair's *The Grave* (1808) bore a dedication 'To the Queen'.
7. *Egremont's Countess*: Sir George O'Brien Wyndham (1751–1837), Third Earl of Egremont, was a munificent patron of living artists at his estate in Petworth, Sussex. He bought several of Blake's pictures. He did not marry the mother of his children for many years, he separated from her not long after they married, and she does not seem to have been generally known as 'Countess'. She bought Blake's *Satan Calling up his Legions* (1808) and *Vision of the Last Judgment* (1808).

'Fayette'

Marie Joseph Paul Yves Roch Gilbert du Motier de Lafayette (1757–1834), Marquis de Lafayette, guardian of the King and Queen of France, was known as 'Fayette' in French Revolutionary terminology.

'Let the Brothels of Paris be opend'

4. *the beautiful Queen of France*: Marie Antionette (1755–93) was Queen of Louis XVI; they were both guillotined in 1793.
17. *The Queen of France just touchd this Globe*: '[S]urely never lighted on this orb, which she hardly seemed to touch, a more delightful vision' than 'the queen of France' (Edmund Burke, *Reflections on the Revolution in France*, second edition, 1791, p. 112).

Motto to the Songs of Innocence & of Experience

The motto was never printed with *Songs of Innocence and of Experience.*

Merlin's prophecy

Merlin's gnomic prophecy to Vortigern is given at length in Geoffrey of Monmouth's *Historie of the Kings of Britain*, Book VII, Chapters 3–4 and Book VIII, Chapter I.

London

The poem was corrected and etched in *Songs of Experience.*

8. *~~german~~ mind*: The manacles were 'german' because Hessian troops had been used to put down civil unrest in England and the American colonies.

To Nobodaddy

'Nobodaddy', representing Jehovah, may be formed from 'Nobody's Daddy'.

The Tyger

The poem was corrected and etched in *Songs of Experience.*

in a mirtle shade

Lines 15–16 were used in the Notebook draft of 'Infant Sorrow', 37–40.

Infant Sorrow

Lines 1–8 were printed under the same title in *Songs of Experience.*

[The Everlasting Gospel]

Part b, 15–26 are adapted in *For the Sexes.*

Part d, 16. *Caiaphas*: Caiaphas was the judge of Jesus.

17–18, 43–4, 47–8. Lines are very similar to *The Marriage*, ¶86.

32. *Woman . . . thee*: Line is repeated in 'To Tirzah'.

Part e, 9. *Socrates . . . Meletus*: The accusers of Socrates were Meletus the poet, Anytus the tanner and Lycon the orator.

Part f, 24. *The Heavens . . . Sight*: '[T]he heavens are not clean in his sight' (Job 15:15).

51. *That have forgot our Ancient Love*: Adapted from 'To the Muses', 13–14: 'How have you left the antient love/That bards of old enjoy'd in you'.

Part k, 39. *Like d*^{r} *Priestly . . . Newton*: Joseph Priestley (1733–1804), radical minister, Francis Bacon (1561–1626), essayist and logician, Sir Isaac Newton (1642–1727), physicist and religious speculator.

59. *Creeping Jesus*: A proverbial expression meaning a favour-seeking hypocrite.

SONGS of EXPERIENCE

Printed in 1794. Many poems etched in *Songs of Experience* were drafted in Blake's Notebook (see 'London', 'The Tyger' and Infant Sorrow' here), and many of the designs appear there too. A number of poems in *Songs of Experience* were conceived as contrasts to specific poems in *Songs of Innocence*:

Songs of Innocence	*Songs of Experience*
'Introduction'	'Introduction'
'Holy Thursday'	'Holy Thursday'
'The Chimney Sweeper'	'The Chimney Sweeper'
'Nurse's Song'	'Nurse's Song'
'A Dream'	'The Angel'
'The Lamb'	'The Tyger'
'The Divine Image'	'The Human Abstract' and 'A Divine Image'
'Infant Joy'	'Infant Sorrow'

Of course this does not mean that poems in *Songs of Innocence* were composed with *Songs of Experience* in mind.

Most of the poems from *Songs of Experience* were etched on the backs of the copperplates for *Songs of Innocence*.

There are twenty-five surviving copies of *Songs of Innocence and of Experience* (plus posthumously printed copies) variously constituted, and all but two of them coloured by the Blakes. The order of the poems varies in most copies before 1818; 'The Little Girl Lost' and 'The Little Girl Found' from *Songs of Innocence* were transferred to early copies of *Songs of Experience*, and 'The School Boy' and 'The Voice of the Ancient Bard' were transferred in later copies. Four copies of *Songs of Experience* survive without any accompanying *Songs of Innocence*, though at least two of these were paginated by Blake as if they were to follow *Songs of Innocence*.

Songs of Innocence and *Songs of Experience* were advertised separately in 1793 (5s each) and 1818 (£3 3s each); it was not until 1827 that they were advertised together (£10 10s). Several copies of *Songs of Innocence* and *Songs of Experience* were issued together before the general title-page for *Songs of Innocence and of Experience* (dated 1794) was combined with them. *Songs of Experience* was often printed and coloured separately from *Songs of Innocence* and later added to copies of *Songs of Innocence*.

Songs of Innocence and of Experience title page represents a man and woman (Adam and Eve) clad only in vine leaves, cowering away from the flames which suffuse the page.

Songs of Experience frontispiece represents a shepherd holding the hands of a winged naked child sitting on his head. The title page represents a girl and a boy weeping over the bodies or effigies of an aged couple.

Introduction

1–2. *Hear the voice . . . sees*: See *Jerusalem*, pl. 15, ll. 8–9: 'I see the Past, Present & Future, existing all at once Before me'.

4–5. *The Holy Word*: Jehovah in the Garden of Eden.

11–16. *O Earth . . . no more*: See *Jerusalem* pl. 49, l. 2: 'Jerusalem! Jerusalem! Why wilt thou turn away'.

Holy Thursday

Above the text, a woman looks down in horror at a dead child stretched on the ground.

Nurse's Song

Below the text, a woman standing in a doorway combs the hair of a standing boy, while another boy sits in the doorway.

The Sick Rose

From the bottom left corner grows a huge, thorny rose-bush, on the branches of which, above the text, are a caterpillar and two tiny crouching women, while below the text is a large blossom from which emerges a woman, with outstretched arms, wrapped in a worm, presumably representing the 'Rose' 'destroy[ed]' by 'The invisible worm'.

The Fly

Beneath the text, a woman in a mob cap bends to hold the hands of a child who is apparently learning to walk. Behind her, a girl is about to hit a shuttlecock with a racquet.

The Angel

Above the text, a woman in a long belted dress lies on the ground, supporting her head with her right hand and holding at bay with her left hand a naked, winged child.

15–16. *For the time of . . . head*: Were drafted in the Notebook in 'Infant Sorrow', 39–40 and 'in a mirtle shade', 17–18.

The Tyger

Below the text, by the trunk of a massive tree, is a tiger walking left. He is certainly not as ferocious as the text describes him, and indeed he looks rather like a child's stuffed toy. He is rarely coloured realistically and is sometimes almost iridescent with yellow, brown, blue, pink, green, black, red and orange.

12. *& what*: Erased and replaced by 'Formed thy' in one copy (P). For drafts of the poem, see Blake's Notebook.

My Pretty Rose Tree

Below the text lies a woman in a long gown with a man crouching at her feet.

Ah! Sun Flower

8. *my Sun-flower*: When Apollo deserted Clytia, 'she pined away and was changed into . . . a sun-flower, which still turns its head towards the sun in his course, as a pledge of love'. Ovid, *Metamorphoses* 4, fab. 3 (J. Lempriere, *Bibliotheca Classica*; or *A Classical Dictionary* [1792]).

The Garden of Love

Above the text kneel a girl and boy with clasped hands beside a tonsured monk with an open book, who gestures down to the open grave before them.

6. *writ over the door*: See *Europe*, 191: 'Over the doors "Thou shalt not" & over the chimney "Fear" is written.' God told the Jews: 'thou shalt write them [the Commandments] upon the posts of thy house, and on thy gates' (Deuteronomy 6:9).

The Little Vagabond

Above the text, in a dark forest, a bearded old man (God), whose head gives off rays, kneels with his left arm over a naked boy kneeling before him.

2. *the Ale-house*: Some extreme dissenters such as Muggletonians held religious meetings in ale-houses and sang popular songs adapted to religious subjects.

London

A small boy leads a long-bearded old man with a crutch. A similar man appears in *For Children: The Gates of Paradise* (1793), pl. 17, *America* (1793), pl. 14, 'Death's Door' in Blair's *The Grave* (1808), *Job* (1826), pl. 6, and *Jerusalem* (1804[–20]), pl. 84, where he is described as 'London blind & age-bent begging through the streets of Babylon'. Notice the paradox of the blind man who 'mark[s] in every face I meet/Marks of weakness'. But most of what he responds to is sounds – cries, voices, sighs and curses.

The draft of the poem in Blake's Notebook is given above.

The Human Abstract

Below the text, a crouching bearded old man lifts a heavy rope above himself, perhaps representing 'Cruelty [as he] knits a snare'.

Infant Sorrow

Below the text, a woman in a long gown and a mob cap bends over a naked, struggling baby on a bed.

The much longer draft of the poem in Blake's Notebook is given above.

A Poison Tree

Below the text lies a naked man beneath the branches of a tree, evidently representing 'My foe outstretchd beneath the tree'.

In the Notebook draft, the poem is entitled 'Christian forbearance'.

A Little Boy Lost

Beneath the text, two figures cower before a roaring fire; presumably they are 'The weeping parents' before the fire where their son was burnt.

A Little Girl Lost

4. *Love! . . . thought a crime*: See 'Soft Snow', 4: 'Ah that sweet love should be thought a crime'.

To Tirzah

Below the text, two women in long gowns endeavour to raise from the ground a limp, naked man, while to the right an old man (the good Samaritan?) offers a pitcher. On the old man's robe are the words 'It is Raised a spiritual body' from Corinthians 15:44: 'It is sown a natural body; it is raised a spiritual body'.

4, 16. *what have I to do with thee*: Repeated in 'The Everlasting Gospel', part d, l. 32. It derives from John 2:14: 'When Mary asked Jesus for wine for the feast, he replied: "Woman, what have I to do with thee? mine hour is not yet come".'

A Divine Image

Below the text, a kneeling, naked man with a huge hammer is about to strike a flaming head (the sun) on an anvil. This plate was never issued by Blake and survives only in copies printed after his death.

EUROPE a PROPHECY

First printed in 1794. Sketches for the designs but not the text of *Europe* are in Blake's Notebook. The work is etched on the backs of the copperplates for *America*. There are nine known copies of *Europe* (all but one of them coloured) plus posthumous prints. Only two copies include pl. 3 with the Fairy Preface. More often than not it was bound with *America*. The order of the plates is the same in all copies except for three full-page plates which appear in two different positions. Blake offered *Europe* for £5 5s in 1818 and £6 6s in 1827.

One of Blake's best-known images, the frontispiece represents a naked old man (Urizen) kneeling in the sun with his beard streaming out to the left in the wind; with his left hand he reaches down into the black chaos beneath him to divide dark from light with rays emanating from his fingers. A sketch of the design in Blake's Notebook is entitled 'Who shall bind the infinite' (*Europe*, 52), and a separate sketch of a side view of the figure is called 'The Ancient of Days'. Blake printed a number of copies for sale separately from *Europe*; perhaps the most splendid of them is the one he coloured on his death-bed for his disciple Frederick Tatham.

On the title page an open-mouthed serpent writhes up and across the design, perhaps representing what was created by Urizen on the facing page; 'Thought chang'd the infinite to a serpent' (143).

6. *stolen joys . . . pleasant*: See Proverbs 9:13, 16, 17: 'The foolish woman . . . saith . . . stolen waters are sweet, and bread eaten in secret is pleasant.'

7. *a streak'd Tulip*: Streaked tulips were expensive hybrids, an affectation of elegance.

30. *I am faint with travel*: The design represents a clothed traveller with a huge pack strapped on his back. He turns a corner around rocks, in a crevice of which hides a crouching naked assassin with a dagger; a similar assassin appears in a watercolour of causeless *Malevolence* (1799). In Blake's time, the word 'travail' could also be spelled 'travel'; Blake writes in his letter of 25 March 1803 of 'the sore travel' of his 'three years' at Felpham.

57. Beneath 'A Prophecy' floats a heavy-winged woman (Enitharmon) with her hands behind her back.

58–60. *The deep of winter . . . eternal day*: This seems to be an echo of Milton's 'Nativity Ode' which Blake later illustrated.

74. The design shows a naked bald man floating in air and strangling two naked men, while another man holding his head flees away through the sky.

81. Below the text are naked, sprawling figures, two of them embracing, while beneath them a far larger nude woman lifts a dark cloth from a naked light-giving youth lying with his face on his arms.

90. Above this line, the design shows a naked man covered with scales wearing a spiked crown and holding a naked sword, while just behind him stand two heavy-winged angels, one with hands clasped as if in prayer or adoration.

90. Below the line come two full-page designs. The first shows two elegantly clothed and jewelled women before a huge arched fireplace with a boiling cauldron, while beside them on the floor lies a naked dead child, whom they are apparently about to put in the pot. The second full-page design shows a black-clad and -hatted bellman walking past a door inscribed 'LORD HAVE MERCY ON US'; behind him a woman falls with upstretched arms and beside him a man supports a fainting woman. A separate similar watercolour represents *Plague* (*c.* 1779).

111. Below this line is a large design of a long-bearded old man stretching his hands to the left as if to ward off a horror, while a kneeling woman grasps his legs.

112. Above this line is a splendid design of a naked man and woman whirling through space as they broadcast plagues and mildews from curling trumpets.

129–30. *ancient temple serpent-form'd . . . Island white*: This is Stonehenge, associated with the Druids.

132. *golden Verulam*: Just north of London, and associated with Francis Bacon (1561–1626), first Baron Verulam, venal Lord Chancellor, whose *Essays* (1798) Blake annotated indignantly: 'Good Advice for Satan's Kingdom'; 'Contemptible Knavery'; 'The Prince of darkness is . . . a Lord Chancellor'.

135. *such eternal in the heavens*: See Corinthians 5:1 for 'our building of God . . . eternal in the heavens'.

143. In the left margin writhes a huge, open-mouthed, light-giving serpent.

159. Above the line, most of the page is occupied by a design of a bat-winged, bat-eared man in a papal tiara, seated on a Gothic throne with a book open on his knees, while below him bowing winged angels hold forth crossed sceptres. The man's heavy, stupid face is rather like that of George III. He clearly represents Urizen and 'his brazen Book' (160–61).

178. *Guardian of the secret codes*: May be Edward Thurlow (1731–1806), first Baron Thurlow and Lord Chancellor, defender of George III's rigidity against the American colonies and of the slave trade, who was driven from office in 1792 (see D. V. Erdman, *Blake: Prophet Against Empire*, 1969, p. 217).

181. *With dismal torment . . . fled*: The line is repeated in *The First Book of Urizen*, 234–5 and *Vala*, p. 54, l. 29.

191. *Thou shalt not*: In 'The Garden of Love' '"Thou shalt not" [is] writ over the door'.

203. *Newton*: Newton may represent not only the mathematician Sir Isaac

Newton (1642–1727) but also John Newton (1725–1807), friend of William Cowper and anti-slavery agitator (see Warren Stevenson, *Blake: An Illustrated Quarterly*, XXIX, 1995, pp. 24–5).

217. Below the line is a large design of a seated naked man chained in a stone cell who raises his hands in horror as he watches a scaly naked jailer with keys climb a dark stairway.

252. *Till morning ope'd the eastern gate*: In a proof version, the line reads: 'till morning ope'd the eastern gate, and the angel trumpet blew'.

255. *Shot from the heights of Enitharmon*: In an early proof, this line read 'Shot from the heights of Enitharmon, before the trumpet blew'.

261. *The Tigers couch upon the prey*: Tigers were thought to live by drinking blood insatiably.

265. Below '*FINIS*' is a design not of Los triumphant but of a naked man carrying a clothed woman on his shoulder as he pulls a child from billowing flames.

THE FIRST BOOK OF URIZEN

First printed in 1794. Most of the plates of *Urizen* were probably etched on the backs of the copperplates of *The Marriage of Heaven and Hell* ([1790]). The work is very extensively illustrated, with full-page designs without text on ten plates (pls 9, 12, 14, 16–17, 21–2, 24, 26–7), and of course the title page (pl. 1) is mostly design. All copies are heavily coloured, most of them colour-printed about 1795.

It is very difficult to understand what its title should be, what plates it should have, and in what order the plates should be arranged. In the first place it is called *The First Book of Urizen* but there is no *Second Book of Urizen* – perhaps *The Book of Ahania* or *Vala* (organized at first in books) was intended to fulfill this role. *The First Book of Urizen* deals with the creation myth in terms similar to Genesis, the first book of Moses. The word 'First' was omitted from the title page and running heads in two copies, including the last copy printed, so Blake's final intention was clearly to call it *The Book of Urizen*.

The constitution of the work is puzzlingly inconsistent. Only two of the eight surviving copies have all twenty-eight plates; the other six copies lack one to four plates. Three of the missing plates (pls 9, 16, 24) consist of designs only, so their absence does not affect the text. However, the other three omitted plates are pl. 4 with ll. 45–93 (the end of Chapter II and the beginning of Chapter III), pl. 7 with ll. 145–53 (the end of Chapter III) and pl. 8 with ll. 154–65 (all Chapter IV[a]). The lack of pl. 4 is particularly anomalous, for the text was never corrected to account for its absence. In at least one copy (G), pl. 4 was apparently omitted because it had been printed slightly crooked.

The logical, consecutive order of the narrative is emphasized by chapter and section numbers (as in the Bible) and by running heads. However, the eight surviving copies are arranged in nine different orders (in one copy, Blake's page numbers do not correspond with the order in which the plates are bound). No two copies are arranged in the same way; the work is as unstable as Urizen's created world, where 'no flesh nor spirit could keep/His iron laws one moment' (ll. 445–6). However, it is mostly the plates with large designs but without text which move.

Text from *The First Book of Urizen* was repeatedly used later, in *The Book of Los* (1795), *Vala* (?1796–?1807), and *Milton* (1804[–11]) – thirty-eight lines in *Milton*.

Urizen was printed in 1795 and 1818 and advertised at £5 5s in 1818 with twenty-eight plates and at £6 6s in 1827. Copy E was sold in 1999 for $2,300,000 (plus $200,000 auction fee and 10–15 per cent agent's fee). (See Elizabeth B. Bentley, '*Urizen* in New York City', *Blake: An Illustrated Quarterly*, XXXIII (1999), pp. 27–30: the price amounted to 'over $100,000 per page'.)

The title page represents an old bearded man sitting on the ground with his feet on an open book, which he is copying with a pen in each hand. This is apparently Urizen writing 'secrets of dark contemplation' in his 'books formd of metals'. A separate print of it is inscribed 'Which is the Way, The Right or the Left'.

Between 'Preludium to' and 'the First Book of Urizen' is a design of a woman in a long swirling dress floating in air (rather like an apsara, a Chinese Buddhist female angel), reaching out to a naked baby who floats towards her.

Above l. 1 and 'Chap: 1' is a design of a naked young man running through swirling flames – perhaps Urizen as he 'fought with fire'. A separate print of it is inscribed 'O flames of furious desire'.

Chap: II

74. The line is erased from the paper in one copy.

Chap: III

93. The line is erased from another copy.
Below the line a naked man sits on the ground and holds his head: The rains 'fell & fell'. This is followed by a whole-page design of a naked, white-bearded man who seems to be rising through deep water. He may represent Urizen when 'his pale visage/Emerg[ed] from the darkness' (ll. 85–6) or Urizen's words: 'strong, I repell'd/The vast waves, & arose on the waters' (ll. 65–6). One copy is inscribed: 'I labour upwards into futurity'.

94. Above the line a white-bearded man holds open an enormous, illegible book; probably he is Urizen 'unclasping The Book of Brass'. One copy is inscribed 'The Book of my Remembrance', echoing Malachi 3:16:

'a book of remembrance was written ... for them that feared the Lord'.

95–6. The lines were deleted in one copy.

109. The line was erased in one copy.

144. *Urizen is a clod of clay*: In *Jerusalem*, pl. 56, l. 27, 'Gwendolen Is become a Clod of Clay'.
Below the line, three naked men wrapped in serpents fall through flames.

153. Below the line is a tormented naked, kneeling man with his arms wrapped around his throat, perhaps representing how 'Los howld in a dismal stupor'.

Chap: IV[a]

163. Below the line is a large skeleton cramped in a fetal position with his arms wrapped around his head; evidently they are the 'bones' of Urizen in the 'first Age'. Following this is a whole page design of a naked, white-bearded man with one knee raised and both hands on the ground who seems to struggle to lift the enormous mass of rocks which seem to press him down. A separate print of the page is inscribed 'Eternally I labour on'.

Chap: IV[b]

166. Above the line, a naked man in the position of a weight-lifter struggles with great rocks which press upon him from all sides. A separate print is inscribed: 'Does the Soul labour thus In the Caverns of the Grave'.

190, 207–208, 210–13, 216, 218, 221–2, 225–6, 229–33, 235–9, 243–9, 251–4 are adapted in *Milton*, pl. b, and some in *Vala*, pp. 54–5.

210–12. The lines are adapted from *Visions*, 53–6.

234–5. The lines are repeated in *Europe*, 181 and *Vala*, p. 54, l. 29.

Chap: V

235. Below the line, half the page is taken up with a design of a partly fleshed chained skeleton (Urizen in 'fetters of iron'), sitting with his knees drawn up and his head raised. Seated to our right is a naked man (Los) with a large hammer, sitting in a contorted position with both hands on the ground: 'In terrors Los shrunk from his task:/His great hammer fell from his hand' (ll. 255–6).

236–54. The lines are repeated in *Vala*, pp. 54–5 and, with substantial changes, in *Milton*, pl. b.

294. Below the line is a whole-page design of a muscular naked man with his back to us, who seems to have floated, head downwards, to rest on his hands on rocks or clouds.

307. Below the line most of the page is taken up with a design of three men staring down from a dark sky at a dark mass which may be the earth. The ones on the right and left have long white beards, and the young man in the centre reaches down to separate one part of the earth from another. Perhaps the scene is of 'The Abyss of Los . . . now seen, now obscur'd to the eyes/Of Eternals' (ll. 299–301).

This is followed by a whole-page design of a naked man crouched in flames with his hands behind his head; in one copy he has a long white beard, and in another there are tears on his cheeks.

A further full-page design shows from the back a female (?) figure with long hair and a red skirt, who covers her ears as she bends downward over a flaming sphere, evidently representing 'The globe of life blood . . . Branching out into roots' embodying the 'female form' of Enitharmon.

308. *The globe of life blood*: In the margin of *Vala*, p. 54, is a note: 'Bring in here the Globe of Blood as in the B of Urizen'.

322. Below the line, most of the page is devoted to a design of a heroic naked man (Los) with outstretched arms, holding a great black hammer as he walks through rocky flames.

323. Above the line, a nude woman with long hair bends away as if in distress from a naked man bowed before her with his head covered by his hands. They evidently represent Enitharmon and Los as 'she wept, she refus'd/In perverse and cruel delight;/She fled from his arms' (ll. 333–5).

Chap: VII

379–90. The lines are adapted in *Vala*, p. 60.

Chap: VIII

421. Below the line is a naked, flame-giving boy with spread arms and legs, falling through darkness. Clearly he is Orc 'Delving earth in his resistless way: Howling . . . with fierce flames' (ll. 366–9).

This is followed by a full-page design of a nude woman (Enitharmon) looking down at a naked, half-grown boy (Orc) who is embracing her, while to the right a naked man (Los) with a great hammer looks down at them. The man's chest is girdled by a large red chain ('the Chain of Jealousy').

Following this is a full-page design of a naked, manacled, white-bearded old man whose head gives off light seated on the ground.

447. Below the line, half the page is filled with a design of a white-bearded man in a long robe carrying a large, light-giving red globe as he strides to the right towards a moderate-sized lion. 'Urizen explor'd his dens . . . With a globe of fire lighting his journey . . . annoy'd/By cruel enormities' (ll. 416–20). The design is repeated on *Vala*, p. 74.

447. *For he saw . . . death*: The line is repeated in *Vala*, p. 87, l. 19.

The next page has a whole-page design of four naked men apparently emerging from their elements. At bottom left is a head in a black sea; to the right a man with a stubble beard climbs from the green earth; across the page floats a man with his hands raised to shoulder height with a red swirl coming from his chest; above him is the head and outspread arms of a man in flames. They represent the creation of Urizen's four sons: 'first Thiriel appear'd . . . Like a man from a cloud born, & Utha/From the waters emerging . . . Grodna rent the deep earth howling . . . then Fuzon Flam'd out' (ll. 431, 433–5, 437–8). In one copy, Fuzon and Grodna are omitted.

448. Above the line is a confusing design which seems to show three nude women in the sea wrapped in the coils of a giant winged worm, perhaps Urizen's 'daughters . . . From monsters, & worms of the pit' (ll. 440–44).

448–9. *The Ox . . . wintry door*: The lines are modified in 'Fayette', 26–27 and *Vala*, p. 36, ll. 3–4.

465. The line is erased in one copy.

494. Below the line is a whole-page design of a boy in a long dress, standing with clasped hands to the right of a dog lying before a door and howling, representing 'The Dog at the wintry door'.

Following this is a whole-page design of the back of a white-haired man in a long robe, fleeing with his hands raised; Urizen 'wanderd in sorrows/Upon the aged heavens' (ll. 454–5).

517. Below the line, half the page is devoted to a design of a man (Urizen) with a long white beard and a long robe sitting with outstretched arms; he is enmeshed in a net of heavy rope representing 'The Net of Religion'. A similar design illustrated 'The Human Abstract'.

THE SONG OF LOS

Printed in 1795. Six copies of *The Songs of Los* were colour-printed in sombre hues while the ink was still wet in about 1795. The work is a companion to *America* and *Europe* in size and in its division into 'Africa' and 'Asia', and it was sometimes bound with them. The order of the plates with text is stable, but pls 5 and 8 with full-page designs move disconcertingly in two copies. The book does not appear in his lists of works for sale in 1818 and 1827.

The frontispiece represents a barefooted man in a long robe, kneeling before an altar over which hovers a huge mottled sphere emitting rays.

On the title page above the imprint lies a bearded man in a long robe, leaning on his left elbow with his hand on a skull and looking upward at the title.

Africa

7. *mountains of Ararat*: On Mount Ararat, in what is now called Turkey, Noah's boat came to rest after the flood.
17. *Mount Sinai*: Where Moses received the Law from God.
18. *Trismegistus Palamabron*: Hermes Trismegistus (the Egyptian god Thoth) was believed to be the author of alchemical and neo-Platonic writings, especially what *Jerusalem*, pl. 91, l. 34, calls 'the Smaragdine [emerald] Tablets of Hermes'.
30. *Odin*: The Norse god of war.
52. The line is repeated from *America*, 'The Prophecy', 1.
Below the line a naked man runs across grass to the right with a woman in a flowing skirt; his left arm is around her waist, and her left arm is around his head.

This is followed by a full-page design of a woman in a long dress asleep in the blossom of a lily, beside a crowned man with a mantle and sceptre. One copy is inscribed 'King and Queen of the Fairies'.

Asia

1. Above the line is a cave in which a naked man squats, holding a limp woman in a long gown.

20–22. The lines are repeated in *Milton*, pl. f, ll. 10–41.

After 'Urizen Wept' is a full-page design of a naked man (Los) with an enormous hammer, crouching over an enormous red light-giving globe.

I Asked a Thief

Composed in 1796. The manuscript, in Princeton University Library, is copied without change from Blake's Notebook, p. 114.

VALA or *The Four Zoa's*

Vala is an immense poem of over 4,000 lines written over a period of ten or more years ([?1796–?1807]) and heavily revised. The poem was never finished, but parts of it were transferred, sometimes scarcely changed, to *Milton* and *Jerusalem*. The earliest extant version, *Vala*, is a fair copy written in 1797 in a very fine copperplate hand (pp. 1–14, 17–18, 23–30) and revised in a modified copperplate hand (pp. 4–5, 14–16, 18, 31–42) on blank leaves of very large paper (32 × 41 cm); it is quite different from the last version, *The Four Zoa's*, written in 1802–1807 in the ordinary hand in which Blake wrote his letters (pp. 19–22, 43–145) on proofs of his engravings, chiefly for Young's *Night Thoughts* (1797). It is organized in nine Nights as in Young's *Night Thoughts*. The later version is dense with references to Christianity, geography and Druidism, references which are virtually invisible in the first version.

Eighty-four pages of the manuscript have sketches for *Vala*. Some of them are highly sexual. On p. 26 is a women with butterfly wings, pendulous breasts and an enormous vulva. On p. 40 is a nude woman lying on her belly holding the hands of a man kneeling above her as in coitus, and on the man's hip is a tiny figure with spurs. On p. 41, a voluptuous nude woman lying on her back stretches backward to what seem to be the enormous penis and scrotum of a man kneeling behind her.

The unfinished nature of the poem is indicated by the facts that there are two Nights called Night the First but none called Night the Second (though the second Night concludes with 'End of the Second Night') and two Nights called 'Night the Seventh' (here distinguished as VIIa and VIIb).

Any version of the text short of a full-size facsimile must be an uneasy compromise. The present compressed text omits most deletions and additions (particularly the late pencil addenda). This necessarily creates some unfortunate anachronisms, for additions (omitted here) in Blake's usual hand on the earlier pages may be of the same date as the earliest surviving versions on pp. 43–145. For instance, the intricate Christian and Hebrew symbolism of pp. 43–145 is visible only in additions to the earlier pages. The narrative current plainly visible in the first four Nights is regularly overlaid with elaborate geographical and theological symbolism, which is at best only implicit in the earliest version. Blake revised and rearranged the poem repeatedly. Occasionally parts of pages or even whole pages are moved to another section, which may make the pagination perplexing. I have tried to maintain the narrative and have included the consciously poetic parts.

The poem, now in the British Library Department of Manuscripts, was first printed, very badly, by E. J. Ellis and W. B. Yeats in 1893. A true-size reproduction appears in *Vala or The Four Zoas*, edited by G. E. Bentley, Jr (Oxford: Clarendon Press, 1963).

The Greek word 'zoa' of the title, meaning 'living creatures' (Ezekiel 1:5), is translated as 'beasts' in Revelation 4:6.

Night the First

P. 23. 'Night the First' was never corrected to 'Night the Second'.

P. 25, l. 3. *The tygers of wrath*: 'The tygers of wrath are wiser than the horses of instruction' (*The Marriage*, Proverb of Hell, 44).

P. 36, l. 13. *Thus could I sing . . . with me*: See Job 9: 34–5: 'Let him [God] take his rod away from me, and let not his fear terrify me. Then would I speak, and not fear him: but it is not so with me.'

Night the Third

P. 39, ll. 17–19, p. 40, ll. 2–11, 13–20, p. 41, ll. 1–4, 10–17, p. 42, ll. 1–6, 9–19 are repeated, mostly as corrected in *Vala*, in *Jerusalem*, pl. 29, ll. 33–82.

P. 41, l. 16. *Coverd with boils from head to foot*: Satan 'smote Job with sore boils from the sole of his foot until his crown' (Job 2:7).

Night the Fourth

P. 48, l. 12. *Hitherto . . . cease*: In Job 38:11, God said to the sea, 'Hitherto shalt thou come, but no further; and here shall thy proud waves be stayed.'

19. *I know . . . gates of heaven*: The same line is in *Jerusalem*, pl. 82, l. 81.

P. 54, ll. 1–30, p. 55, ll. 1–9, 43–6 are repeated from *Urizen*, 184–256 and adapted in *Milton*, pl. b, ll. 6, 10–14, 16–27.

P. 55, ll. 8–9. *And his feet . . . woe*: The lines are a variant of *Urizen*, 251–2.

P. 55, l. 50. Below the line is a note: 'Bring in here the Globe of Blood as in the B of Urizen.'

Night the Fifth

P. 60, ll. 11–13, 16–18 are adapted from *Urizen*, ll. 379–90.

P. 64, l. 27. *The stars threw down their spears*: In 'The Tyger' 'the stars threw down their spears'.

Night the Seventh [a]

P. 79, l. 23. *Kneed bread of Sorrow*: See Psalm 127:2: Without God, 'It is vain for you . . . to eat the bread of sorrows'.

P. 80, ll. 12–13. *And when his children . . . overrun*: This is the argument of Thomas Robert Malthus (1766–1834) in his *Essay on the Principle of Population* (1798).

Night the Seventh [b]

Pp. 88 and 89 have no written text.

P. 91 (second version, p. 201), ll. 6–9. *As when the Earthquake . . . shoulders huge/Appear*: The metaphor appears in *Tiriel*, ll. 246–9.

l. 13 is repeated from *America*, Preludium, l. 21.

ll. 25–9. *Sound the shrill fife . . . night*: Blake probably heard the thundering drum, the shrill fife, and the trumpet, terrified, and saw the folding banners of the mounted First Regiment of Royal Dragoons (so-called because their musket was called a dragon) when they were quartered in 1803 in Blake's Sussex village of Felpham. Later, after a fracas with a dragoon, Blake was tried for sedition but acquitted.

P. 92, l. 3. *the black bow draw*: In *Jerusalem*, pl. 52, ll. 17–18: 'Satan first the black bow bent/And the Moral Law from the Gospel rent', perhaps referring to Blake's trial.

P. 92, ll. 11–13, 15–37, 19 are in a slightly different form in *Jerusalem*, pl. 65, ll. 6–8, 10–32, 37–55.

P. 95, l. 9 is repeated in *Milton*, pl. 34, l. 1.

Night the Eighth

P. 100, l. 37. *the Synagogue of Satan*: See Revelation 3:9; 2:9: 'the synagogue of Satan, which say they are Jews, and are not, but do lie'.

P. 113, l. 49. *They anoint his feet . . . hair of their head*: See Luke 7:38 (and John 12:3): Mary 'did wipe them [Jesus' feet] with the hairs of her head, and kissed his feet, and anointed them with the ointment'.

P. 104, l. 56. *Lord Jesus, come quickly*: See Revelation 22:20: 'come, Lord Jesus'.

P. 105, ll. 31–54. *O thou poor . . . Vegetation*: Lines are adapted from *Jerusalem*, pl. 67, ll. 44–50, 52–61, pl. 68, ll. 3–9.

P. 105, ll. 32, 45, 49, 51. Mahlah, Noah, Milcah, Hoglah and Tirzah, the daughters of Zelophehad (Numbers 26: 33), reappear in *Milton*, pl. 16, l. 11.

P. 105, l. 48. *bind him down on Ebal*: Moses directed Reuben, Gad, Asher, Zebulun, Dan and Naphtali to 'stand upon Mount Ebal to curse' the people (Deuteronomy 27: 13). 'Ebal' is Hebrew for cursing.

P. 113, ll. 27–8. *I am that shadowy . . . bosom*: Are in *Milton*, pl. 20, ll. 15–16.

P. 115, l. 24 is in *Milton*, pl. e, l. 22.

P. 115, ll. 33–4 are in *Milton*, pl. 6, l. 46.

P. 115, ll. 36–7. *And Satan . . . Pity*: Are adapted in *Milton*, pl. 7, ll. 46–7.

P. 115, ll. 42–4, 47–9 are in a somewhat different form in *Milton*, pl. 11, ll. 17–19, 22–4.

P. 115, l. 45. *Elohim*: Blake made a separate design of 'Elohim Creating Adam'.

P. 108, ll. 11–12. *Will you erect . . . hungry grave*: Lines are adapted from *Visions*, ll. 152–3.

P. 109, l. 21. *Awake! The bridegroom*: In the parable of the wise and foolish virgins, 'Behold, the bridegroom cometh' (Matthew 25:6).

Night the Ninth

P. 119, ll. 32–8, 42–3, p. 120, ll. 1–3 appear in a slightly different form in *Jerusalem*, pl. 19, ll. 1–7, 9–14.

P. 123, ll. 27–8. *And after the flames . . . great Glory*: Man shall 'see the Son of man coming in a cloud with power and great glory' (Luke 21:27).

P. 123, ll. 34–9. *Above . . . Eternity*: Blake's watercolour of 'The Four and Twenty Elders Casting Their Crowns before the Divine Throne' (1805), based on Revelation 4:6–10, shows the 'throne . . . surrounded by twenty four venerable patriarchs/And these again surrounded by four wonders of the Almighty'.

P. 133, ll. 21–3. *Ephesians iii c. 10 v*: Paul preached to the Gentiles, 'that now unto the principalities and powers in heavenly places might be known by the church the manifold wisdom of God'.

P. 134, ll. 18–24. *Let the slave . . . dream*: Lines are repeated from *America*, 'A Prophecy', ll. 42–8.

P. 136, ll. 16–40, p. 137, ll. 1–4 are rearranged in *Milton*, pl. 24, ll. 2–7, 11–14, 16, 19–20, 25–41.

P. 138, ll. 20–21. *The Sun . . . night*: Lines are from *America*, 'A Prophecy', ll. 49–50.

Letters

Written between 1800 and 1803. In Blake's time, letters were paid for by the recipient, at so much per sheet compounded by distance: Chichester (the Felpham post office) to London was sixty-three miles and cost 6d. Within London, letters were normally delivered on the day of posting; from London to Chichester took overnight. To save money, the sheet of paper was folded so as to make its own envelope (as it were). Mail was expensive – 6d would pay for a good dinner – and thus was used sparingly.

Blake's letters to the Flaxmans of 12 and 14 September 1800 are in the Pierpont Morgan Library (New York); those to Thomas Butts of 2 October 1800, 22 November 1802 and 16 August 1803 are in Westminster Public Library (London). See *Letters from William Blake to Thomas Butts 1800–1803*, printed in facsimile, edited by Geoffrey Keynes (Oxford: Clarendon Press, 1926).

12 September 1800

Blake was grateful to Flaxman, particularly for the introduction to William Hayley which resulted in Blake's move in September 1800 to Hayley's seaside village of Felpham in Sussex to work under Hayley's patronage.

3. *Flaxman was taken to Italy*: Flaxman was in Italy in 1787–94.

7. *Paracelsus & Behmen*: For Paracelsus and Behmen, see *The Marriage*, ¶81.

14 September 1800

7. *On the Turret*: Hayley referred to his house as 'The Turret' and to himself as 'The Hermit'.

11. *My Brother*: Robert Blake who died in 1787; 'My Friend & Thine' may be Hayley's illegitimate son, Thomas Alphonso Hayley, who had been Flaxman's apprentice and who had died on 2 May 1800.

2 October 1800

Thomas Butts had been and, after Blake's return from Felpham, was to become again, Blake's chief patron, eventually commissioning hundreds of watercolours, generally at a guinea each. His wife Betsy had a school for girls.

41. *My Sister & Friend*: Blake's sister was called Catherine, like his wife.

22 November 1802

7–8. *Verses that Hayley sung*: May be Hayley's translation of Tasso's *Le Sette Giornato del Mondo Creato*, called *Genesis*, which Blake wrote out – or almost any other volume of Hayley's voluminous poetry.

11–16. *With Silver Angels . . . mone*: Blake's father James (d. 1784), his brothers Robert (d. 1787) and John, who ran away to join the army about 1793; this is the only known reference to John's death.

33ff. *For here does Theotormon*: This is the only place where Blake refers to his mythological characters in his letters.

53–9. *So I spoke . . . Los in his might*: This is the central action of Blake's *Milton*; see particularly pl. 20, ll. 5–11.

16 August 1803

Blake was writing for advice which Butts might be able to give because of his position as a clerk in the office of Commissary General of [military] Musters.

> I am at Present in a Bustle to defend myself against a very unwarrantable warrant from a Justice of Peace in Chichester, which was taken out against me [today] by a Private in Captn Leathes's troop of 1st or Royal Dragoons for an assault & Seditious words. The wretched Man has terribly Perjurd himself . . .

A 'True Bill' was found in October 1803, but Blake was acquitted at his trial in January 1804.

1–2. *O why . . . race*: Blake used these two lines in a slightly different form in 'Mary', ll. 21–2, *William Blake Writings*, ed. G. E. Bentley, Jr (1978).

MILTON

Blake dated *Milton* '1804', but it cannot have been printed before about 1811. *Milton* is about 'the deceits of Natural Religion' (pl. 36, l. 25). Its central event (pls 20–21, 40), perhaps of September 1801, is described in the poem in Blake's letter of 22 November 1802 to Thomas Butts (see pp. 236–8). In a later letter of 25 April 1803 Blake writes of:

> the Spiritual acts of my three years Slumber on the banks of the Ocean ... [described in] My long Poem descriptive of those Acts ... an immense number of verses on One Grand Theme Similar to Homer's Iliad or Milton's Paradise Lost, the Persons & Machinery intirely new to the Inhabitants of Earth (some of the Persons Excepted). I have written this Poem from immediate Dictation twelve or sometimes twenty or thirty lines at a time without Premeditation & even against my Will.

And on 25 July 1803 he speaks of:

> A Sublime Allegory which is now perfectly completed into a grand Poem. I may praise it since I dare not pretend to be any other than the Secretary; the Authors are in Eternity. I consider it the grandest poem that this World Contains. ... This Poem shall by Divine Assistance be progressively Printed & Ornamented with Prints & given to the Public.

But *Milton* cannot have been 'perfectly completed' in 1803, for the title page is dated '1804', and the poem represents some events which did not take place until even later.

The quarrel of Palamabron (Blake), Elynittria (Catherine Blake) and Satan (Hayley) on pl. 3–11 (not included in this volume) took place in 1802–1803. The references to 'South Molton Street' must be from when Blake lived there from late 1803 to 1821. 'Scofield' is John Scholfield who accused Blake of sedition in August 1803, leading to Blake's trials in October 1803 and January 1804. The complaints in the Preface about low prices given for works of genius and the 'expensive advertizing boasts' about them seem to refer to R. H. Cromek's purchase in 1805 for £21 of twenty designs by Blake for Blair's *The Grave* (published 1808). The three-headed 'Hand' on pls 17 and 22 seems to represent Leigh Hunt and his two brothers, who attacked Blake as 'an unfortunate lunatic' in their *Examiner* (7, 28 August 1808, 17 September 1809); their anonymous essays were signed by a pointing hand. Pl. 43 condemns those who 'mock [inspiration] with aspersions of Madness'.

Compared to his other works in Illuminated Printing, Blake's *Milton* is not densely illustrated; there are ten full-page designs, but most plates have few designs or none.

The poem is inconsistently arranged from copy to copy. The title page calls it 'a Poem in 12 Books', but, as T. G. Wainewright wrote anxiously on 28 March 1826, 'The title says in *12* books. My copy has but *3*! yet "*Finis*" is on the last page! How many should there be?' All four known copies, including Wainewright's, have two books, and in two copies the title page has been altered to '2 Books'.

Further, the number and order of the plates change. The first two copies with pls 1–45 are in the same plate order, but in the two later copies pl. 21 (a full-page design) and pl. 24 move to new positions, pl. 2 (the Preface) was withdrawn, and pls a–e (or a–f) were added, sometimes as late afterthoughts; in one copy pls c and e were intercalated as '8*' and '32*'.

The four surviving copies were apparently printed and coloured in 1811 and 1818. *Milton* was offered with fifty prints at £10 in 1818 but was not listed with the other works Blake offered for sale in 1827.

On the title page, a naked man seems to break the word 'MILTON' in two with his outstretched hand.

In two copies, the title page says 'a Poem in 12 Books', though all copies have just two books. The epigraph comes from *Paradise Lost*, I, 26.

Preface

The Preface was omitted in the last two copies Blake made. The 'Jerusalem' lyric was set to music by Hubert Parry and has become a kind of second national anthem in Britain. The question it poses was answered with an explicit 'Yes' in *Jerusalem*, pl. 27.

9–10. *Bring me my Bow . . . desire*: Blake writes in his letter of 22 November 1802 of 'the bows of my Mind & the Arrows of Thought'.

12. *Chariot of Fire*: See 2 Kings 2:11 for 'chariots of fire'.

Book the First

Pl. a, l. 5. Palamabron (Blake) speaks.

Pl. a, ll. 6–14. *Not to show . . . wrath*: Blake's 'Defiance' of Los is given in different terms in the poem in his letter of 22 November 1802.

11. *Newton's Pantocrator*: The organizer of a mechanical universe.

Pl. f, l. 19. *Ah weak . . . form*: The song is that of the Males at the Furnaces as the 'Females prepare the Victims'.

Pl. 7, ll. 46–47 are in *Vala*, p. 115, ll. 36–7 in a slightly different form.

Pl. 12, l. 3. *To whom be Glory . . . Amen*: See Jude 1:25: To God 'be glory and majesty, dominion and power, both now and ever. Amen.'

13. *He took off the robe of the promise*: Below the line is a full-page design of a naked man (Milton) with a nimbus standing with raised arms holding white garments.

15. *Gods of Priam*: Those of Troy.

28. *Emanation*: Milton's emanations were his three wives and his three daughters.

Pl. 17, ll. 15–21 are repeated substantially in *Milton*, pl. 34, ll. 32–9, along with 'Milton's track'. On Pl. 32 is a design of an egg shape labelled 'Adam' at the top and 'Satan' at the bottom. It is intersected by four circles labelled 'N Urthona', 'E Luvah', 'S Urizen', and 'W Tharmas'. At the south-east corner is 'Milton's Track'. An analogous design of 'This World' is in *Jerusalem*, pl. 54.

15–25 are in a somewhat different form in *Jerusalem*, pl. 59, ll. 10–13, 15–21.

Pl. 18, ll. 27–30. *Seest thou . . . rich array*: For similar ideas, see 'The Fly' in *Songs of Innocence*.

Pl. 19, l. 56. *I am with you alway*: In Matthew 28:20, Jesus said, 'lo, I am with you alway'.

Pl. 20, ll. 4–8. *what time I bound my sandals*: Lines are illustrated on Pl. 21 in a whole-page design of a naked man (Los) stepping from the sun, while before him on grass kneels another naked man (Blake), wearing a sandal on his right foot and looking up over his shoulder at Los.

5–11. *On: to walk . . . Los descended to me . . . wishd me health*: The same scene is described in the poem in Blake's letter of 22 November 1802.

15–16. *I am that Shadowy Prophet . . . Years*: The same lines are in *Vala*, p. 113, ll. 27–8.

55. *Whitefield . . . Westley*: George Whitefield (1714–70) was a Methodist evangelist and John Wesley (1703–91) was the father of Methodism.

57–8. *Faith in God . . . Cross*: Jesus 'took upon him . . . the likeness of men . . . and became obedient until death, even the death of the cross' (Philippians 2:7–8).

Pl. 23, l. 71. *Spirit of Prophecy*: For Los as 'the Spirit of Prophecy', see *Jerusalem*, pl. 44, l. 31, pl. 90, l. 39 and Revelation 19:10: 'The testimony of Jesus is the spirit of prophecy'.

Pl. 24, ll. 2–7, 11–14, 16, 19–20, 25–41 are repeated with some change of order in *Vala*, p. 136, ll. 16–40, p. 137, ll. 1–4.

Pl. 25, l. 48. *Jerusalem's Inner Court, Lambeth ruin'd*: Blake lived at Hercules Buildings, Lambeth (1790–1800); a little to the north were Apollo Buildings and the recently defunct Apollo Gardens. The ruins of Lambeth may be the decaying Vauxhall Gardens a little way upriver.

49–50. *Asylum . . . bread*: Near Blake's house was the Royal Asylum for Female Orphans, a workhouse on the site of the former Hercules Tavern. Lambeth Palace was the seat of the Archbishop of Canterbury.

61. *Supper of the Lamb*: For 'the marriage supper of the Lamb', see Revelation 19:9.

Book the Second

Pl. 31, l. 54. *the White-thorn lovely May*: Also celebrated in Blake's poem in his Notebook.

Pl. 39, l. 55. *Seven Angels bear my Name*: In *Jerusalem*, pl. 55, ll. 30–32, those who wished 'to make a Separation . . . Elected Seven, calld the Seven Eyes of God; Lucifer, Molech, Elohim, Shaddai, Pahad, Jehovah, Jesus'. In the Kabbala, the 'tradition' of the Jews referred to in *Jerusalem*, pl. 27, God (En Soph) is manifested in creation by seven Sephiroth including Shaddai.

Pl. 42, l. 34. *The Negation is the Spectre; the Reasoning Power in Man*: Substantially repeated in *Jerusalem*, pl. 54, l. 7 and pl. 74, l. 10.

Jerusalem

Blake dated *Jerusalem* '1804' but it cannot have been printed until about 1820. Blake made a number of references to the creation of *Jerusalem*. *Milton*, pl. 4, ll. 14–15, refers to 'Lambeth's Vale Where Jerusalem's foundations began', and in *Jerusalem*, pl. 38, ll. 40–42 he wrote:

I heard in Lambeth's shades [where he lived 1790–1800]:
In Felpham [1800–1803] I heard and saw the Visions of Albion.
I write in South Molton Street [1803–21] what I both see and hear.

The Preface to *Jerusalem* speaks of how he chose the 'Cadence' 'When the Verse was first dictated to me'. In his *Descriptive Catalogue* (1809), ¶75, Blake wrote that 'the human sublime', 'the human pathetic', and 'the human reason'

> were originally one man, who was fourfold; he was self-divided, and his real humanity slain on the stems of generation, and the form of the fourth was like the Son of God. How he became divided is a subject of great sublimity and pathos. The Artist has written it under inspiration, and will, if God please, publish it; it is voluminous, and contains the ancient history of Britain, and the world of Satan and Adam.

The poem was long in gestation, probably from 1804, the date on the title page, until 1820. Some of the evidence for its date is internal to the poem. The characters in *Jerusalem* called Scofield, Cock, Hulton, Brereton, Peachey and Quantock refer to Blake's accusers and Justices of the Peace at Blake's trials for sedition in October 1803 and January 1804. The character called 'Hand' seems to be the three Hunt brothers who attacked Blake in their *Examiner* articles in 1808–1809.

Other kinds of evidence are external. In the summer of 1807, Blake's friend George Cumberland wrote in a notebook: 'Blake has eng^{d} 60 Plates of a new Prophecy!' (*Blake Records*, 2004, p. 246), which must refer to *Jerusalem*, Blake's only known work with more than fifty plates. On 19 December 1808 Blake told Cumberland that he had 'now so long been turned out of the old channel' of 'my former pursuits of printing' 'that it is impossible for me to return to it'. The poet laureate Robert Southey saw *Jerusalem* in its incomplete state in 1811 and thought it 'a perfectly mad poem'. In 1812 Blake lent 'Detached Specimens' of *Jerusalem* to the exhibition of the Watercolour Society. It was not listed among Blake's works for sale in 1818, but two copies of Chapter I may have been printed in 1818, and Linnell bought Chapter II for 14s on 31 December 1819. (He may have bought Chapter I and III ('Prints') for £1 on 10 December 1820 and the 'Balance of Jerusalem' for 15s on 4 February 1821.) Every copy contains leaves with watermarks of 1820 or later, and the imminent publication of the whole was announced in a jocular piece by Blake's enthusiastic patron Thomas Griffiths Wainewright in the *London Magazine* of September 1820:

> an ancient, newly discovered, illuminated manuscript, which has to name 'Jerusalem the Emanation of the Giant Albion!!!' It contains a good deal anent one '*Los*', who, it appears, is now, and hath been from the creation, the sole and fourfold dominator of the celebrated city of *Golgonooza*! The doctor assures me that the redemption of mankind hangs on the universal diffusion of the doctrines broached in the M.S.

By the time he came to etch *Jerusalem*, Blake's income had become very limited, and he had to save money on the expensive copperplates. Most of the *Jerusalem* plates probably had other *Jerusalem* plates etched on their versos. At least seven of them exhibit the disfiguring marks which the copperplate-maker put on the backs of his copperplates, and six others seem to be etched over other designs.

The work is very generously illustrated, both with full-page designs marking the beginnings and endings of chapters (pls 1–2, 26, 76, 100) and with extensive designs on pages with text. Only fourteen plates have little or no design.

The order of the plates is invariable in Chapters I, III–IV, but it changes strikingly in Chapter II (pls 26–50). In two early copies, pls 42, 29–32 follow pl. 46; in the last three copies they are in the standard order of 26–50.

There were also less obvious changes in the poem as it grew. Chapter I, which now ends on pl. 25, once ended on pl. 14. Twenty-one plates were apparently once in different positions or are late additions.

There are five surviving complete copies of *Jerusalem* printed by Blake, plus at least three posthumously printed copies. One complete copy plus one consisting only of Chapter I are gorgeously coloured by Blake.

Blake wrote to George Cumberland on 12 April 1827, a few weeks before his death:

> The Last Work I producd is a Poem Entitled Jerusalem the Emanation of the Giant Albion, but find that to Print it will Cost my Time the amount of Twenty Guineas. One I have finishd [i.e. coloured]. It contains 100 Plates but it is not likely that I shall get a Customer for it.

He did not get a customer for this coloured copy, and it was not sold until long after his death.

On the frontispiece a traveller (Los), wearing a short belted coat and a flat-brimmed hat and carrying in his right hand a round object which gives off light, enters an arched doorway in a stone wall ('the Door of Death').

On the title page surrounding the title are five women with moth or butterfly wings, the largest of whom vegetates on a wing-like leaf decorated with stars.

Pl. 3, ll. 1–2. *Reader! lover of books*: Blake deleted from the copperplate the words 'lover' (l. 1, twice) and 'all books are given' (l. 2).

Chap: I

Above 'Jerusalem' heading appears the Greek for 'Jesus only' (Mark 9:8, Luke 9:36, John 8:9).

Pl. 5, ll. 16–17. *Trembling I sit . . . my great task*: Blake wrote to Flaxman on 12 September 1800: 'My Angels have told me that Seeing such visions I could not Subsist on the Earth But by my conjunction with Flaxman who knows to forgive Nervous Fear.'

Pl. 22, ll. 1, 10–12, 14–15, 20–24 are in *Vala*, p. 4, ll. 18–21, 27–8, 30–34.

4. *Cush his Son*: Cush and his son 'Nimrod the mighty hunter before the Lord' (Genesis 10:8) do not perform in the Bible the actions narrated here in *Jerusalem*.

9. *Valley of Vision*: See Isaiah 22:5.

Pl. 25–26 appear between Pl. 24, l. 56 and Pl. 27, l. 1. Below Pl. 25 is a large design of a naked man kneeling with his hands behind his back and his head on the right knee of a nude seated woman; on his thighs, shoulder and belly are stars, a flaming face, a crescent moon, and from his belly extends a bloody cord held by a nude woman seated to the right. Over the scene broods a nude woman from whose outstretched hands depend bloody lines.

Pl. 26 is a splendid whole-page design of a naked man (labelled 'HAND') in flames with outstretched hands with spikes in the palms looking back at a woman ('JERUSALEM') in a long dress standing with her hands raised to waist-level. Sideways beside the figures is written:

SUCH VISIONS HAVE APPEARD TO ME
AS I MY ORDERD RACE HAVE RUN:
JERUSALEM IS NAMED LIBERTY
AMONG THE SONS OF ALBION.

[Isaac D'Israeli], *Vaurien* (1797), I, xviii, wrote: 'Liberty is awefully loved by a Briton; it forms his national religion'.

Pl. 27 has the introduction to Chapter II, addressed 'To the Jews'.

17. *She walks upon our meadows green*: This is the answer to the question posed in *Milton*, pl. 2, l. 4.

Chap: 2

Pl. 31, l. 30. *I could not dare*: The speaker is Los.

Pl. 33, l. 8. *fortuitous concourse of memorys*: 'Fortuitous concourse of atoms' is a common phrase deriving from Cicero's description of the atomic theory of Democritus.

18. *Mighty Ones*: Nimrod was 'a mighty one in the earth' (Genesis 10:8).

Pl. 34, l. 23. *I hear the screech*: Los speaks.

Pl. 35, l. 9. *Albion goes to Eternal Death*: Los speaks.

11. *No individual . . . are death*: In *The First Book of Urizen*, 444–6,

Urizen 'saw That no flesh nor spirit could keep/His iron laws one moment'.

Pl. 38, ll. 17–21 are in *Vala*, p. 21, ll. 2–6.

23. *He is the Good shepherd*: Is in *Vala*, p. 8, l. 10; see John 10:11, 14: 'I am the good shepherd'.

40–42. *So spoke London . . . South Molton Street*: Blake lived in Hercules Buildings, Lambeth (1790–1800), in Felpham, Sussex (1800–1803), and in South Molton Street (1803–21).

Pl. 49, ll. 32–5, 40–41 are in *Milton*, pl. f, ll. 19–23, 25–6.

Pl. 52 is the preface to Chapter III addressed 'To the Deists' who 'charge the poor Monks & Religious [like the Methodist Whitefield] with being the causes of War'. The poem was drafted in a more extensive form in Blake's Notebook, and a few stanzas appear in 'The Grey Monk' in the Ballads Manuscript.

Chap 3

Pl. 54, l. 14. Below the line is a design of nude figures floating around a bumpy sphere labelled 'Reason' at top (north), 'Wrath' at right (east), 'Desire' at bottom (south), 'Pity' at left (west), and 'This World' in the centre. See *Milton*, pl. 17, ll. 15–21 for a similar design.

19. *Friend of Sinners*: The Pharisees accused Jesus of being 'a friend of publicans and sinners' (Matthew 11:19).

Pl. 55, ll. 27. *Stars in their courses*: In Judges 5:20, 'the stars in their courses fought against Sisera'.

31. *And they Elected Seven*: Is repeated in *Vala*, p. 19, ll. 9–10.

69. *Who will go forth*: See Isaiah 6:8: God said, 'Whom shall I send, and who will go for us?'

Pl. 60, l. 67. *lo I am with thee always*: See Matthew 20: 'lo, I am with you alway'.

Pl. 61, l. 6. *Art thou more pure*: See Job 4:17: 'shall a man be more pure than his maker?'

19. *That Debt is not Forgiven*: On 7 December 1826, Blake told Crabb Robinson that the 'Atonement . . . is a horrible doctrine – If another man pay your debt I do not forgive it' (*Blake Records*, p. 453).

22. *Is without Money & without Price*: See Isaiah 55:1: 'come, buy wine and milk without money and without price.'

27. Cf. Matthew 1:18: 'Mary was . . . with child of the Holy Ghost'.

Pl. 65, ll. 6–8, 10–32, 37–55 are in a slightly different form in *Vala*, p. 92, ll. 11–13, 15–37, p. 93, ll. 1–19.

Pl. 67, ll. 44–50, 52–61, pl. 68, ll. 3–9 are in a slightly different form in *Vala*, p. 105, ll. 31–54.

Pl. 74, l. 14. *Testimony of Jesus*: See Revelation 19:10: 'the testimony of Jesus is the spirit of prophecy'.

Pl. 76 is a splendid whole-page white-line design of a naked man (labelled

'Albion') with outspread arms and legs looking upward at a figure ('Jesus') with a nimbus nailed to the forked branches of a huge tree.

Pl. 77 is the preface 'To the Christians' to Chapter IV: 'I know of no other Christianity and of no other Gospel than the liberty both of body & mind to exercise the Divine Arts of Imagination.'

12. *a Watcher & a Holy-One*: In Nebuchadnezzar's dream, 'a watcher and an holy one came down from heaven' (Daniel 4:13; see also 4:14, 23).

C[hap:] 4

Pl. 84, l. 12. Below the line is a design of a bearded old man on crutches led through city streets by a child, a scene echoed from 'London' in *Songs of Experience*.

15–16. *The Corner of Broad Street*: Blake grew up at the corner of Broad and Marshall Streets (1757–72); he lived in Poland Street (1785–90), and he served as an apprentice with James Basire in Great Queen Street, Lincoln's Inn Fields (1772–9).

Pl. 86, l. 61 is repeated from *Vala*, p. 30, l. 48.

Pl. 88, ll. 40, 42. *Continually building . . . because of love & jealousy*: A design on pl. 72 represents angels in flames weeping on either side of a globe inscribed in slightly different form: 'Continually Building. Continually decaying because of Love & Jealousy'.

Pl. 91, ll. 7–12. *the Worship of God . . . cup*: Lines are very similar to *The Marriage*, ¶83.

24–5. *You smile . . . time*: Lines are adapted from *Milton*, pl. 43, ll. 19–20.

Pl. 97, l. 17. Below the text is a splendid design of a naked man carrying a large circle of fire, clearly echoing the design on Pl. 1. A sketch for it is labelled 'Journey of Life'.

Pl. 99, l. 5. Below the text, occupying nine tenths of the page, is a design of a bearded man in a long robe pressing to him the loins of a nude woman with open arms. A similar design on Pl. 96 clearly depicts the scene in l. 2 there: 'England who is Brittannia enterd Albion's bosom rejoicing'.

Appearing after Pl. 99, Pl. 100 is a whole-page design of a naked man with a great hammer in his right hand and fire-tongs in his left; to our left a naked man carries the sun on his shoulder away from us, and on our right a nude woman holds up a spindle in her left hand and in her right hand she holds lines from which depend a crescent moon. In the background is the serpent temple.

'To the Queen'

Composed in 1807. 'To the Queen' was printed as the dedication to Robert Blair, *The Grave, A Poem, Illustrated by Twelve Etchings* [by Louis Schiavonetti] *Executed from Original Drawings* [by William Blake] (London:

R. H. Cromek et al., 1808). These copperplates, the designs by which Blake was best known in the nineteenth century, were reprinted in 1813, 1826, 1870 and 1926 and printed in reduced size in 1847, 1858 and 1879.

The only known published contemporary comment, in *The Antijacobin*, XXXI (1808), 234, said that the poem

> is one of the most abortive attempts to form a wreath of poetical flowers that we have ever seen. Should he [Blake] again essay to climb the Parnassian heights, his friends would do well to restrain his wanderings by the strait waistcoat. Whatever licence we may allow him as a painter, to tolerate him as a poet would be insufferable.

A facsimile of 'To the Queen' appears in *William Blake's Works in Conventional Typography* (1984).

The Ballads (or *Pickering*) *Manuscript*

The work known as the Ballads or Pickering Manuscript (Pierpont Morgan Library, New York) derives its conventional title from B. M. Pickering, who bought it in 1865 and published it in 1866; but a more intrinsic title is the Ballads Manuscript because of the paper on which it is printed and the character of some of the poems. The Ballads Manuscript consists of twenty-two leaves made from unsold leaves of the first of Wiliam Hayley's *Designs to a Series of Ballads* (Felpham: William Blake, 1 July 1802), with Hayley's text cut off, leaving the wide inner margins to write on. (Blake used other leaves from Hayley's *Designs* for scrap paper from about 1805 to at least 1824.) The poems in the Ballads Manuscript were probably composed in 1800–1804 (at least three were drafted in 1803) and transcribed here after 1807.

A facsimile appears in *The Pickering Manuscript*, edited by Charles Ryskamp (1972).

The Mental Traveller

8. *Which we in bitter tears did sow*: See Psalm 126: 'They that sow in tears shall reap in joy.'

Auguries of Innocence

37–8. *The Caterpiller . . . grief*: Lines are echoed in 'The Keys' to *For the Sexes: The Gates of Paradise*, ll. 1–2.

125–6. *We are led . . . the Eye*: Appear also in 'The Everlasting Gospel', part k, ll. 103–104.

127. *Born in a Night . . . Night*: The gourd which God made to shade Jonah 'came up in a night, and perished in a night' (Jonah 4:10).

THE GHOST of ABEL

Printed in 1822. This little dramatic scene is etched on the front and back of a single sheet of copper. It is clearly a response to the iconoclasm of Lord Byron (to whom it is dedicated), especially his *Cain, A Mystery* (1821).

Only four complete copies are known, probably given away by Blake to his friends. He did not colour it or list it with his other works for sale in his letter of 1827.

To LORD BYRON in the Wilderness: Blake apparently refers to Byron's mordant play, *Cain, a Mystery* (1821). 'The Voice of one crying in the wilderness' (*All Religions are One* [1788], referred to in the imprint) applies to John the Baptist in Matthew 3:3, Mark 1:3, Luke 3:4, John 1:23 (echoing Isaiah 40:3).

What doest thou here, Elijah: From I Kings 19:9, 13.

4–5. *Woman's Seed . . . Serpent's head*: 'The Lord God said unto the serpent . . . I will put enmity between thee and the woman, and between thy seed and her seed; it shall bruise thy head, and thou shalt bruise his heel' (Genesis 3:14–15).

8. *O Earth, Cover . . . Blood*: See Job 16:18: 'O earth, cover not thou my blood' and the prayer for the slave in Erasmus Darwin, *Botanic Garden* (1791), I, 96: 'Earth! Cover not their blood!'

29. *a Contrite Heart*: See Psalms 51:17: 'The sacrifices of God are a broken spirit . . . and a contrite heart'; see also Psalms 34:18.

For the Sexes: *The Gates of Paradise*

Printed in (?) 1826. The first form of the work was *For Children: The Gates of Paradise* (17 May 1793) and consisted of eighteen uncoloured prints with very brief captions (e.g., 'Water', 'Fire'). The designs were chosen from many emblems in Blake's Notebook. Only five copies of *For Children* are known. It was advertised at 3s in Blake's Prospectus of 1793 but was not named in his letters of 1818 and 1827.

For Children was revised and extended in *For the Sexes: The Gates of Paradise* (?1826). Three new plates were added with explanatory poems, and the captions were extended. The ideas and some of the phrases resemble those in Blake's 'The Everlasting Gospel'. Five copies and a surprising number of fragments are known, most of them probably printed posthumously.

Above the text of pl. 1 is a design of a baby in a cocoon on a leaf with a caterpillar hovering above.

What is Man!

Pl. 2, ll. 3–4. *Against . . . Stones of Fire*: In *Jerusalem*, pl. 49, ll. 73–4, it is 'the Eternal Human That walks about among the stones of fire'.

The Keys

Pl. 19. The numbers at the beginnings of lines refer to the designs first etched as *For Children: The Gates of Paradise* and later included in *For the Sexes: The Gates of Paradise.*

1–2. *The Caterpiller . . . Grief*: Lines are echoed in 'Auguries of Innocence', 37–8.

Of the Gates

13–15. *Two Horn'd . . . We stood*: For similar ideas and phrases, see 'The Everlasting Gospel', part k, ll. 97–8 and *Jerusalem*, Pl. 64, ll. 27, 31.

To The Accuser

Pl. 21. Below the text is a design of a naked man, the dreaming traveller, outstretched on the hillside, while over him hovers a black, bat-winged figure with stars, sun and moon on his wings. A very similar figure appears in 'The Flight of Moloch' for Blake's illustrations to Milton's 'Nativity Ode'.

Index of Titles and First Lines

THE STORY OF PENGUIN CLASSICS

Before 1946 ...'Classics' are mainly the domain of academics and students, without readable editions for everyone else. This all changes when a little-known classicist, E. V. Rieu, presents Penguin founder Allen Lane with the translation of Homer's *Odyssey* that he has been working on and reading to his wife Nelly in his spare time.

1946 *The Odyssey* becomes the first Penguin Classic published, and promptly sells three million copies. Suddenly, classic books are no longer for the privileged few.

1950s Rieu, now series editor, turns to professional writers for the best modern, readable translations, including Dorothy L. Sayers's *Inferno* and Robert Graves's *The Twelve Caesars*, which revives the salacious original.

1960s The Classics are given the distinctive black jackets that have remained a constant throughout the series's various looks. Rieu retires in 1964, hailing the Penguin Classics list as 'the greatest educative force of the 20th century'.

1970s A new generation of translators arrives to swell the Penguin Classics ranks, and the list grows to encompass more philosophy, religion, science, history and politics.

1980s The Penguin American Library joins the Classics stable, with titles such as *The Last of the Mohicans* safeguarded. Penguin Classics now offers the most comprehensive library of world literature available.

1990s The launch of Penguin Audiobooks brings the classics to a listening audience for the first time, and in 1999 the launch of the Penguin Classics website takes them online to a larger global readership than ever before.

The 21st Century Penguin Classics are rejacketed for the first time in nearly twenty years. This world famous series now consists of more than 1300 titles, making the widest range of the best books ever written available to millions – and constantly redefining the meaning of what makes a 'classic'.

The Odyssey continues ...